# FREEMIUM

# FREEMIUM

How Zoom, HubSpot, Atlassian,
and Other Top Companies Use
Product-Led Growth ... for Low-Cost
Customer Acquisition and Expansion

### DAVE BOYCE

**STANFORD BUSINESS BOOKS**
An Imprint of Stanford University Press • Stanford, California

Stanford University Press
Stanford, California

Special discounts for bulk quantities of Stanford Business Books are available to corporations, professional associations, and other organizations. For details and discount information, contact the special sales department of Stanford University Press by emailing sales@ www.sup.org.

ISBN 9781503640399 (cloth)
ISBN 9781503643055 (electronic)

Library of Congress Control Number: 2024049143

Library of Congress Cataloging-in-Publication Data available upon request.

Cover design: Jan Šabach
Typeset by Newgen in 10.75/14 Arno Pro

The authorized representative in the EU for product safety and compliance is: Mare Nostrum Group B.V. | Mauritskade 21D | 1091 GC Amsterdam | The Netherlands | Email address: gpsr@mare-nostrum.co.uk | KVK chamber of commerce number: 96249943

To My Family.
Lisa is my chosen partner in life.
*You have inspired me, supported me, led me, and sustained me. We have sought and found many life adventures; may we find many more.*

Zach, Rose, Calvin, Jacob, Katherine, and Davey
I live in awe of your talent, your determination,
your compassion, and your honesty.

*I thank my God for entrusting me to be your father.*

XOXO,
—dave

# Contents

## PART TWO
### PRODUCT-LED GROWTH IMPLEMENTATION AND TACTICS

**PART FOUR SUMMARY:** The Next Generation of Product-Led
      Growth

# Glossary of Key Concepts in Product-Led Growth (PLG)

**Key Concepts in the PLG Bowtie Model** (listed in chronological order, through a customer journey):

**FIGURE 0.1.** PLG Bowtie

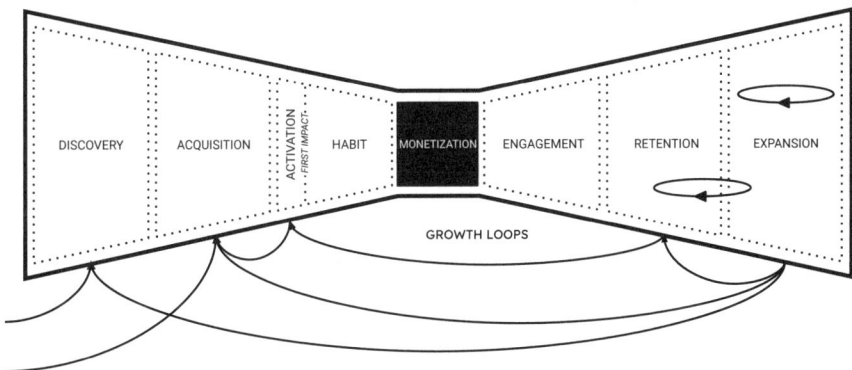

**PLG Bowtie:** A data model describing the stages of progression through a product-led growth customer journey. The PLG Bowtie is a variation of Winning by Design's Recurring Revenue Bowtie Data Model. The two variants can be used together.

**Acquisition:** In PLG, Acquisition refers to the process of getting a new user to experience the product for the first time. An acquired customer may or may not have created a user account.

**Activation:** In PLG, Activation refers to the process of guiding new users to experience First Impact, the moment when they experience the product's core value. "Active" is a defined user state used in measuring daily active users (DAU), weekly active users (WAU), and monthly active users (MAU), based on how recently the user has experienced a defined impact moment.

**First Impact:** First Impact is the moment a new user first experiences the core value of the product. In PLG, this generally occurs before paying for the product.

**Habit:** In PLG, a Habit is a repeated user behavior that occurs naturally and frequently, indicating that the product is delivering ongoing value without requiring external nudges.

**Monetization:** In PLG, Monetization is the process of converting active users into paying customers. Product-led growth has four basic Monetization archetypes: freemium, free trial, reverse trial, and product-led sales.

**Engagement:** Engagement is the depth and frequency of user interaction with a product that indicates perceived value and progress toward desired impact.

**Retention:** In PLG, Retention most often refers to usage retention. Usage retention is the act of continuously engaging users so they remain active within the product. Retention may also refer to the retention of customers or of contract value.

**Expansion:** In PLG, Expansion refers to any increase in usage for existing users or in users acquired within the same account. Expansion may also refer to the expansion of contract value.

**Growth Loops:** Growth Loops are tactics that leverage current users' product usage to drive even more usage. Loops leverage product mechanics to further engage current and prospective users. Types of Growth Loops include: Acquisition Growth Loops, Activation Growth Loops, Monetization Growth Loops, Retention Growth Loops, and Expansion Growth Loops.

## Other Key Product-Led Growth Terms

**Growth Team:** A Growth Team is a small, self-contained team that includes Product, Engineering, Marketing, Design, and Analytics. Growth Teams are organized by growth objective. They are typically small (5–7 people), and they are designed to work at speed. Types of Growth Teams include: Acquisition Growth Teams, Activation Growth Teams, Monetization Growth Teams, Retention Growth Teams, and Expansion Growth Teams.

**Job To Be Done (JTBD):** When capitalized or abbreviated, Job To Be Done refers to Clayton Christensen's Jobs Theory. According to the theory, customers "hire" products or services to help them make progress on a particular job.

**Product-Market Fit (PMF):** The degree to which a product satisfies a strong market demand. PMF can be quantified using the First Impact Success Rate, which represents the percentage of new users who achieve First Impact within a target timeframe.

**Go-To-Market Fit (GTMF):** The degree to which a repeatable go-to-market motion is able to achieve scalable and sustainable growth. "Scalable" refers to the ability to grow quickly, and "sustainable" refers to the ability to achieve favorable unit economics and therefore grow profitably.

# Foreword

After working for decades with some of software's leading brands (Canva, Do-cuSign, HubSpot, and Adobe), I can confidently say that having a great product is necessary but not sufficient. The best products often fail because they cannot establish a meaningful connection with customers. In my experience, the best long-term solution is the "freemium" strategy (which tech insiders call Prod-uct-Led Growth, or PLG). At Canva we used the freemium strategy to build a multi-billion-dollar company. In a nutshell, freemium/PLG means designing a phenomenal product that delivers true value to customers and then giving that product away. At Canva, our strategy is to deliver value first—before we make any effort to monetize. If the free version of the product can deliver enough value, it can market itself, drive user adoption, upsell to the right customers, and fuel expansion. Doing this well (like HubSpot, DocuSign, and Adobe—all PLG power-houses) is difficult. It's also become a critical success factor in the software space, and PLG is expanding beyond software to other industries.

*Freemium* is a defining book for PLG, because not only is Dave Boyce a good thinker and writer, he's also been personally involved in dozens of companies, large and small, using PLG to achieve dramatic growth. His book explains the key tactics and strategies for using product-led principles to transform every stage of your customer's journey, from initial discovery to expansion and advocacy. This holistic perspective is crucial, since PLG is a full-customer-journey growth strategy, not just a tactic for bringing in new customers. Dave also tackles the (sometimes painful) organizational and cultural shifts required to truly embrace a product-led, customer-centric mindset. These are insights you only get from being inside companies while the PLG change is happening.

I found the book's discussion of how freemium strategy/PLG intersects with and supports a traditional sales team particularly valuable. At HubSpot and DocuSign, balancing our PLG strategy with enterprise sales was crucial to our growth. Dave offers nuanced perspectives on when and how to take this hybrid approach.

Maybe you are a startup founder or product team leader looking to build a unicorn PLG company from the ground up, like we've done at Canva. Or maybe you are a leader at an established company seeking new growth. Either way, *Freemium* will help you understand what it takes to get customers excited about your free product, happy to pay for your premium version, and eager to tell others.

*Rob Giglio*
CHIEF CUSTOMER OFFICER, CANVA

# FREEMIUM

## INTRODUCTION

# How "Freemium" Became "Product-Led Growth"

Most people have heard the term *freemium* and understand the basic strategy behind it. A smaller group of tech marketers and leaders are familiar with the evolution of "freemium" into "product-led growth" (PLG). These strategies have supported dozens of initial public offerings (IPOs), thousands of high-growth companies, and the creation of billions of dollars of shareholder value—and yet very few books have been published on the topic. I should know—I did a comprehensive search when I launched the world's first course on freemium/PLG at the masters in business administration (MBA) level.

The word *freemium* was coined in 2006 to describe the strategy of providing a basic product for free and then charging money for extensions and upgrades. Freemium tactics have been in use since the 1980s in shareware—software that was distributed via online bulletin boards and was free to use for an initial evaluation period, after which the user would purchase a license to continue. The term *freemium* was popularized by the venture capitalist Fred Wilson, and it quickly became a handy way to describe early internet successes such as Skype (2003), LinkedIn (2003), Spotify (2008), and Candy Crush Saga (2012).

By 2016, freemium was being "rebranded" as product-led growth, and the concept was expanded to include all the ways software could be reconceived to remove expensive and unnecessary sales and marketing labor by "hiring" the product to execute sales, customer onboarding, and sales expansion tasks previously performed by humans.

This expanded PLG business model grew quickly, as firms discovered the advantages of deploying lower-cost approaches to customer Acquisition, Retention, and Expansion. Dozens of successful companies in the 2010s built their entire enterprises using PLG, including Zoom, Dropbox, DocuSign, HubSpot, Slack, and Atlassian. At the time of this writing, forty companies have gone

1

from startup to IPO using PLG as their primary go-to-market (GTM) strategy, dozens of public companies have verified PLG motions, and dozens more private companies are queued up for IPO. In all, 72% of the Forbes Cloud 100 top private software companies use PLG to "de-labor" their go-to-market processes.[1] Thousands of startups use self-service models (built into their software), for customer Acquisition, onboarding, and retention. In other words, these companies use the product to sell and deploy itself.

Non-software companies are also getting into the game, embedding software, near-field communication (NFC), and internet of things (IoT) functionality so their "smart" products can perform go-to-market tasks without human assistance (for examples of PLG adoption by non-software companies, see Chapter 18: Product-Led Growth Beyond Software).

With the mainstream adoption of artificial intelligence (AI), this trend of de-laboring has intensified. In recent years, AI has begun to execute countless tasks formerly performed by humans. This trend will be as significant in go-to-market initiatives as it is in other parts of the economy.

How broadly can the AI-driven freemium/PLG strategy extend? Will it apply beyond software? Can products sell themselves? Install themselves? Grow their own market share?

Yes, yes, and yes. We see it everywhere: e-commerce, self-service grocery checkout, self-service rental cars, self-service financial advice, self-service developer tools, self-service business-to-business (B2B) software, hands-off industrial reordering, self-service network upgrades, smart tractors, smart building management, smart irrigation systems, smart utilities....

**CASE STUDY**

### Smart Utilities

Utility companies are transforming customer experience through automated go-to-market strategies that streamline sales, renewals, configurations, upsells, and service orders. Automation simplifies these processes, reducing the need for manual interaction.

Smart meters and advanced metering infrastructure offer real-time monitoring and automated readings, allowing providers and customers to easily track energy usage. Energy management systems enable demand response and peak load management, reducing costs and improving reliability through automated fault detection and predictive maintenance.

Advanced data analytics and customizable alerts help customers make automated decisions about energy consumption, systems upgrades, maintenance, and fault recovery. Proactive management of energy use and maintenance saves the provider selling time and saves the customer money without requiring them to be deeply ingrained in analysis. In other words, the product is able to "sell itself." By leveraging automation and smart technologies, utility companies offer a more efficient, cost-effective, and user-friendly service.

To deliver these benefits, utility companies often give away smart monitoring devices, the software that runs them, and in some cases energy capture and storage hardware. This is the freemium strategy, in the sense that free products and services are provided in order to improve customer experience, extend customer loyalty, and more effectively Monetize the relationship via optimized and automated transactions. Customers are charged only for features and services that extend beyond the free base platform.

---

The examples of software and non-software self-service approaches listed above represent a trend toward freemium and product-led growth. AI will accelerate this trend by automating even more of the buying and selling experience.

Most customers don't want to deal with salespeople or stores or the telephone when they're buying something, especially software. They prefer the "self-service" model of doing the research themselves, downloading a (typically) "freemium" version of the product, and discovering for themselves if they can quickly get real value from it. If so, they are often willing to pay for upgrades. Self-service is not only the preferred buying method for most consumers; it is also trending in that direction for business purchasing.

I believe 70% of sales and marketing as we know it today will be replaced by computers. Either AI/freemium/PLG will replace the salesperson, or these technologies will work together with a human to create a better buying and selling experience.

Since buyers want self-service and since the technology to support self-service is improving daily, we should expect to see more of this in the future, not less.

So why write a book on the freemium strategy now? PLG has been with us for fifteen years, and freemium even longer; isn't this entire domain old news?

Definitely not. We are just getting started.

As all trends point toward more self-service, more freemium, more automation, more AI-assisted buying and selling, and more product-led growth, marketers, product leaders, product teams, and business leaders need a comprehensive, authoritative guide to the single most important strategy for bringing tech products to market. We need to deeply understand product-led strategies that de-labor the go-to-market process. We need a framework for implementing products that sell themselves. What can we learn from the forty companies that went public, leveraging PLG? What can we learn from the thousands of private companies currently de-laboring their go-to-market motions (GTMs)[2] using PLG and AI? We need a definitive book that outlines the blueprints, strategies, and tactics for bringing this to life, not only for software startups but also for companies of all types and sizes.

This is why I wrote *Freemium*.

It's crucial that every marketer, business leader, designer, engineer, and product team member understand things like:

- What is the role of freemium in product-led growth strategies?
- How does PLG apply to my industry?
- How can I apply the freemium/self-service idea to lower my marketing, sales, and training costs?
- How can I leverage these capabilities to advance my company and/or my personal career?
- What is the role of AI in freemium strategy, PLG, and self-service?

Business leaders and entrepreneurs need a definitive book with answers to these questions and more. Serious professionals in companies across the economy need the frameworks, tools, and blueprints that have previously been locked away in high-growth companies in Silicon Valley. *Freemium* brings PLG strategies to light and presents an easy-to-follow path for implementing them in your own company.

My personal story with PLG is punctuated with ups and downs. After growing and selling a Software as a Service (SaaS) startup, ProfitLogic, to Oracle in 2005, I spent almost five years watching the B2B world change before my eyes while I continued to work for Oracle—a company that was the embodiment of old B2B paradigms. Tired of watching the freemium revolution from the sidelines, I left Oracle to help found Fundly, an online fundraising platform for nonprofit organizations.

Fundly first built an online application for political fundraising. Our software was used to raise money for candidates in the 2008 U.S. midterm elections, including candidates on both sides of the aisle (e.g., Mitt Romney (R) for President;

Barbara Boxer (D) for Senate). Since political fundraising is seasonal, we also began selling our platform to nonprofit organizations to fill the gaps between political campaigns.

Using direct sales and demos, we landed impressive nonprofit clients, including Habitat for Humanity, Teach for America, the American Heart Association, and the Miami Children's Hospital. Neither political nor nonprofit organizations have large budgets. Our business model, therefore, was to charge a nominal monthly fee for the software and then collect a small percentage of each donation processed.

For political organizations, this worked brilliantly—we launched thousands of campaigns and processed hundreds of millions of dollars. The money we spent paying salespeople to pursue political organizations could be easily recouped in a few months of fundraising on the Fundly platform. For nonprofit organizations, however, the economics worked differently. We expended the same effort selling to nonprofits and helping them launch Fundly campaigns, but the nonprofit fundraising volume was so low that we often failed to recoup our selling expenses.

We were stuck. Should we (a) charge nonprofits a larger monthly subscription fee so that we would make a profit whether or not they raised significant money on our platform? This seemed unlikely to succeed, as nonprofit organizations are notoriously reluctant to commit to large software fees; in many cases they have become accustomed to highly discounted software from other providers like Salesforce and Microsoft.

Or (b) should we invest in personnel to help our customers succeed more reliably with fundraising? This would require paying salaries to customer success people who can directly help nonprofits with fundraising campaigns. But would these campaigns ultimately succeed in raising large amounts of money, like political campaigns?

We decided to take a third route. We removed people from the selling process and the customer success process altogether. Instead of charging *more* money for the platform, we decided to make it *free*.

If we could attract new customers with zero selling effort and help them successfully raise money with zero customer success effort—in other words, make the platform 100% self-service—any amount of fundraising success would generate pure profit for Fundly.

Begin for free, build out a fundraising page for free, get a merchant account for free, connect your social network, market your fundraiser, and spread the word, all for free. Then only pay for success if and when your fundraising efforts succeed.

Freemium.

This worked. Success didn't come immediately, because it took many weeks to adjust the user experience to be simple and intuitive enough. But once we had fine-tuned the experience, new customers could get a fundraising page built, launched, and accepting donations within three minutes.

Before we knew it, people were finding their way to Fundly.com on their own and launching campaigns with no assistance from us. We began optimizing for this freemium journey, and we built a marketing engine to attract self-service customers to the platform. Our freemium business generated thousands of new account starts each day, whereas the nonprofit business (where we still used direct sales) was selling one account at a time.

Our political campaigns had raised a median amount of $150,000 each (with some raising tens of millions of dollars), but these new freemium customers only raised on average $300 each. Since we expended no human effort to acquire or activate these accounts, however, the yields from these small campaigns were pure profit. Furthermore, with almost 10M formal nonprofit organizations in the world and virtually endless possibilities for personal fundraising campaigns, the total addressable market for a freemium fundraising platform was orders of magnitude larger than the political fundraising market.

It had taken almost two years to retool the business, but at this point we didn't have to look for customers; they came looking for us. A freemium offer that was easy and fun to use met the needs of small and large customers alike. At this point, I tracked new customer additions not by managing a sales forecast in customer relationship management (CRM) software but by reading the list that auto-updated as the freemium product itself gained new customers. Contracts, transactions, upgrades, and usage were all managed on a self-service basis. This was much easier than the manual work of selling, implementing, onboarding, and supporting customers manually. I was hooked.

Since that time I have been involved in freemium, enterprise, and hybrid GTM models. I have worked in and invested in dozens of companies, and I have made friends with and learned from people who have built some of the largest and most highly valued freemium-driven companies in the world. I am convinced the future of software belongs to freemium, self-service, and product-led growth—in both software and traditionally non-software markets alike.

In 2021, after selling InsideSales to Aurea Software, I made the decision to go heads-down on freemium, learn everything there is to know about it, network my way into the best examples of PLG, decode its secrets, discover its limitations, and bring it into the light. If freemium/PLG had been that hard for me to figure out—living in the heart of Silicon Valley—how hard must it be to study from afar?

One of the first things I did was call Brigham Young University, where I was an adjunct professor of B2B sales and marketing. After eight years of teaching these topics, I was increasingly convinced that I was teaching the past, not the future. Would BYU support me in developing an MBA-level class on freemium/PLG? They agreed.

Now all I had to do was look up the PLG cases in Harvard Business School's case library, and I was off to the races, right?

Wrong.

The number of PLG cases in Harvard's catalog: 0.

I called Mark Roberge, who teaches at the Harvard Business School and was HubSpot's first chief revenue officer:

Me: *"Is it really true there are no cases on PLG?"*

Mark: *"Yeah. . . . It's pretty much true."*

Me: *"Then how do you teach PLG?"*

Mark: *"There's a Dropbox case you can repurpose. And I've built a simulation you can use. But if you're going to build an entire class, you will need to do some work."*

As it turned out, my class would be the first-ever MBA-level class on PLG.

The cool thing about building an MBA-level class from scratch is that anyone will talk to you. It's been no problem securing guests for the class, and it's been relatively easy to source cases and materials. Building this class, I have been able to meet the brightest minds in PLG and get an up-close view of what they have figured out and how they figured it out. My students have benefitted from this insider view, and now I'm bringing it to you.

This book is full of stories of building freemium companies from the ground up. We have also included stories of mature companies, adding freemium as an additional GTM after already being at scale. We delve into the combination of product-led and sales-led strategies to create what is now known as product-led sales (PLS). And we look at applications of PLG outside software altogether.

I've had the privilege of interviewing dozens of executives who have built these models and succeeded with them at companies like DocuSign, HubSpot, MongoDB, Cloudflare, Figma, John Deere, Stryker, Chatbooks, and more.

And while freemium/PLG in its purest form is not for every company, studying it *should be* mandatory for every manager. Some of the principles outlined in this book will be applicable to your business directly, while some PLG principles will help build understanding of how competitors are operating. Some principles might be adopted wholesale, while others are adapted and applied in specific situations and within specific businesses.

> To understand and compete in nearly every industry today
> requires an understanding of the principles of PLG.

I am grateful to the students, the teachers, the executives, the practitioners, the academics, the coaches, the researchers, the editors, and the designers who helped bring *Freemium* to life.

I hope reading the book is as fun to read as it is practical. And I would love to hear your stories as you apply these principles in your own work.

*XOXO,*
*—dave*

# PART ONE

## How Billion-Dollar Companies Are Built Using Product-Led Growth

# ONE

# Why Freemium Is a Powerful Strategy for Every Company with Digital Products

> Or, "What Is Product-Led Growth, and Why Should I Care?"

Young Turk: *"I think we should go PLG."*

CEO: *"What does that stand for?"*

Young Turk: *"Product-led growth."*

CEO: *"I believe we already do that. I love our product, and we lead with it every day."*

Young Turk: *"No, product-led growth, like where the product sells itself."*

CEO: *"Totally agree."*

Young Turk: *"No, not like 'It jumps off the shelf.' . . . I mean like Zoom or Slack, where there is no salesperson."*

CEO: *"So we should fire our salesforce?"*

Young Turk: *"No . . . but we should give our product away for free."*

CEO: *"Son, that is funny."*

Young Turk: *"Not forever. . . . You give it away for free until people want to pay you for it."*

CEO: *"Like drugs?"*

Young Turk: *"Um. . . . Yes, like drugs."*

CEO: *"Okay, I'm listening."*

Slack became the fastest-growing software company in history by launching a free product that was easy to find and use without consulting a salesperson. The company reached almost $100M in revenue before its first sales hire.[1] Atlassian, the Australian software company, grew to over $300M in revenue without a single salesperson. The less well-known Helsinki company Supermetrics grew to €5M before adding its first salesperson.[2] They scaled to €10M in annual recurring revenue (ARR) with three sales reps, who contributed only 8% of monthly revenue. One year later, they reached €20M ARR with twenty sales reps, who contributed only 19% of monthly revenue. In other words, Supermetrics had a product that could sell itself. Today, the Supermetrics ARR exceeds €50M ARR, with the majority contributed via a digital-first, sales-assist strategy.[3]

> These are exceptions, right?
> The kind of Silicon Valley companies that get lucky
> and hit the right timing to catch a trend?

Not exactly.

Atlassian was founded in 2002. DocuSign, whose growth also depended on a product that was initially free to use, was founded in 2003. Dropbox was founded in 2007, Twilio in 2008, and Zoom in 2011. Thousands of companies have been built using a go-to-market strategy that the world knows as "freemium" but that tech industry insiders now call "product-led growth" (PLG). With a freemium product, the entry-level version is free to use forever. Users are able to solve problems and experience positive impact using the free product, no questions asked. At some point, the user reaches a limitation in the product that can only be unlocked by upgrading to a paid version. This pricing strategy dates back to the shareware services of the 1980s and 1990s, and the name *freemium* was suggested by Jared Lukin, who at the time was working for a company in Fred Wilson's venture capital portfolio. "I hope the name sticks, because I love it," commented Wilson.[4]

Freemium/PLG has grown dramatically since then. The venture capital firm OpenView tracks over three hundred product-led growth companies as of 2023.[5] Seventy-two percent of the Forbes Cloud 100 software companies in 2023 have PLG initiatives.[6] And 91% of software companies surveyed by Gainsight in 2022 indicated that they intended to increase their investment in PLG.[7]

### Freemium Forces You to Know Your Customers Better

Upon launching a new product, the first objective is to establish what is known as Product-Market Fit (PMF). PMF is generally understood as the degree to which a product satisfies a strong market demand.[8]

When a product is sold and implemented by fallible humans, the assessment of PMF can be clouded with false positives. Human salespeople are good at convincing customers to buy, and customer success people are good at helping customers succeed with a product—even when the product itself falls short of expectations.

In the case of these false positives, a product might indeed be sold and implemented (a positive signal of PMF) but then not renewed at the first or second anniversary (a negative signal). These dynamics are normal and are to be expected. Salespeople, after all, work on commission. One can imagine a conversation between salesperson and customer along the following lines:

Customer: "Can your product do _____?"
Salesperson: "That's a good question. I never really thought about it . . . but I suppose it could. Yes! I see your point—I think this could work!"

In this scenario, the salesperson is being creative. The use case proposed by the customer is clearly not the use case for which the product was designed, but the salesperson is designing her way to making it work in the service of the customer. And so the deal closes, but it carries with it expectations around customization and support that the product and customer success (CS) organizations will struggle to meet. This puts additional pressure on the customer experience and on any future contract renewal.

By contrast, product-led purchases include no salesperson. In PLG, the customer uses the product on his own, with no one whispering in his ear, coaching him, or helping him. And he does this all before purchasing—a sort of pre-purchase evaluation. Each step of consideration, activation, and usage is self-directed and opt-in. If at any stage while using the free product, the product does not live up to expectations, the customer may opt out. By the time a PLG customer decides to commit to a paid version of the software, he has already assessed whether the product is a good fit for his needs. Since customers who purchase via PLG have the opportunity to use the product and assess fit prior to purchasing, they are less vulnerable to future attrition.

The advantages of launching a new product using PLG are demonstrable. First, no salespeople are required, with their attendant salaries and commissions. This saves money on sales compensation, but it also avoids the complexities of recruiting, training, and motivating salespeople to sell a new product. Customers acquired via PLG are also less likely to be attrition risks.

Finally (and for some this is most important), a large base of free or "low-commitment" customers is a perfect testing ground for fine-tuning new features, onboarding journeys, and in-app workflows. Many companies with large enterprise books of business explicitly *also* maintain a large base of PLG customers for this very reason. These low-paying customers are highly forgiving. They partner well. Their users and admins care. This is a perfect development and refinement ground for building amazing products.

> "A large base of PLG customers is the lifeblood of the company. Protect it. Grow it. The PLG of today is the enterprise of tomorrow."
>
> —Anil Somaney, SaaS executive (Splunk, Cloudflare, Chargebee)

The rise of PLG as a strategy for bringing products to market without dependence on direct sales is partially due to advances in software's ability to distribute itself and partially motivated by economic advantages to the selling company, but it also supports a fundamental shift in customers' preferred buying processes.

### Younger Generations Prefer Not to Buy from Salespeople

Today's buyers behave differently than a generation ago. Gen Alpha, Gen Z, and Millennials have little interest in dealing with salespeople.[9] They have everything they need to discover, evaluate, try, purchase, and upgrade their products and services.

What would a Gen Alpha need from a salesperson? They grew up with smartphones, the internet, Alexa, Siri, Reddit, TikTok, and Discord. They're tied into a whole host of social channels for information and validation that goes beyond what any formal marketing or sales channel could deliver.

They don't trust marketing and sales anyway.

When these generations (and digital-savvy members of preceding generations) want to buy or consume something, they go directly to sources they trust: their peers and social media influencers/reviewers.

And then they try it out/try it on/trial it on their own.

If they like it, they keep it. Otherwise, they drop it like it's hot.

This is true for clothes, appliances, entertainment, consumables, food, travel, technology, furniture, cars, sports equipment—virtually every category you can imagine. So forward-thinking producers of these products have figured out how to meet current generations where they live, and nowhere is this truer than in software.

Ask a member of Gen Z about the software on her phone, her laptop, her gaming console. . . . Ask her about the software she uses for her job, her school, her hobbies, her side gig. . . . You will likely not find a single piece of software that was purchased from a salesperson.

> So what does this mean for the future of
> purchasing? For the future of selling?

Given the current state of technology, it will not come as a surprise that products are smart.

- Google and Apple know where you are at all times, because you permit them to track this.
- Your Tesla knows where it is at all times.
- Alexa is monitoring conversations for keywords.
- Your Apple Watch anticipates your next move and makes suggestions (what to swipe, what to type, what to listen to, where to drive, when to set an alarm, etc.).
- ChatGPT can follow directions, make adjustments per your instructions, and carry out tasks at a college-educated level.
- As data collection, data management, and artificial intelligence (AI) capabilities have become more modular and easier to use, their use has extended well beyond large tech companies. Companies of all sizes now incorporate intelligence and data collection into their products.

So if products are smart, can they sell themselves?

Of course they can! And if you thought that was true today, just hold on to your seat. It all starts with bottom-up adoption of a free product, leading to monetization of individuals, teams, and enterprise accounts.

**CASE STUDY**

**How Zoom Beat WebEx and GoToMeeting**

"Should we hop on a WebEx?"

"Let's schedule a GoToMeeting."

In 2017, the terms *WebEx* and *GoToMeeting* were synonymous with videoconferencing. The choice of term depended only on the platform that was standard at your company.

WebEx was a product of Cisco, and in early 2017, LogMeIn bought GoToMeeting from Citrix for approximately $4B.

Competitors like BlueJeans, Join.me, UberConference, and 8x8 had been fighting for share in the videoconferencing market, but they had been unable to unseat the two reigning leaders, which had essentially split the enterprise videoconferencing market.

Zoom was also a competitor, and for WebEx and GoToMeeting they were easy to ignore—until they weren't.

Zoom's entry price, after all, was "free," and even its top paid plans were only $19.99 per user per month.

Zoom's strategy was based on ease of use and organic, bottom-up adoption by end users. Within one month of launching, Zoom's free and-easy-to-use video conferencing service had four hundred thousand users. Five months later, its user base was over one million. Most of these users had adopted the free version of the product, but that was not the end of the story.

The first time I used Zoom, I was pulling into a parking lot outside my dentist's office, early for my appointment, but just in time to dial into an executive meeting at which I was expected.

When I looked at the meeting on my phone's calendar, I realized that my company had recently switched our remote meeting software from GoToMeeting to Zoom. To my discredit, I had not yet created a Zoom account, nor installed the app on my phone.

**FIGURE 1.1.    Zoom Pricing**

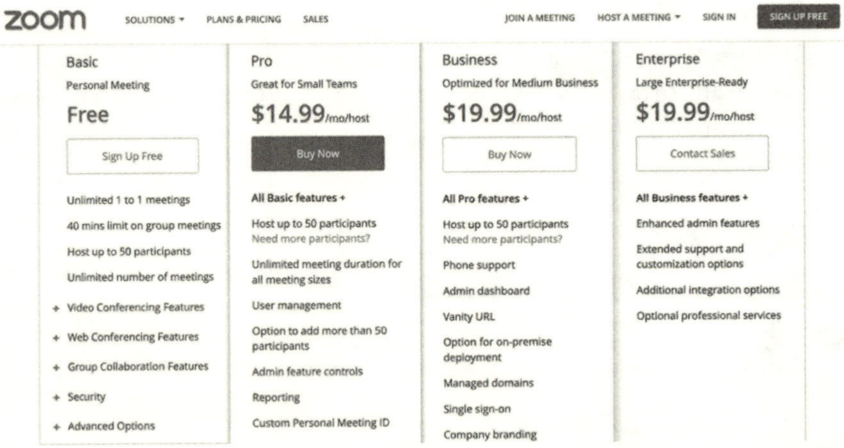

*Source:* "Plans and Pricing," Zoom, archived Feburary 1, 2017, https://web.archive.org/web/20170201052319/zoom.us/pricing

"Great," I thought to myself. "Once again I have pushed the limits of time management too far, and I'm going to miss this executive meeting entirely."

I knew from past experience that installing a video conferencing app was a pain to accomplish on a laptop—not to mention on a phone. And who knew how much more difficult it would be if I didn't have an account at all?

15 seconds later I was on the call—fully dialed in, with perfect video and sound.

"What?"

"Video conferencing never works that well. And I'm on a mobile phone outside my dentist's office!"

The only words I could think of to describe this experience were, "It just works!"

At the time, WebEx and GoToMeeting had multi-year contracts with most of the Fortune 500, and their enterprise, security, and network functionality was robust. But the software was not easy for end users to use. It was this opening that Zoom exploited.

Since Zoom was built from the beginning for end users, and since the bulk of Zoom's early user base were free users—tenants at will—the experience had to be perfect to compel these freemium users to remain on the platform and eventually upgrade to a paid plan. Zoom's ease of use, user delight, and zero-friction onboarding allowed it to break free of the pack of competitors in the mid-market. Within five years of launching, Zoom had eclipsed both market leaders.

**FIGURE 1.2.**   Video Conferencing Software Market, 2016–2019

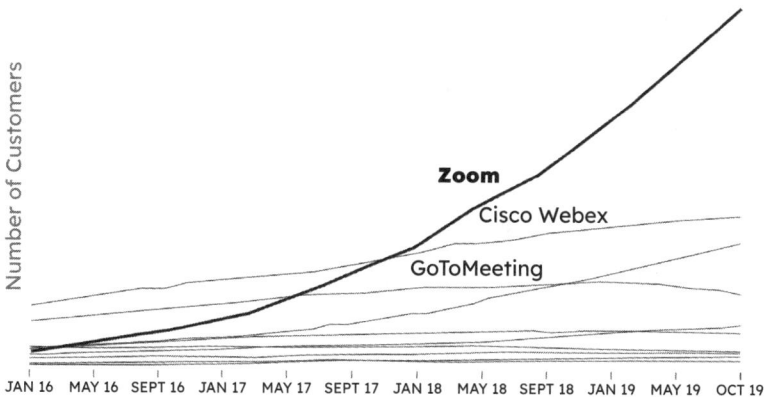

*Source:* "How Zoom Conquered Video Conferencing," Forbes, effective April 14, 2022, https://www .forbes.com/sites/rogerdooley/2020/09/30/how-zoom-conquered-video-conferencing/

Zoom's mission statement was simple: "Make Video Communications Frictionless."

The source of Zoom's ascendency can reliably be attributed to its successful execution of this mission. Current generations barely remember WebEx and GoTo-Meeting; they "hop on a Zoom." Zoom's revenue growth accelerated during COVID-19 and eventually topped $1B and 50% market share,[10] but the origins of Zoom's success clearly predate the COVID pandemic, and they are firmly rooted in the freemium strategy.

---

## Freemium's Flipped Model: "Seek First to Create Value, Then to Extract Value"

Can you think of software products you use today that you were able to discover, launch, and use, all without assistance from another human?

Perhaps you thought of Google Drive, Slack, Calendly, DocuSign, Notion, Netflix, Instagram, or Superhuman. Each of these products goes to market via freemium, and each embraces a core tenet of that strategy:

Seek first to create value, then to extract value.

At the beginning of the user's experience with these products, there is no emphasis on contracts or payment. The sole focus during the Activation phase is helping a user achieve what they came for: "Seek first to create value." Once a user has become convinced that the product is indeed meeting their needs and creating value—and only then—an opportunity arises to begin paying for the service. In some instances this Monetization event happens after a user has been realizing value for months or even years. The freemium strategy lies at the core of most PLG customer Acquisition approaches.

## How Large Companies Leverage PLG for Hypergrowth

Of the seventy-two Forbes Cloud 100 private software companies that have a verified PLG motion, 100% *also* have an enterprise offering, which they sell and deploy to the largest companies on the planet. Among the companies on this list that have PLG *and* enterprise motions are:

- Stripe ($95B valuation)
- Databricks ($38B valuation)

- Plaid ($13B valuation)

- Snyk ($8.6B valuation)

- Intercom ($1.27B valuation)

- Lucid ($3B valuation)

In addition to these private companies, dozens of multi-billion-dollar public companies have been built using PLG, including:[11]

- Atlassian ($47B)

- Snowflake ($40B)

- Datadog ($29B)

- Zoom ($26B)

- MongoDB ($17B)

- HubSpot ($13B)

All of these companies also sell to enterprises. All boast customer contracts stretching up to over $1M. Yet all go to market using a product-led strategy, where the product is *able* to sell itself.

Going to market via PLG vs. selling to enterprise-scale companies is not an either-or decision. PLG is used by small companies and large companies alike. PLG is used for new products and mature products. Product-led strategies can be used to acquire small customers as well as large customers. Enterprise-scale companies employ both product-led and human-led go-to-market (GTM) motions, often for the same product. PLG can also be used to facilitate upgrades, renewals, and Expansions—even when the initial sale is completed by a salesperson. In this book we explore all these angles, outlining when and where PLG makes sense and how it fits into a holistic GTM approach.

### Can Freemium Apply to Non-Digital Products?

Giving away products to attract new customers is nothing new, and it is not limited to digital products. Gyms and yoga studios give away the first month free. Consultants give away initial workshops. Coffee shops give away free Wi-Fi, manufacturers give away sample products, and restaurants attract new customers via various samples and promotions (see the Oak Wood Fire Grill case study in Chapter 18).

Innovations in PLG, however, have brought new possibilities and new sophistication to the strategy.

Implementing PLG can lead to significant organizational changes. For example, if your company's revenue is driven primarily by sales, you may want to brace yourself. Today your company may manage a sales bookings forecast, working with the head of sales to ensure enough pipeline to cover the forecast for this quarter. You may actively consider whether you have a large enough sales team, carrying enough quota to hit future targets. You may apply human effort to customer onboarding, product adoption, subscription renewals, and Expansion sales. But adopting the techniques in this book could shift portions of that traditional, human-led, go-to-market strategy to be more product-led.

Even with non-digital products, self-service and e-commerce can play a large role in acquiring new customers. Content-rich e-commerce experiences can incorporate interactive demos, AI agents, and calculators/estimators/configurators to help a buyer better understand the implications and benefits of purchase. These tactics not only help a buyer along the buying journey, they also "de-labor" portions of the customer Acquisition process. Implementation, installation, and adoption can similarly be accelerated via digital tutorials and AI agents. And embedded technology—including software, artificial intelligence, near-field communications, and internet connectedness—can allow your products to be "smarter." Smart products can have awareness of where they are, how they are being used, and when to suggest an upsell, extension, renewal, repair, or other value-added service. Consider these examples:

- Smart TVs enable content subscriptions.
- Smart exercise equipment bundles in content subscriptions.
- Electric vehicles deliver new features via software.
- Agricultural machinery tracks movements, optimizes efficiency, collects data on soil conditions, and sells aggregated data back to farmers (see the John Deere case study in Chapter 18).
- Building management systems regulate and optimize energy consumption.
- Irrigation systems detect leaks, regulate water consumption, and suggest maintenance and upgrade schedules.

If you are in the software industry, these dynamics have already played out. Sales-led organizations are struggling with the cost of acquiring new customers and expanding revenue. In some cases these companies are incorporating the same freemium and PLG tactics used by their competitors as a way of defending their market share (see the SAP case study in Chapter 17).

If you are in a non-software industry, the changes may not be immediate, but they are coming. Over the first four chapters of this book, I hope to demonstrate that aspects of product-led growth will feature not only in software but in all industries (see non-software examples in Chapter 18).

If I succeed, you will want to read the rest of the book, grab your management team, and have a heart-to-heart chat. You will want to rally managers from across your team to help you embrace your product-led future.

## How to Read this Book If You Are a CEO or General Manager:

You can skip Part Two, but I recommend you read Parts One, Three, and Four. Here's a quick overview:

### PART ONE: HOW BILLION-DOLLAR COMPANIES ARE BUILT USING PRODUCT-LED GROWTH

This section covers the theory and frameworks of PLG. We include plenty of re-al-world examples of high-growth public and private companies that have proven these theories in the real world.

### PART TWO: PRODUCT-LED GROWTH IMPLEMENTATIONS AND TACTICS (OPTIONAL)

These tactical chapters are written at a level of detail appropriate for the teams that will implement PLG in your company. Check chapter titles and descriptions and read only the chapters that interest you.

### PART THREE: PRODUCT-LED GROWTH FOR LARGE ENTERPRISES

In this section we discuss how, when, and why PLG is deployed within enter-prise-scale companies. We cover not only the mechanics of adding PLG to an existing sales-led model but also the politics of the transformation as well as the dynamics of operating multiple GTMs in parallel.

### PART FOUR: THE NEXT GENERATION OF PRODUCT-LED GROWTH

If you are a forward-looking non-software executive, you may want to consider how and when PLG models will apply to your industry. Part Four delves into next-generation applications of PLG today and in the future.

At the end of each chapter is a "Manager Minute" page, where we ask you to reflect on questions about your product or business. Be thoughtful and write down answers to these questions—your notes will help you evaluate the current state of your business and how to advance your company in the direction of PLG.

## How to Read This Book If You Are in Product, Marketing, or Engineering

Part Two is where you will likely live.

### PART ONE: HOW BILLION-DOLLAR COMPANIES ARE BUILT USING PRODUCT-LED GROWTH

Even though Part Two is where the meat is, you should probably not skip Part One. Part One sets up the argument for PLG, and it will be a useful source of information when communicating with upper management.

### PART TWO: PRODUCT-LED GROWTH IMPLEMENTATION AND TACTICS

Part Two contains details on how to implement, measure, and optimize PLG within your business. You may want to read Part Two twice.

### PARTS THREE AND FOUR (OPTIONAL)

These sections describe specific situations that may or may not apply to you (PLG within large enterprises and PLG for non-software companies). Read these as applicable.

Be sure to write down your answers to all the questions on the "Manager Minute" pages—doing so will help you reflect on your own journey.

If you are launching a PLG effort from scratch, you will want to surround yourself with resources and experts beyond the scope of this book. Seek knowledge and expertise from the best books and guides, and don't be shy about asking for help from someone who has been there before (see the Resources section, Appendix A).

## Chapter 1 Summary

- Gen Alpha, Gen Z, and Millennials are less interested in dealing with salespeople. Everything they need to discover, evaluate, try, purchase, and upgrade their products and services they prefer to find online.

- These "online-only" customer purchasing preferences have carried over from business-to-consumer (B2C) to business-to-business (B2B), opening a huge opportunity for companies (especially B2B SaaS) companies to build self-service purchase options for their products.

- Large companies like Dropbox ($9B valuation), Zoom ($20B valuation), and Slack ($26B valuation) were built from the ground up with a freemium go-to-market strategy oriented to "end-user-first/self-service."

- These changes are also coming to non-software markets, where intelligence and ancillary services are increasingly bundled.

## Manager Minute

Thinking about your own company, take time to reflect on the following questions:

1. In what ways have customer purchasing processes changed in our market?

_____

_____

_____

2. How are end users participating in the selection and purchase of our products? Our competitors' products?

_____

_____

_____

**3.** Where in our market do I see freemium/product-led growth gaining traction?

_____

_____

_____

**TWO**

# The Paradigm-Shifting Cost Savings and Customer Experience of Product-Led Growth

> How Digital Products Now Seamlessly
> Do the Work of Marketing, Sales,
> Onboarding, and Customer Success

**Case Study: How Atlassian Built a $3B Company with No Sales Force**

At the time of this writing, Atlassian is a $47B software company with $3B in revenue, headed toward $10B. Revenue has grown 30%+ year over year for twenty years. Atlassian's growth chart is a work of art (Figure 2.1).

> "You have to believe in the product-led system. Could we grow faster with sales led? Perhaps for a time. But we built a system that is consistent and long-term. Next milestone is $10B. And I sleep fine at the end of each quarter."
>
> —Cameron Deatsch, Atlassian chief revenue officer (CRO)

How many CROs of $3B revenue companies "sleep fine at the end of each quarter?" And how many companies have a growth pattern this consistent? How does Atlassian do it?

The answer is that growth is "programmed into" Atlassian's business model itself. The product is designed to facilitate growth, and everything else centers around that.

FIGURE 2.1.    Atlassian Growth

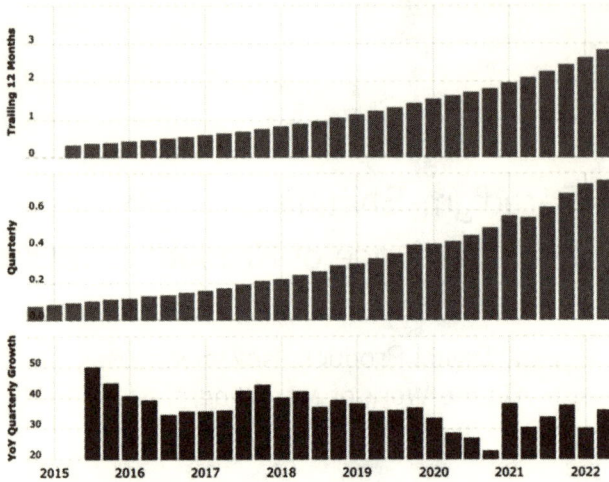

*Source:* SEC Filings

So how do people buy Atlassian's products?

Point and click.

Although Atlassian sells enterprise software—often costing the customer over $1M per year—it all starts with an individual user or manager making a decision to set up an account and begin using it for their own team. These contracts grow over time as usage spreads within a given company, until the aggregate usage reaches its natural limit.

In 2002, when Atlassian was founded, the product-led growth (PLG) business model was novel. Co-founders Mike Cannon-Brookes and Scott Farquhar had the idea of building a tool for software developers, but they had no money. They realized that building a successful company meant two things:

1. They had to quickly create useful tools—to win market share.

2. They had to find a way to sell them—without paying for a sales team.

Since they were themselves developers, Cannon-Brookes and Farquhar saw the need for developer-specific tools around issue tracking and collaboration. They built these functions into their first two tools—Jira and Confluence.

No one had built project management or collaboration tools for software developers before, and the founders knew from their own work that other developers would want these tools. All they had to do was get programmers to try it. They decided to use a freemium plan to allow people to test out the tools risk-free and realize for themselves how useful they were.

This model allowed people to start using the tools quickly for free before converting to paid plans. Without sales overhead, Atlassian onboarded more customers and grew revenue. Atlassian's rapidly growing revenue base allowed it to start acquiring other software companies and adding to its developer offerings very early in the company's lifetime.[1]

Atlassian is famous for not having a sales team until it was over $300M in revenue. Even now, with a sales team, its salespeople are not allowed to speak to non-customers.

*What? How does it get new customers, then?*
*The same way it always has.*
*Point and click.*

Cameron Deatsch had served in a number of executive roles at Atlassian before, but he had never been a CRO at Atlassian or anywhere else. When Atlassian decided it needed a CRO and asked Cameron to take the role, he agreed, and he brought to the job a completely different perspective.

Atlassian's customers prefer to experience the product before buying and purchase only what they need when they need it. So, Cameron decided not to disrupt that model but rather to build on top of it.

Instead of hiring a traditional sales team, he assembled a group of people he calls "advocates." Advocates are not allowed to sell to non-customers—they can only engage with existing customers who already have an annual contract value of $30K or more. That is true even if the potential customer's name is Chevron, even if they are already spending $5K, and even if they are waving a big check.

Once an advocate is engaged, the topic becomes how to scale the existing success. Advocates have four sales "plays" only, and each play is optimized for a minimum annual contract value of $100K. The thinking is, if it is easy to renew and expand usage online, then let people do it online. We will engage in the things that are worth our time—the large, enterprise-scale deployments.

Despite what one might expect, Altassian's advocates never discount . . . ever. Even for the large enterprise contracts, advocates sell off the price list. If a customer wants a discount at the end of the quarter, Atlassian walks away until the next quarter, when that customer can choose to buy at full price or not at all.

What in the world are they selling—the fountain of youth?

Yes, the product is good. It has to be. Because of how the company was built, the product has had to carry its weight from day one. It has to be easy to find, easy to use, easy to purchase, and easy to expand. Atlassian built that into the business model as a default requirement, and because it hasn't relented, all Atlassian products follow this pattern.[2]

## How PLG Became the Dominant Go-to-Market (GTM) Model for Emerging Software Companies

Atlassian is an early pioneer in PLG, but we've seen dozens of examples since. Basecamp was founded in 2004. Then Dropbox (2007), Zendesk (2007), Yammer (2008) . . .

Some other companies[3] to consider:

- Twilio ($3.83B revenue, 34.64% year-over-year growth)[4]
- Canva ($1B revenue, 42.86% YOY growth)[5]
- Slack ($974M revenue, 39.74% YOY growth)[6]
- Airtable ($100M revenue, 198.51% YOY growth)[7]
- Monday.com ($519M revenue, 68.43% YOY growth)[8]
- Asana ($547M revenue, 44.60% YOY growth)[9]
- Notion ($43.5M revenue, 35.94% YOY growth)[10]
- Cazoo ($1.4B revenue, 182.74% YOY growth)[11]
- MongoDB ($1.3B revenue, 46.95% YOY growth)[12]

Each of these companies acquires some or all customers without a sales team. Each is currently worth over $1B, and each is still growing at over 30%.

In the world of enterprise software, high-paid sales reps and systems integrators once controlled the entire distribution chain. Now "enterprise" software has transformed from being sold by expensive salespeople to being sold over the internet.

In 2016, OpenView Partners dubbed this strategy "product-led growth"—a moniker that subsequently became immensely popular.[13]

> *"Product-led growth is a go-to-market strategy, whereby product usage drives customer Acquisition, Retention, and Expansion."*
>
> —OpenView Venture Partners

---

**CASE STUDY**

**Technology-Powered Life**

Imagine the following scenario.

You wake up to your alarm.

- "Hey, Siri. Turn off alarm."

You get dressed for a workout.

- Peloton suggests your workout for this morning.

- You join a group and take a ride.

- You review stats from your ride, compare them to others in your group, check your max heart rate, and towel off.

You walk into the bathroom.

- "Alexa, play NPR."

- "Would you like to thank your Amazon driver for the most recent delivery?"

- "Yes."

- "Done. Now playing NPR."

You go downstairs, where coffee is waiting, freshly brewed according to the programmed schedule.

Now you walk into your home office.

- "Alexa, shuffle music by Stan Getz."

You fire up your laptop, and . . .

- You check your Slack.

- You check your email using Google Workspace.

- You check your LinkedIn.

- You review summaries of yesterday's calls using Grain.

- You get ready for your first meeting on Zoom.

- How many of these software products were sold to you by a salesperson?

  Likely zero.

  How many were sold to your company by a salesperson?

  Also, likely zero (unless you have a large company).

  How many were installed using help from another human?

  Again, zero.

  How many of these products required personal training?

  Zero.

---

In the entire scenario above, it is likely that not a single software product was sold or implemented by a human. Of the nine pieces of software, five are business-to-business (B2B) software: Slack, Google Workspace, LinkedIn, Grain, Zoom. In each case, you found the product on your own, fully implemented it, and trained yourself to use it with no human assistance.

This is the PLG revolution.

*How did this come to be?*
*Where does it go from here?*
*Why must the rest of the world sit up and take notice?*
*If my company is not doing these things, are there lessons I can apply, even if it*
*didn't start that way? Even if my company is not a software company at all?*

If you work in a company that did not build your success using PLG, count yourself among the 99% majority. Most of the world's successful and valuable companies were built in an era that predated PLG.

Consider, however . . .

Business dynamics are shifting, and your company will be vulnerable if you ignore these developments. The ability of generative artificial intelligence (AI) to provide a helpful self-service option to virtually every sales and support interaction only expands the possibilities. These trends will continue, and they will eventually become relevant to every segment of every industry in every corner of the world.

✘ Not just software companies.

✘ Not just technology companies.

✘  Not just companies in Silicon Valley.

✔  Every product company in the world.

When business dynamics shift this significantly, leaders must sit up and take notice. Fundamental shifts create both opportunity and peril, depending on businesses' ability to respond. Some companies at the time of the Industrial Revolution were able to pivot and leverage new means of production to send them on new and ascendant trajectories. Others were overtaken by competitors, bankrupted and forgotten.

The PLG revolution has auspicious parallels with historical business shifts that had the potential to make or break businesses. We present these here for your consideration: The Industrial Revolution, E-commerce, and Cloud Computing.

## Why PLG Is Software's Industrial Revolution

### THE INDUSTRIAL REVOLUTION

Before the first Industrial Revolution, people accomplished much of their work via manual labor. They separated cotton, weaved fabric, and manufactured goods using only simple tools. Via clever innovation, these same people discovered they could make their lives easier by using machines to do those jobs. Machines' output was also more uniform, and maintaining and operating machines cost less than paying for manual labor.

Whole classes of jobs were created to design, build, operate, and maintain machines. People didn't lose their jobs—they got better jobs.

### E-COMMERCE

In July of 1995, Jeff Bezos boxed up and shipped the first book ever sold on Amazon.com. That same year, Pierre Omidyar, a software programmer, started coding a simple web site he called AuctionWeb; it eventually became eBay. Shopping would never be the same. Forrester forecasts the US online shopping market will exceed $1.6 trillion of the total $5.5 trillion in US retail by 2027, accounting for 29% of the total market.[14]

E-commerce is revolutionary because of accessibility and ease. These are the same products, filling the same needs, but now they are far easier to access. In a world where e-commerce allows me to make a few clicks on my phone and have something delivered to my front door on the same day, the major innovation is ease.

### CLOUD COMPUTING

In the late 1990s, business-to-consumer (B2C) e-commerce was accelerating, and B2B e-commerce was close behind. If we could use the internet for B2B e-commerce, why couldn't we use it for B2B functionality beyond purchasing? How about resource planning? Logistics optimization? Sales funnel management?

In 2000, I joined ProfitLogic as its first head of product and marketing. We used hosted computing infrastructure to run optimization models for retail pricing at the stock keeping unit level by individual store. Also in 2000, we began seeing billboards for a new company, Salesforce.com, which had built a customer relationship management (CRM) platform in a hosted environment. Industry analysts initially called this software delivery model "application service providers," and then in 2001, the term *SaaS* emerged (Software as a Service) and quickly became ubiquitous.[15]

ProfitLogic's decision to host our software paid off, and in 2005 we sold ProfitLogic to Oracle, where we became one of its very first SaaS offerings.

Early on it wasn't always clear that SaaS would be triumphant. Many industry observers doubted the potential of SaaS:

> *"SaaS can be used for B2C and simple B2B purchasing—but not complex, highly configured, and negotiated B2B purchase contracts."*
> *"SaaS can deliver isolated functionality, but it will not replace highly connected systems within corporate data centers."*
> *"SaaS cannot be trusted with proprietary or sensitive data— that will be the limiting factor for how far it can spread."*
> *"SaaS will apply to highly developed applications. It will not be able to meet the needs of custom development."*

Of course, these voices were wrong. SaaS has indeed become the primary delivery mechanism for delivering software services and benefits to most business segments.

And just like e-commerce, nothing seems to have changed: same product, same benefits. But also like e-commerce, the major innovation here is ease. Because B2B software has become easier and quicker to access from anywhere, the world will never go back.

So what do **cloud computing**, **e-commerce**, and the **Industrial Revolution** have to do with PLG?

- **Cloud computing** democratizes access to powerful B2B functionality, and PLG further democratizes access by eliminating the need to deal with salespeople or commit to minimum contract sizes. PLG makes it easier for end users to access solutions to their problems where, when, and in the quantity they need.

- Similar to **e-commerce**, PLG makes achieving impact easier—customers can even achieve impact before purchase, and they can do so without help from sales or implementation personnel. Just as e-commerce eliminates the inconvenience of traveling to a store and navigating the physical space, PLG eliminates the inconvenience associated with purchasing: salespeople, contract minimums, manual installations, etc.

- And similar to the first **industrial revolution**, PLG "hires" the product to do jobs previously performed by humans. PLG products do their own selling, their own onboarding, their own success tracking, and their own Expansion. In this sense, we have become more efficient, and we have also become more humane.

*Why more humane?*

Prior to PLG, GTM professionals filled their days with the details of orders, contracts, pricing, terms, features, and other mundane topics. With the product now handling many of those tasks independently, the same GTM professionals can focus on higher-order aspects like strategy, process, and priorities. They can turn more of their attention to how customers achieve and scale impact.

In software's Industrial Revolution, workers add value by skillfully operating the machines rather than being the machines.

Imagine a world where a software salesperson is able to focus on how her customer can achieve impact and scale it across the company. Imagine that the contracting is automated, the implementations are seamless, and the salesperson's focus is mostly on identifying additional use cases for the product to deliver maximum impact. This salesperson isn't a paper pusher. She isn't chasing contracts and signatures, explaining features, or negotiating terms. She isn't a human order-getter. This salesperson is a strategic partner. The software demonstrates its own functionality, manages its own trial, and communicates its own terms. Purchasing is automated. Renewals and Expansions are automated. Access, provisioning, and scaling are automated. So this salesperson focuses on the big picture. She partners with the managers and executives who are making business decisions. She helps align the software with the Jobs To Be Done in her customers' businesses. She advises on where, when, and why her product might be the right answer to advance her customers' objectives.

Now consider the salesperson's colleague in customer success (CS). If the product is easy to install and use, with self-service being the standard, where does the CS professional spend his time? He's not managing the details of an implementation or setting up and provisioning access to the product. He's not teaching people how to use the software's features or helping them get oriented—the software does that on its own. So what does the CS professional do? He coaches. He advises. He identifies additional opportunities to leverage the software to achieve impact for the customer. He educates his customers on best practices and helps them benchmark their performance against industry peers. This CS professional is not a mechanic—he is a consultant, a concierge. His activities focus on scaling impact across the company.

> "Product-led growth is the de-laboring of the GTM process. It's about making it as easy as possible for users to find, understand, adopt and achieve value with your product, without the need for a lot of manual intervention from your sales and marketing teams."
>
> —OpenView Venture Partners

In this world, knowledge workers are allowed to play at a level equal to their capability. Rather than serving as a human conveyor belt to fill in for processes that haven't been automated, they now let the product do what it was designed to do, while they direct, optimize, and orchestrate. These professionals truly leverage their knowledge of business and strategy to create a better experience for their customers. They let the software take care of itself.

More efficient.

More humane.

Better experience for the customer.

Better experience for knowledge workers.

Software's industrial revolution.

PLG.

## Chapter 2 Summary

- Product that can sell itself (product-led growth, or PLG) is a revolution similar to the industrial revolution.

- Dozens of billion-dollar-plus software companies have been built using PLG as a primary go-to-market strategy.

- Whether businesses produce software or not, they can likely make finding, buying, and succeeding with products easier by taking advantage of self-service, simplification, and automation.

## Manager Minute

Thinking about your own company, take time to reflect on the following questions:

1. I could "de-labor" my current go-to-market process in the following areas:

 

 

 

2. I am watching the following competitors in my space, whose product is either (a) easier to find, (b) easier to use, or (c) both:

 

 

 

3. If I were starting a new business to compete with my own, I would leverage the ideas in this chapter in the following ways:

 

 

 

# THREE

# First Principles of Product-Led Growth: Empathy, Generosity, and Metrics

> ## How Freemium Products Are Built Differently Than Typical Enterprise Software

*"How much do I owe you?"*
Nothing.
*"When do I pay you?"*
Never.
*"Wait. That's a business?"*
Yes, it is.

Product-led growth (PLG) companies lead with generosity. They seek first to create value, then to extract value. PLG businesses are engineered from the ground up with this philosophy at the center.

Think of the first time you used:

- Zoom
- Slack
- Calendly
- HubSpot
- Google Suite
- Bill.com

What did you think of the experience?

I admit, the first time I used Bill.com I approached it reluctantly. I am not an enthusiastic software user. Having spent more than my fair share of late nights poring over spreadsheets as a young analyst, I respect the functionality of software. But I am also wary of that functionality. Functionality can suck you into black holes of perfectionism. I have spent hours on the details of perfecting a design, a calculation, or an automation—and when considering using Bill.com to manage invoices, I was concerned that the same thing might happen. I was sure Bill.com could be set up with all sorts of automations and configurations and integrations that in theory would make my life easier—once I figured out how to use them. But at that moment I just wanted to set up an invoice that could be paid via electronic funds transfer (EFT)—that's all I needed.

I created an account on Bill.com. I connected my bank account using a seamless authentication workflow. I used the standard template to build an invoice, and within five minutes I had sent the invoice to my client. *Voilà!*

Is more functionality available on Bill.com? Of course it is. And since that first experience, I've come back to the product to figure out recurring billing, automatic payments, and other advanced features. But when I just needed to create a single invoice, payable by EFT, Bill.com made it easy.

### Why Freemium Products Are Built for the End User, Not the Buyer

PLG businesses are built from a different vantage point. They are built expressly for the end user.

*"Isn't that true of all software?"*
Patently not.

Many business-to-business (B2B) software products evolve in such a way that the considerations of the *buyer* are prioritized over the needs of the *user*. After all, in order to sell software, B2B salespeople must identify a decision-maker who has the budget and authority to make a purchase on behalf of their company. This person is the buyer of the software—but not necessarily the user.

The dynamic can play out as follows (illustrative):

VP:  *"General Mills is interested in our software."*
CEO:  *"No way! That's amazing."*
VP:  *"They just need us to upgrade a few things to be 'enterprise ready.' But they are willing to pay $10M per year if we can make that happen for them."*
CEO:  *"Okay—we would do pretty much anything for $10M. What's their list?"*
VP:  *"Here is their list:*
   • *GDPR compliance*

- *CCPA compliance*
- *SOC2 compliance*
- *Tiered administration permissions*
- *Single sign-on with their core system*

*That's it!"*

CEO: *"That seems pretty reasonable for a customer of that size, right?"*

VP:   *"For sure. Any enterprise company will want these same features."*

Harmless enough, right?

Wrong.

Now X% of the development budget goes toward developing new features for this $10M customer. And Y% of ongoing engineering is pre-committed to supporting, maintaining, and upgrading these new features. Then enterprise customer #2 comes and asks for flexible reporting and archived logging—also reasonable enterprise requirements. Another X% and Y%.

Before you know it, more than 50% of engineering's capacity is *pre-committed* to features that satisfy the *buyer* but have *nothing to do* with the *end user*.

By default we have now optimized for the *buyer* and the *approver*. We have optimized for revenue *Acquisition,* but not necessarily revenue Retention, Expansion, or growth.

We have become dependent on up-front $10M checks in exchange for enterprise features and forward-commits on our roadmap. And as the percentage of roadmap available for usability decreases, so do the chances of the end-user experience being delightful. Without user delight, we have to work harder for Renewals, Expansions become unlikely, and growth encounters significant headwinds.

This type of bespoke business can work for a while, but it has a natural limit in terms of scale. If each new deal comes with its own set of custom commitments, the business begins to look more like a services business, and it loses some of the inherent advantages of being able to use the same product—without customization—over and over again.

One of the tricks with PLG is to welcome customers who love your product *as-is* and to invite other customers to either adopt the standard product or go another way.

Remember our example of Zoom from Chapter 1? Zoom is generous. It offers all end users a forever-free version of their software that facilitates unlimited video calls of up to forty minutes each. Not only does this offer exist—Zoom promotes it. It makes it easy to find and easy to adopt. It makes the experience for the end user delightful.

"It just works."

WebEx and GoToMeeting had been focused on enterprise *buyers* for so long, they had let their *user experience* deteriorate. At a certain point, WebEx and GoToMeeting were ripe to be disrupted by something that is delightful and generous toward the end user. Zoom answered that call.

No doubt, the best PLG businesses are profitable and provide an excellent return for shareholders, but they are built from the ground up with the end user in mind. Not the manager, not the administrator, not the purchaser, not the approver—the user reigns supreme.

With no irony whatsoever, PLG companies are built on 3 pillars:

1. Empathy

2. Generosity

3. Metrics

## Empathy—Who Is My User, What Does She Care About, and How Does She Measure Progress?

Empathy means "the ability to sense other people's emotions, coupled with the ability to imagine what someone else might be thinking or feeling."[1]

When building a PLG software product, empathy means understanding the end user intimately. We want to know what she's thinking, how she's feeling, and how she approaches her work.

We understand that the end user has multiple demands on her time and more work to do than she likely can accomplish. Our challenge is to understand how she prioritizes the demands on her attention and how she thinks about making progress on her Jobs To Be Done (JTBD).

Clayton Christensen introduced the Jobs To Be Done framework (or Jobs Theory) as a way of understanding the situation in which someone would "hire" a product or service to help them make progress in a particular aspect of their life.[2]

When we develop PLG products, this is the level of understanding we need:

- Who has a Job To Be Done?
- In which situations would it be advantageous for them to . . .

  hire my product . . .
  . . . vs. any alternative options (such as direct or indirect competitors) . . .
  . . . to help them accomplish the job at hand?

I recently worked with a large provider of WhatsApp chatbot functionality for corporations. Its customers could customize the platform to automatically handle routine questions and route WhatsApp conversations to live agents when questions became too specialized. For large corporations, this company's product was the premium choice.

But what about small companies? What did small companies need?

At first we assumed they needed the same things as larger companies, only simpler. To test our hypothesis, we reviewed the opportunity records of small-company prospects and customers who had chosen not to buy or renew our service. The data showed that our hypothesis was partially correct. Midsize companies needed an enterprise-like solution that was easier to configure and quicker to deploy. But the smallest companies needed something different.

As we interviewed owners of very small businesses, three things became clear:

1. Communication with customers started on Instagram, not WhatsApp. But Instagram was not ideal for managing ongoing conversations—they needed to quickly move valid conversations from Instagram to WhatsApp.

2. They had very specific use cases for what the product should do with these messages, none of which resembled the enterprise use cases for the core product.

3. They were worried about artificial intelligence (AI) handling their primary WhatsApp number ("we don't want robots to take over"). They needed to build personal relationships with customers.

As we continued to interview very small business owners, we narrowed in on two use cases they encountered every day. We shadowed them in their shops, and we prototyped possible solutions to their problems.

After several weeks, we had a simple design that business owners loved.

From there we moved first to a prototype, then to a minimum viable product (MVP), then through further refinement, and finally to a full-blown launch.[3]

To get to this level of understanding, we had to get out of the office. We had to deprioritize our own ideas and begin developing empathy for the customer, and learn how she experiences the world.

Empathy.

### Generosity—Leveraging "Free" to Build Momentum

Once we understand who the user is, how he characterizes his JTBD, and how we can help him make progress against that JTBD with an MVP, the next step is to give it to him.

For free.

In PLG, the focus is on the end user, and the aim is to first create value and only thereafter extract value.[4]

There will be a time to charge the customer money, but remember the definition of PLG we put forward at the beginning of the book?

> *"Product-led growth is a go-to-market strategy, whereby product usage drives customer Acquisition, Retention, and Expansion."*
>
> —OpenView Venture Partners

Product *usage* drives purchase, not the other way around.

We want the user to experience the product *before* purchasing. In fact, we want the user to achieve **impact** before purchasing. If, as Winning by Design founder Jacco van der Kooij reminds us, "Recurring revenue is the result of recurring impact," then PLG takes that one step further:

*All* PLG revenue is the result of impact.

No impact, no revenue.

So we must be generous up front. Hand customers the keys—let them take it for a drive. Let them experience real impact.

The most forward-leaning PLG companies provide a free product that delivers real impact with no expiration date: "forever free."

- Zoom has a forever-free version.
- Google Drive, Dropbox, and Box have forever-free versions.
- Calendly has a forever-free version.
- As does DocuSign.

- As does Lucid.

- As does Canva.

If we can help the user succeed with our product, we will have developed a fan. True impact that has genuinely helped our user make progress against his JTBD is value delivered. As a result, the user comes to love and appreciate our product and our generosity.

At some point, our user becomes a power user. He is now an expert, and he begins to depend on our product in his day-to-day life. The product becomes an essential part of his routine.

When a user gets to the point where usage exceeds the limits of the free version, he will ask for an upgrade. In a PLG freemium strategy, this is the moment of Monetization, and it happens *after* Acquisition and *after* Activation. There are various types and strategies for Monetization, which we discuss in Chapter 9: How to Convert Free Users into Large Paying Contracts.

For now, it's important to focus on the principle of generosity.

1. Many PLG models, users experience the product before purchasing.

2. All PLG revenue is the result of impact.

We need our customers to use the product and experience impact—for free—before we ask for anything.

Generosity.

## Metrics—The Criticality of Instrumentation and Metrics in Building and Scaling PLG

Since no one is in the room when the customer activates on the product . . .

. . . and no one is there to see how hard or easy it is to get started and achieve impact . . .

. . . and no one is personally observing the customer's ongoing experience with the product . . .

. . . we need information to tell us how the process is going. All PLG products are instrumented by design to provide information about how the product is being used. Key events are tagged, such that when they are triggered, a log is created. Product managers analyze these logs to understand which features are being accessed and how often. We refer to the information in these logs as "signal."

Instrumentation gathers metrics on the users' experience, organizes it, and presents it as signal we can use to analyze product usage patterns. If users are getting stuck in a certain place, we will see it. Then we can run experiments to see if we can make that part of the experience easier or less confusing. Once we have tuned that experience such that users fly through it, we move on to the next bottleneck and then to the next.

> *"PLG companies maniacally focus on metrics that quantify user value and user experience, and optimize for those in the knowledge that they are leading indicators for future monetization."*
>
> —Ben Williams, growth advisor

PLG product managers have an existential interest in the metrics collected via instrumentation. It is the lifeblood of their businesses.

The singular way for a PLG company to make money is to ensure that customers can find its product, activate their account, achieve impact, and continue using the product—all with no assistance. If there is any friction whatsoever in this process—if the user is getting stuck or frustrated at all—we need to know.

When working on growth, PLG product managers look for the compound effects of many small improvements across the user experience. In this quest, metrics and the analysis they enable are the go-to inputs for diagnosis, hypothesis generation, experiment design, and results measurement.[5]

We've covered the first principles of PLG:

1. Empathy. PLG begins with a deep understanding of the end user and empathy for how she approaches making progress on her jobs.

**FIGURE 3.1.    First Principles of Product-Led Growth**

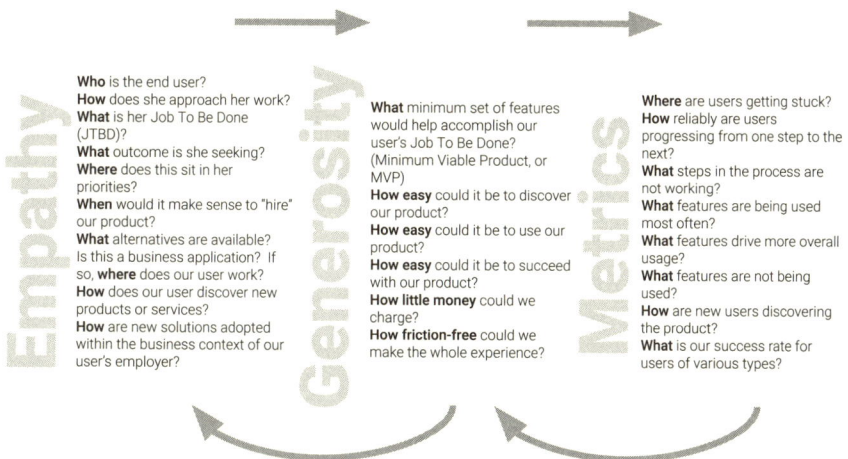

**Empathy**

Who is the end user?
How does she approach her work?
What is her Job To Be Done (JTBD)?
What outcome is she seeking?
Where does this sit in her priorities?
When would it make sense to "hire" our product?
What alternatives are available? Is this a business application? If so, where does our user work?
How does our user discover new products or services?
How are new solutions adopted within the business context of our user's employer?

**Generosity**

What minimum set of features would help accomplish our user's Job To Be Done? (Minimum Viable Product, or MVP)
How easy could it be to discover our product?
How easy could it be to use our product?
How easy could it be to succeed with our product?
How little money could we charge?
How friction-free could we make the whole experience?

**Metrics**

Where are users getting stuck?
How reliably are users progressing from one step to the next?
What steps in the process are not working?
What features are being used most often?
What features drive more overall usage?
What features are not being used?
How are new users discovering the product?
What is our success rate for users of various types?

**2.** Generosity. Product-led approaches allow users to experience impact from the product before purchase. Generosity is at the heart of how a PLG product is built and distributed.

**3.** Metrics. Information about customers' lived experience with the PLG products comes by way of instrumentation. Instrumentation collects signal that lets product managers know which portions of the product are working as intended and which are not.

To put these principles into action in the context of a new product or a product reimagined for PLG, we insist on a foundational understanding of the user and the user persona. We want to know how she approaches her work and how and when and why she might look for help from an outside product or service. In the service of that understanding, we ask a series of questions and seek answers to those questions through any means available, insisting on a good understanding at each step of the process and revisiting it as necessary. It will not pay to skip a step or gloss over a key question—we want to be as in sync with our end user as possible as we work through the process of developing a product that can meet her where she is and help her achieve the outcomes she seeks.

PLG is a labor of love. It runs on empathy, generosity, and metrics.

We who build and manage PLG products care a lot about our end users. We breathe empathy and generosity, and we live and die by metrics and analysis.

We know when users are succeeding and when they are struggling. We know that when users are suffering, the business will also suffer.

To this end, we iterate, iterate, iterate. Growth is the compound result of thousands of little improvements. And once this flywheel is turning, it is very hard to stop.

### Chapter 3 Summary

- Product-led companies lead with *empathy* for the end user. Because the end user is the first engagement point for a PLG product, the product must be fine-tuned to her priorities. This requires a deep understanding of her psychology, her decision processes, and her Jobs To Be Done.

- *Generosity* is a core tenet of PLG. PLG products give away value and allow customers to experience the product before purchase.

- *Metrics* are indispensable for B2B growth product managers—this is where we get signal about what is working and what isn't.

**Manager Minute**

Thinking about your own company, take time to reflect on the following questions:

1. My company is currently empathetic (*vis-à-vis* the end user) in the following ways:

_____

_____

_____

2. My company is currently generous to the end user in the following ways:

_____

_____

_____

3. My product is currently instrumented in the following ways, such that I get signal back on usage patterns:

_____

_____

_____

# FOUR

# Product-Led Growth Is a Long-Term Growth Strategy, Not a Short-Term Sales Tactic

Securing Top Management Support for a
1-to-3-Year PLG Roadmap, Plus Leading
Indicators to Track Success Along the Way

Product-led growth (PLG) is not for every product or every market. If sold internally as a panacea, PLG will understandably be met with skepticism. The number one criterion when considering PLG as a growth strategy is "fit." Is PLG a good fit for our company? The answer to this question is not always affirmative (see Chapter 17: Can PLG Work at a Company Like Mine?). And if you believe PLG is a good fit, what is the strategy most likely to contribute positively to growth? If you are casual about your assessment of "fit," your internal proposals will fall flat. To make a strong case for PLG, you need a clear hypothesis for how and where it can help your company grow.

### Gaining Executive Alignment Via a PLG Business Case

If you have assessed fit and identified a clear hypothesis for how PLG might contribute to your company's growth, it is time to sketch out a business case. We say "sketch," because the business case does not need to be fancy. It merely needs to "add up." In other words, when you pencil out the inputs and throughput and outputs, the math needs to work, the assumptions need to be believable, and the impact needs to be significant.

- If your hypothesis revolves around "freemium," be prepared to pencil out how many more new customers you could get with a free service and then how those free customers could convert to paying customers, resulting in a significant contribution to revenue growth.

**FIGURE 4.1.   Go-to-Market (GTM) Growth Calculations**

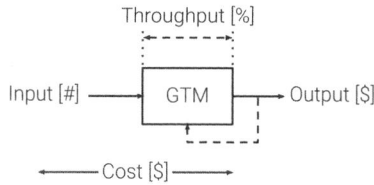

E.g., *"I've identified an underserved market for an XYZ service. I believe if we made a free XYZ offering, we could capture # customers over t years. If these free customers converted to paying customers at a rate of % and a price of $, the overall contribution to our business would be $."*

- If your hypothesis revolves around self-service, be prepared to show how de-laboring a particular portion of the customer journey could not only reduce cost but also improve the experience for customers.

E.g., *"Our onboarding process is too manual and too unreliable. I believe if we automated certain portions of the onboarding process, we could reduce cost from $$ to $, and we could improve the success rate of customers achieving First Impact within 30 days from % to %."*

Whatever the crux of your business case, you need to pencil it out all the way. In strategy work, this is called a "What would we have to believe?" analysis. What would we have to believe to make this a hypothesis worth pursuing? If the answer is reasonable—in other words, if we don't have to believe anything extraordinary—then the hypothesis may be worth testing. This is your business case, and this is the first step toward securing organizational support.

## The CFO's Model for Investing in Innovation

Does your organization have a history of innovation? Is there an established pattern for how innovations come about? Are innovations funded and staffed in a reliable or structured way? If so, then use your company's existing innovation language and structure to describe the PLG project you are proposing. This is the most likely way to get a PLG experiment scoped, resourced, and approved.

If your company has no history of innovation, or if innovation is haphazard, consider this an opportunity to make the innovation case to your chief financial officer (CFO). For the CFO, the argument for innovation goes as follows:

1. All growth at our company—current and expected—is already priced into the valuation of the company.

2. The only thing that can raise the valuation of our company is to do something that is *not* expected that increases growth and surprises investors positively.

3. Therefore, it is worthwhile investing *some amount* of time, energy, and money into initiatives that have a shot at paying off big.

Unexpected innovation is sometimes called "disruptive" or "breakthrough" innovation. In a basic management theory called aggregate project planning, breakthroughs are planned and resourced explicitly according to a 70/20/10 rule of thumb:

- **Core or existing projects** typically receive an allocation of ~**70%** of investment resources.

- **Adjacent or platform projects** receive ~**20%** of investment resources.

- **Breakthrough projects** receive ~**10%** of investment resources.

In their book *Managing New Product and Process Development,*[1] Kim Clark and Steven Wheelwright describe breakthrough projects as having the highest risk and highest reward of the project archetypes. They recommend breakthrough projects be given leeway to work outside of normal and existing operating techniques.[2]

Once your company has decided to allocate resources (time, attention, and capital) to breakthrough projects, half your job of securing commitment to PLG is done. Now the task is to convince the organization that your business case for PLG has more breakthrough potential than other proposals. In other words, PLG is the most likely to produce unexpected growth.

## The Resourcing Required for a PLG Initiative

So you want to build a product that sells itself? On the one hand, that will be easy to do. The patterns have been established, books have been written (including this one), and good examples exist in almost every category of software, with an increasing number of PLG examples extending beyond software. All you have to do is copy what has worked elsewhere, right?

Right!

But here's the rub—it turns out what's worked elsewhere was neither simple nor fast. Although PLG involves a new way of bringing products to market, it is more involved than merely spooling up a new GTM motion. For PLG to work, we need to make changes in our product as well as our GTM motion. We need to iterate both product and marketing toward success in a coordinated way (for more on Growth Teams, see Chapter 5: Creating and Managing Growth Teams).

### The Only Three Big Decisions You Must Make to Launch a Credible PLG Initiative

This takes time and focus and dedication, yes, but the good news is it's not open-ended. Your business case (see above) has expected positive results, and it also has a bounded set of investments required to achieve those results.

For an executive sponsoring a PLG strategy, there are three big investment decisions. After you've committed to these three decisions, the rest of your PLG pursuit is as simple as following the formula and pattern matching.

- Mindset: First, get in the right mindset—one that puts the customer at the center.
- Talent: Next, dedicate 5–7 of the very best people you have (take them off of their current assignments).
- Timeline: Then work on it for 1–3 years.

### For Business Leaders:

If you are running an existing, successful business, perhaps this level of investment sounds too extreme, and that is fine. It may not be the right time for you, and this may not be the right investment at the moment. Maybe your current business has burning issues that demand the attention of your 5–7 very best people. Perhaps you cannot afford to take them off what they are doing and dedicate them to something new. This is understandable and a legitimate reason not to launch PLG. In general, I recommend stabilizing each phase of your growth before launching the next, and if your current GTM strategy is still evolving, let your people continue working on that until you can get it repeatable and scalable.

## For Founders:

Perhaps you are the founder of a new venture, and you are worried about cash flow. If pursuing PLG takes 1–3 years to produce significant revenue, how will you keep your team fed in the meantime? Some venture capitalists invest in pre-revenue startups, but many venture capitalists want to see revenue early in a startup journey, and some base their company valuations on early-stage revenue growth. Virtually all ventures start out using founder-led sales techniques to secure their first customers. But founder-led sales aren't scalable, and they aren't generally sufficient to secure a Series A round of funding. For that you will need a repeatable and scalable go-to-market motion.

At this point you can choose sales-led or product-led growth. It may seem easier to employ a few salespeople and sell a few deals for $20K each to get some early cash flowing. Yes, you can always get early cash flowing by selling a few higher-dollar contracts. Here is the thing to note: the larger the contracts you sign early in your product's life, the more likely you are to make roadmap commitments to support those early customers. And the more commitments that stack up, the more "sold out" your roadmap will be. If you decide to launch a sales-led motion to get your product to market, that is a legitimate choice. But bigger contracts are not always better—especially in the beginning. Even for a sales-led motion, never hand over control of the product roadmap to early paying customers. Deliver the same product, via the same GTM process, over and over again. Build a repeatable, scalable business. Contracts can be larger in a sales-led model than in PLG, but you will also pay salaries to salespeople, and you will need to manage salespeople within a defined system. Revenue may show up sooner, but it will also cost more, and the main challenge you will face is variability within your system, due to unruly humans running sales and working hard to hit their quotas.

If you decide you would rather program GTM actions into your product instead of salespeople, this book is for you. As a founder, you will focus more on product in the early years, and even though revenue won't flow as quickly, once it begins, it is relatively unstoppable. Because in PLG you program GTM into your product, it is performed automatically and reliably. Repeatability and scalability are built into the code, and you can leverage a solid PLG foundation going forward when adding on subsequent GTM motions, like product-led sales (see Chapters 13, 14, and 15).

### Does It Really Take 1–3 Years to Build PLG?

In the hypercompetitive markets where we all play, 1–3 years can seem like an eternity—a bet we can't reasonably make, in light of many other pressing concerns. When considering an investment in freemium, self-service, or product-led GTM, I recommend insisting on a clear statement of the business case (i.e., a "What would we have to believe?" analysis) as well as a statement of the timeframe required to see the experiment all the way through. If we do not clearly articulate these expectations, we do not give ourselves a reasonable chance of success.

This journey—building competence in PLG and logging initial wins—takes time. It requires new skills, new processes, and new habits. It is not unlike learning a new sport. While a championship soccer team may be full of excellent athletes, we could not expect that same team to launch a successful foray into volleyball—at least not immediately. And if a subset of the best athletes on the team were to try, we would give them enough time to learn the game, develop the skills, recruit some help, and perfect their play before deeming the experiment unsuccessful.

Launching PLG is not dissimilar. The team will need full executive support and commitment to secure the time they need to succeed at building a PLG GTM. Of course, we will not be irrational. If we have legitimate reasons to believe our PLG strategy is not working, we will adjust accordingly. In this chapter, I provide metrics for use along the way to monitor whether continuing makes sense. Even though significant revenue may take 1–3 years to achieve, we should be able to see leading indicators of success in the operating metrics of our PLG engine. This can give us the confidence we need to continue investing.

Consider our soccer team that is learning volleyball. The team may struggle to win games in the first few years. Meanwhile, the team is developing skills, learning plays, and gaining experience. It may be making progress, even if we can't yet see it in the win/loss record. The challenge is to acknowledge that progress as being directional toward winning games.

Consider these three legends' revenue growth during their initial years.

All three companies had fully dedicated and undistracted teams working on product-led growth. They were staffed with undisputed "best and brightest" product and engineering talent. If they were only able to achieve minimal revenue through the first three years of iteration and effort, how would we "beat" that without our own fully dedicated team of the best and the brightest?

We wouldn't.

But look what happened once these companies' iterations and incremental improvements began to pay off! The investments in product-led capabilities and systems began to produce repeatable customer Acquisition, Activation, Monetization, and Expansion—the kind that compounds without the need for salespeople or customer success people. This type of nonlinear growth is the prize that gets us all thinking we would like to explore product-led GTM for our own businesses.

**FIGURE 4.2A.   PLG Company Revenue Growth Patterns—Gitlab**

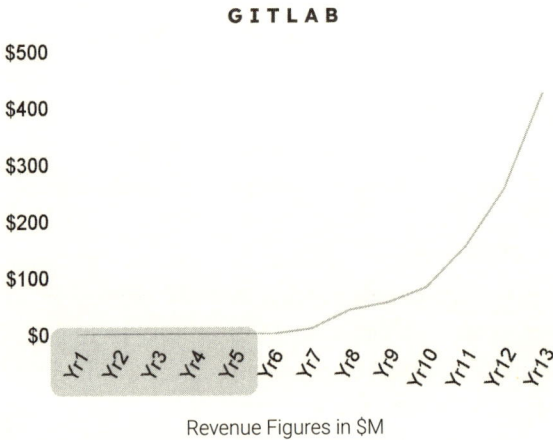

GITLAB

Revenue Figures in $M

**FIGURE 4.2B.   PLG Company Revenue Growth Patterns—Twilio**

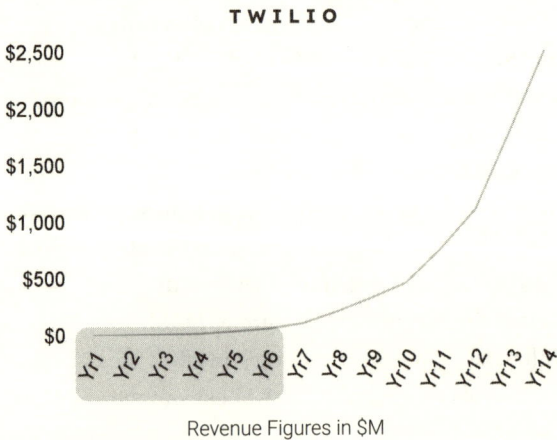

TWILIO

Revenue Figures in $M

**FIGURE 4.2C.   PLG Company Revenue Growth Patterns—Canva**

CANVA

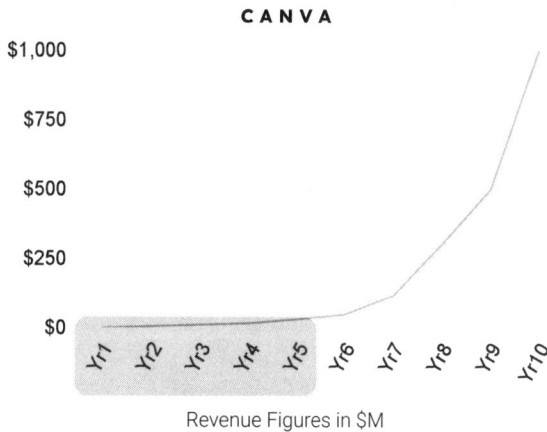

Revenue Figures in $M

## PLG Strategy Considerations for Founders: How and When to Choose PLG as Your Initial GTM Motion

After an initial phase of selling the product yourself, every founder must consider what GTM to pursue for repeatable, scalable growth. If this describes your situation, consider these three arguments for PLG as your initial GTM (more on the pros and cons of PLG in Chapter 17: Can PLG Work at a Company Like Mine?).

- **Defensive**: If any of your competitors has figured out how to make self-service work in your industry, you must also pursue this strategy or leave yourself exposed to disruption coming your direction from the low end of the market.
- **Offensive**: When you have a product that sells itself, you spend less money and energy on hiring and managing a sales team. Once a product-led growth engine is moving, it can grow faster and with more attractive unit economics.
- **Strategic**: With PLG, you are able to invest the money you would have spent on sales back into your product to make it as good as possible. These investments can either be in user features or in product-led growth capability, but either way, you are putting distance between yourself and your competitors.

## PLG for Executives: How to Think About the Investments, Returns, and Strategic Implications of Launching PLG

If you are an executive at a larger firm that goes to market via sales-led motions, you may have similar considerations as the founder's considerations listed above. But since you already have a going-concern business, you must consider all options for breakthrough innovation. Given a reasonable probability of a good outcome with a PLG experiment, does PLG rise to the top in terms of producing unexpected growth? If this is your best opportunity to unlock unexpected growth, how do you give your team the best chance of succeeding? Can you reasonably resource this bet by investing in the mindset, talent, and timeline required?

- **Mindset**—"Can I get a team thinking more about empathy, generosity, and mindset" than about revenue and profits? Will my organization organ-reject that mindset, or can I protect it?"

- **Talent**—"Can I afford to dedicate 5–7 of my best and brightest people to this effort and remove all distractions to let them build?"

- **Timeline**—"Can I allow the team 1–3 years to show significant annual recurring revenue (ARR)? What if I could see leading indicators of success before I began seeing the ARR? Would that be enough to stay the course?"

If you can make these three commitments, the rest of PLG is relatively straightforward. Across the number of successful examples of PLG companies we highlight in this book, the mechanics and success patterns of PLG are fairly well understood. But you cannot execute the known playbook until you have committed the required resources and support. Below we outline what it means to commit to mindset, talent, and timeline. In Chapter 16 we provide examples of companies that have done this at scale. Get your head around this, and the rest will flow.

### The PLGTM Cheat Code: How to Get PLG Results in Half the Time

Maybe your company is already at scale, and you want to see PLG results in half the time? If your company is already at scale, with existing products and an ongoing flow of subscription customers, here is a cheat code:

PLGTM

Not all product-led GTM strategies need to take three years to implement.

You can cut this time in half if you expand your view of GTM to include more than just new-customer Acquisition. Full-lifecycle PLG opens up a world of possibilities for PLG. Product-led renewals can de-labor and streamline a part of the customer journey that causes unnecessary friction. Certain types of product-led Expansion can be similarly easy to implement. We call this PLGTM (product-led go-to-market), and we cover these strategies in depth in Chapters 16 and 17.

## Mindset: The PLG Mindset Required for Success

In Chapter 3 we discussed the first principles of PLG:

**1.** Empathy

**2.** Generosity

**3.** Metrics

These are not things you simply announce in an all-hands meeting and then promptly forget. This is a mindset that goes deep. This mindset underpins decisions large and small. It colors who you hire, who you promote, and what victories you celebrate.

I once worked with a company that took empathy so seriously, it had everyone "meet" the target customer. It did this by having all engineers, designers, marketers, and product managers participate in live interviews with customers. The company then aggregated their findings into a persona. Designers chose a name for their persona (Gretel) and created a backstory for her. They chose stock imagery to represent Gretel, and they used these images on posters they hung on the walls of the office. The posters included key details about her title, function, and Job To Be Done. In that office it was impossible to forget who we were designing for: Gretel.

Generosity must similarly sink in. If you are on a high-functioning Growth Team, you channel empathy for Gretel (as an example) and design products and experiences that will add value to her life and help her make progress on her Job To Be Done (JTBD). In this mindset, it is not helpful if your reviews with upper management are exclusively focused on "how will we make money?" Yes, we need to figure out how to make money. But generosity first. Our mindset must be, "Seek first to create value, then to extract value." And management can't always be pulling in the opposite direction. We need a generosity mindset that supports building a PLG product. We will make money—no doubt—but only by way of being generous first.

If our culture doesn't insist on metrics, that also must change. Early in my career I worked at the strategy consulting firm Monitor Company. We took pride in being data-driven, even to the point of obsession. Directors at Monitor were known to send young analysts back to the drawing board with the following phrase:

"In God We Trust. All others, bring data."

PLG teams must similarly insist on data. Opinions are nice, but they are opinions. We must be empathetic and generous in our ideation about what might create the most impact for a customer. We design empathy and generosity right into the product. But all our intuition and product ideas are just ideas until they get tested. Usage metrics tell us what features users are actually able to discover and are inclined to use. If our intuitions and designs were correct, we might see confirming usage data. If usage data is disappointing, there may be an aspect of the design we need to adjust, to make specific features easier to find or use. Alternatively, we may have misread the need for a feature altogether, in which case we rethink core functionality. But insistence on measuring everything, and depending on data and metrics to validate each step of our journey? That's a PLG "must."

1. Empathy

2. Generosity

3. Metrics

With these principles firmly established in the mindset of those sponsoring the PLG effort, we are prepared to assemble a team.

## Talent: How to Identify the Right Talent for the PLG Team

Some people were built to do PLG, but not all people. The growth function within a company is similar to a scientific laboratory in the sense that it involves asking questions, posing hypotheses, and testing those hypotheses rigorously. Most experiments don't work. Only certain personalities are okay with putting time and energy into things that don't work. Most people would get discouraged. But the successful growth professional is able to continuously develop new questions and new ideas. Once something begins to work, they are also able to engineer it into a process and put it into production. This begins to describe the personality type (more on that later), but it doesn't describe the actual roles needed to make a growth motion work.

### ROLES ON A GROWTH TEAM

In this book we use *PLG Team* and *Growth Team* interchangeably. Often *PLG Team* would be used to describe the team responsible for building a new PLG product, including the ongoing product-led growth objectives, whereas *Growth Team* refers to a team driving product-led growth for a product that already exists. Either way, the roles are the same.

FIGURE 4.3.    Roles on a Growth Team

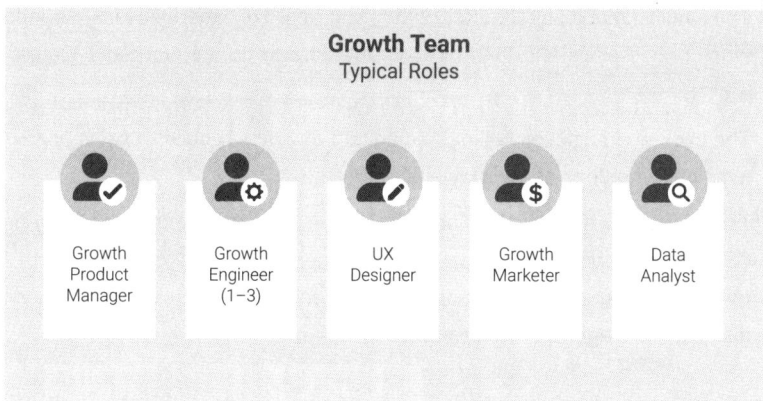

To execute PLG in your business, you need a dedicated team whose sole objective is growth. This team must be small so it can remain nimble. And it must be cross-functional and fully empowered to make changes in the product and marketing experiences that impact customer behavior.

The growth product manager organizes and prioritizes the work for the team. The marketer builds Loops and funnels, the designer designs, the engineers build, the analyst tests. We cover these roles in detail in Chapter 5: Creating and Managing Growth Teams.

Whether you are a startup or a mature company, to execute a PLG strategy effectively, you need to staff the roles on a Growth Team and protect them from other core responsibilities. This team needs to be able to channel the PLG mindset of empathy, generosity, and metrics. And you need to give it time. Not unlimited time, and not time without an expectation of results, but it needs time to do its work. We dive into that in the next section.

## THE GROWTH MINDSET

When considering who will be best to head up your PLG effort, deprioritize current titles and roles. Deprioritize tenure or seniority. Pay attention to technical skills and past experience, but don't make that the sole basis of your selection.

We are looking for a specific mindset, combined with natural talent and instinct. Regardless of the role someone will play on our team, we need them to be naturally curious, intrinsically confident, non-defensive, quick to adapt, and results-oriented. Perhaps the easiest way to understand what we are looking for is to characterize what we are *not* looking for.

We are *not* looking for:

- The tenured marketing director with fifteen years of experience in your industry who creates plans and then hires contractors to do the work and "return and report."

- The back-end engineer willing to dive into any new rebuild to solve hard problems but who does not work well on a team.

- The designer whose designs are so pristine, they are featured regularly on the CEO's own work. Her designs are awesome, but she will only take input from the CEO, and she needs time and space to complete her designs and cannot be disturbed during her creative process.

These are impressive humans with impressive profiles, but they will not be a fit for our PLG team. PLG is more iterative. In PLG, objectives are clear, but problems can be loosely defined, approaches are multitude, and solutions are elusive. A team may have to try seven or ten different approaches for moving one metric before it finds something that works. The solution may end up being technical, design-related, or marketing-related. And we won't know until we've tried.

Imagine a scenario where we struggle to get active users to invite other members of their team to join them on our platform. We have a goal that each active user invites at least three others to join the platform, but our metrics show that even the most active users are inviting fewer than one person on average.

What ideas could we come up with that might unlock this impediment?

- Could we prompt the user to seek collaboration on her work product?

- Could we ask the user to publish or share her work?

- Could we ask the user at some point for team members' names so that we can proactively suggest people, by name, she could invite to join her?

- Should we have the user authenticate to one of her social networks so that we can suggest friends to invite?

- Should we suggest assembling a review committee up front, before the user begins her work?

- Can we invite current users to comment on other current users' projects, thus cementing in their minds the notion of giving and getting input?

- Can we provide blank input fields that encourage users to solicit input?

- Can we score work based on outside collaboration?
- Are there approvals we could build into the workflow?
- What if we required three names at the outset of people who need visibility to this project?

We could probably brainstorm a list twice as long. Some of these ideas will be easy to test, and others may be more difficult. Some have a high likelihood of making an impact, and others are less likely. The PLG team will work through them in a prioritized way, testing each idea to see what works, discarding the ideas that don't work, and then hardening and productizing the ones that do.

Since we know we will be iterating quickly, discarding ideas on a regular basis, we need team members who can incorporate feedback, learn from it, and move ahead without missing a beat. If they can lead with curiosity rather than defensiveness or passiveness, they are most likely to be able to succeed on a PLG team.

### Timeline: What to Measure When, and How to Know When PLG Is Working

#### ARR IS A THING, BUT NOT *THE* THING

Ask any sponsor of a new venture—whether a brand-new company or a new product within an existing company—"What is your measure of success?" Nine times out of ten the answer will be "revenue" or, in the case of a subscription product, annual recurring revenue. Indeed, this is a macro measurement for a successful new business. But not all ARR is the same.

**FIGURE 4.4.   Alternate Paths to $1M ARR**

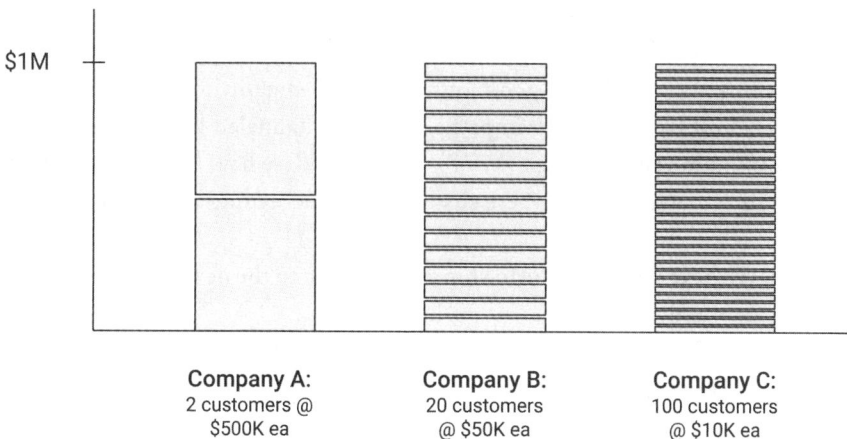

Company A: 2 customers @ $500K ea

Company B: 20 customers @ $50K ea

Company C: 100 customers @ $10K ea

Let's take a hypothetical new product with $1M in ARR. Would you rather see 2 customers @ $500K each, 20 customers @ $50K each, or 100 customers @ $10K each?

That may not be the right question. Better questions are:

- How did you acquire those customers? What did it cost? How repeatable is that process?
- At what rate will you retain those customers? What will that cost? How reliable is that process?
- At what rate will you expand those customers? How much will that cost? How bankable is that result?

When establishing a new PLG product, we are likely not to see significant ARR for 1–3 years. If ARR were our North Star—it's not—we could sell large contracts with custom commitments attached, but that is not a SaaS business, and it is certainly not a PLG business.

In PLG we are looking for new, self-service customers at a low customer acquisition cost (CAC). Company A in the figure above is a different business. Company A has large deals acquired via face-to-face selling. Those deals often come with a healthy dose of customization—both in terms of deal parameters and in terms of promises of functionality or integration. If those are the first two customers for our new product, we are most certainly in a non-PLG business.

To build Company B or Company C, we must build machinery that is repeatable and reliable. Building this in a self-service way takes time. It requires deliberate architecture, building, testing, and iterating.

## WHAT TO MEASURE WHEN?

Let's assume we have done a good job at building empathy for our prospective customer. And based on that empathy, we have channeled healthy generosity into a minimum viable product (MVP) version. And we have instrumented that product such that we can see where customers are succeeding and where they are getting stuck.

"Yes! We have built it! Time to ship and move on to the next thing, right?"

No, not exactly.

Unlike traditional sales-led models, where marketing and sales sell the MVP to early customers, then based on feedback from those customers a roadmap

FIGURE 4.5.    **PLG Metrics That Matter by Stage of Development**

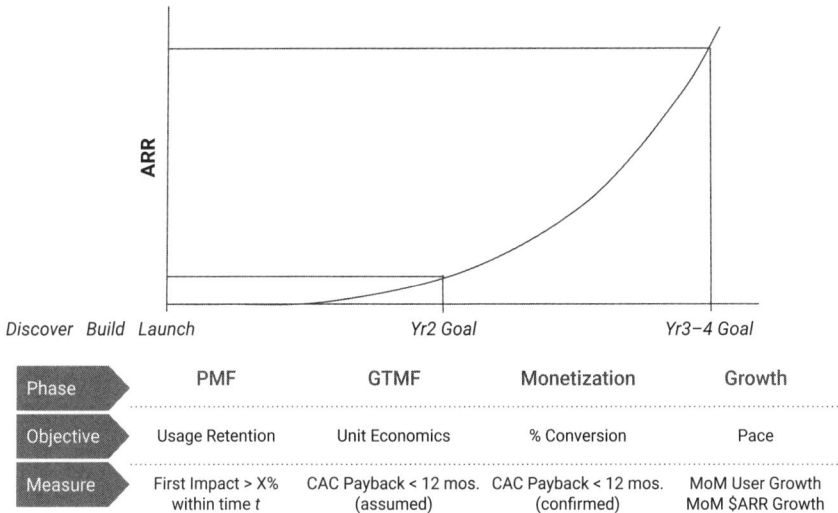

| Phase | PMF | GTMF | Monetization | Growth |
|---|---|---|---|---|
| Objective | Usage Retention | Unit Economics | % Conversion | Pace |
| Measure | First Impact > X% within time $t$ | CAC Payback < 12 mos. (assumed) | CAC Payback < 12 mos. (confirmed) | MoM User Growth MoM $ARR Growth |

backlog full of requested features is created, this is a bit different. Yes, we have early customers, and yes, we may have acquired them via founder sales or some other unscalable method. We may even know these customers by name, and we are certainly getting feedback on the product. But in a PLG model we are likely counting on annual contracts of less than $10K, which will not support custom responses to customer requests. No, if we are to build a profitable PLG business, we will need everything to be standardized and automated, such that the average customer will succeed without help: the "self-service happy path." Figuring out how to make the product experience easier for all customers is an exercise in careful iteration and testing.

In rough terms, after we have an MVP, we will likely spend the first year on Product-Market Fit (PMF), the second year on Go-To-Market Fit (GTMF), and the third and fourth years on monetization and scaling.

### YEAR 1: PMF

During Year 1, our core objective is Product-Market Fit, which we measure in terms of usage Retention.

*"Wait, it takes more than a year to achieve PMF? Good luck with that!"*

Yes, it does take more than a year to achieve PMF, but we are starting our clock at the launch of an MVP. We are assuming that we have already done a good job of developing empathy for our end user, understanding her JTBD, and building a set of minimally viable features to help her achieve her objective. Now we pursue rapid iteration toward PMF, and our key impact metric is usage Retention.

We have an MVP, but we don't yet know if it hits the mark. We instrumented the product for this very purpose—to monitor how it's going. Metrics provide signals indicating where and when users might be getting stuck or confused. Metrics help us pinpoint places in the product where we may be able to remove friction and make the product experience more seamless and intuitive. At this point we are not worried about growth or unit economics; we are only concerned with usage Retention. If users are achieving their objectives with our product, they will come back.

But also—we can't wait months to know if people come back. Measures like daily active users (DAU), weekly active users (WAU), and monthly active users (MAU) are great for ongoing tracking, but in the beginning, we need signal faster than that. So we take a shortcut and look for a leading indicator of long-term usage Retention:

1. First, we define an event in the first minutes or hours of usage that we believe correlates positively with long-term Retention. This should be a measurable event, whereby the user sees demonstrable value in the solution and hopefully becomes convinced she has made the right choice to adopt your product. We call this event First Impact.

2. Then we track the timing of First Impact for each new account owner.

3. Next we organize this information into cohorts:

In this example, each cohort contains all users created in a given month. Each row represents a single cohort, with the number in each cell representing the percentage of users in that cohort that had achieved First Impact by that point in their lifetime. The columns represent the first twelve days of a customer's experience with the product.

As we can see in Figure 4.6, our first launch was not great. For our first cohort of new users, launched in January, only 14% achieved First Impact on Day 1, and only 22% achieved First Impact by Day 12.

FIGURE 4.6.    First Impact by Cohort

| | Day 1 | Day 2 | Day 3 | Day 4 | Day 5 | Day 6 | Day 7 | Day 8 | Day 9 | Day 10 | Day 11 | Day 12 |
|---|---|---|---|---|---|---|---|---|---|---|---|---|
| Jan | 14% | 16% | 18% | 19% | 20% | 20% | 21% | 21% | 21% | 22% | 22% | 22% |
| Feb | 17% | 20% | 21% | 22% | 22% | 22% | 22% | 23% | 23% | 23% | 23% | |
| Mar | 26% | 29% | 33% | 34% | 34% | 35% | 36% | 36% | 36% | 36% | | |
| Apr | 31% | 34% | 37% | 38% | 40% | 40% | 41% | 41% | 41% | | | |
| May | 42% | 43% | 43% | 44% | 44% | 44% | 45% | 45% | | | | |
| Jun | 49% | 52% | 54% | 55% | 55% | 56% | 56% | | | | | |
| Jul | 51% | 54% | 56% | 56% | 57% | 57% | | | | | | |
| Aug | 62% | 65% | 67% | 68% | 70% | | | | | | | |
| Sep | 63% | 66% | 69% | 70% | | | | | | | | |
| Oct | 65% | 68% | 69% | | | | | | | | | |
| Nov | 67% | 71% | | | | | | | | | | |
| Dec | 72% | | | | | | | | | | | |

As we identify and remedy issues that may be confusing or blocking our users, the experience improves. By June, 49% of new users are achieving First Impact on Day 1, and by December we are at 72%.

This means out of one hundred users who created a new account in December, seventy-two were "succeeding" (achieving First Impact) on their first day.

Depending on your target user, your product's value proposition, and the requirements to get started with your product, your threshold for PMF will vary. But a rule of thumb might be, "70% of users achieve First Impact within time t." The percentage of new users who achieve First Impact within the specified timeframe is called the First Impact success rate.[3]

### *YEAR 2: GTMF*

Having achieved PMF quantitatively, you can be confident that most new users you send to the product will succeed. Now it is worthwhile to look for a scalable and sustainable source of new users.

"Scalable" means a large source of potential users, and "sustainable" means that we can acquire these new users at a reasonable cost.

"Reasonable" is relative to the expected revenue from a customer. The rule of thumb here is that we want the net revenue from a new customer to pay back all the expenses we incurred in acquiring that customer within twelve months. This measure is called CAC payback (customer acquisition cost payback), and it is measured in months (on acquisition unit economics, see Chapter 7: How to Acquire Self-Service Customers).

Organic traffic is always the least expensive source of new users, but organic traffic is hard to trace back to specific actions we take. Search engine optimization (SEO) is also inexpensive, but it takes a long time to establish the necessary credibility for key search terms that can drive significant traffic. Content marketing is the next least expensive, and it too has a long lead time. Search engine marketing (SEM) and display advertising are expensive, but since they are easy to track, they lend themselves to quantitative experimentation (ad X on platform Y drove Z results at $CAC). Partner marketing, community marketing, events, and other tactics can round out our Acquisition marketing strategy. Not each channel must perform independently on a CAC payback basis, but the blended results across all Acquisition channels must perform, or we are building a money-losing machine instead of the opposite.

Achieving reliable CAC payback is the quantitative indicator of Go-To-Market Fit. Just as with PMF, your threshold for the target CAC payback that signals GTMF may vary, depending on your product, price point, target market, and target user. Twelve months is a rough rule of thumb. Some business-to-consumer (B2C) products target shorter CAC paybacks, and some enterprise-focused SaaS products target CAC paybacks of two years or even longer (see OpenView's 2023 SaaS Benchmarks Report for benchmarks on CAC payback and other SaaS metrics).[4]

### YEAR 3: MONETIZATION

With PMF and GTMF established, we need to confirm the assumptions we incorporated in our initial build. What did we assume?

1. We assumed that we could continue to acquire new users for a certain CAC.

2. We assumed that users would convert from free to paid at a certain rate.

3. We assumed that users would pay a certain amount for our product.

4. We assumed that paying users would retain at a certain rate.

These were all best-guess assumptions, made and documented using the best knowledge we had at the time. But before we start pouring lots of capital into this Acquisition engine, we want to test these assumptions—especially our assumption around who will be willing to convert to a paid plan. This phase of experimentation is focused on Monetization.

Most of our experimentation during this phase is around the conversion of free to paid. Getting this right might entail adjusting pricing, adjusting feature bundles, tweaking messaging, updating upgrade cadences, etc.

Beyond conversion, we also must test pricing, Retention, and scaled Acquisition. Adjustments resulting from these tests are critical, as they constitute the last remaining "untested" portions of our funnel. You can find detailed explanations of how to think about and pursue Monetization in Chapter 9: How to Convert Free Users into Large Paying Contracts.

### YEAR 4: GROWTH

Finally, three years after beginning this journey (longer if you count the initial discovery and build phases), we are able to begin focusing on what we wanted to focus on all along: ARR growth.

At this point (assuming we have been able to confirm the numbers used in the examples above), we know that 70% of new users are succeeding. One in ten new users is converting to a paid user, and each paid user nets us $1,000 in the first year of use. Because of this, we can afford to spend $100 per new activated user. We have developed a blended new-user Acquisition strategy that reliably gets us new activated users for less than $100 each, including all marketing and sales costs.

So what now?

Fuel up and go faster! This engine is tuned and ready to go. Now we methodically expand our efforts to gain more and more users, being careful to monitor performance metrics as we go. As long as we can operate within these parameters, we are happy to "spend money to make money."

At around $10M in ARR we may consider other opportunities to innovate and expand on this motion. A popular extension to this "self-service happy path" is product-led sales (PLS), whereby we leverage our self-service, new-user Acquisition to generate new qualified leads for sales (on the self-service happy path and PLS, see Chapter 14: Crossing the Chasm from Pure PLG to PLG-Plus-Sales).

## PLGTM Cheat Code Reprise

Remember the cheat code from the beginning of the chapter? If you want PLG results but you can't dedicate the 1–3 years necessary to build product-led Acquisition from scratch, consider self-service-enabling one of the other stages of the customer journey. A full-customer-lifecycle purview (PLGTM) gives you the latitude to aim product-led techniques anywhere along the Bowtie. Some of these investments can pay dividends in less than a year. You still need to commit to the mindset and talent portions of the formula, but investments in post-Acquisition stages of the customer journey could pay dividends sooner than the full product-led Acquisition strategy outlined above.

## Final Thoughts

PLG is not complicated. The playbook has been written, and the steps and mechanics are clear. There are only three difficult decisions to make. These three decisions are made in advance and sponsored by executives. We have focused on these decisions in this chapter:

1. Mindset: Put empathy, generosity, and metrics front and center.

2. Talent: Dedicate 5–7 of your best and brightest people. Remove distractions and clear the way.

3. Timeline: Give it three years, and measure the right things along the way.

If you make these decisions and stick to them, you may have the same results as HubSpot, Unity, and MongoDB—all of whom added PLG to their existing businesses after they were already over $100M in ARR. These companies dedicated highly talented teams to the PLG effort. They gave these teams license to focus on the customer and how she achieves impact (empathy and generosity). And then they gave the teams time to iterate toward a profitable business (metrics). The result?

- HubSpot achieved $10M in PLG ARR within 3 years for a brand-new product, focused on a brand-new user (sales).

- Unity transitioned its "free download" marketing engine into a $100M self-service subscription business within four years.

- MongoDB launched a brand-new cloud product to begin monetizing its open-source community and achieved $20M in ARR within eighteen months.

Each of these projects was sponsored by the CEO. Each of them had a strong team dedicated to achieving results. None of them measured ARR too early—they all worked on tuning and perfecting the funnel so that revenue could be the inevitable outcome (for these case studies, see Chapter 16: Lessons from Building PLG Within Large, Established Companies).

PLG is not complicated. It takes time, talent, and mindset. Follow the playbook, and insist on the results. You will be amazing.

## Chapter 4 Summary

- The number one consideration when deciding if PLG is for you is "fit": Can we develop a hypothesis for PLG that pencils out into a viable business case, from number of new customers all the way through monetization, retention, and expansion?

- The next consideration is whether we can resource it. Consider this a "breakthrough" project and allocate the appropriate time and talent: typically 1–3 years and 5–7 of your best people (take them off current assignments).

- Mindset starts from the top—any PLG effort needs CEO-level sponsorship of a mindset: empathy for the end user, generosity in solution design, and metrics-based experimentation.

- Building the right cross-functional growth team is essential for rapid iteration.

- The appropriate metrics of success shift over time: first PMF, then GTMF, then monetization, and finally growth.

## Manager Minute

Thinking about your own company, take time to reflect on the following questions:

1. We have a hypothesis about how and where PLG would work within our company:

   Underserved Market: _____

   Persona and JTBD: _____

   Target # of Free Customers: _____

   Target % of Paid Customers: _____

   Price for Paid Offering: _____

   Total 5-Year Business Case: _____

2. When considering how much empathy and generosity are embedded in my company, the following are true (check all that apply):

_____ We have developed named personas for our customers.

_____ We understand the JTBD for each of our personas.

_____ We track our customers' success with our product.

_____ Our leadership makes our customers' success a primary focus behind closed doors (not just in company-wide meetings).

3. I know the people I would assign to my growth team:

Growth Product Manager: _____

Growth Engineers (1–3): _____

UX Designer: _____

Growth Marketer: _____

Data Analyst: _____

4. To maintain focus and commitment over a 1–3-year timeline, I will need to consider the following:

_____

_____

_____

## How Billion-Dollar Companies Are Built Using Product-Led Growth

In Part One we described the last thirty years in software—the evolution from locally installed software to cloud-hosted software to product-led models, where end users and teams begin using software without much involvement from marketing or sales. This GTM strategy is called product-led growth (PLG).

We demonstrated that PLG is the "de-laboring" of GTM functions, making products and services easier to access via self-service, resembling the Industrial Revolution. GTM professionals who used to "be" the GTM machine no longer need to perform the manual tasks of demoing the product, explaining features, writing contracts, collecting signatures, negotiating terms, etc. The product handles most of these GTM functions and more. Instead of *being* the GTM machine, these professionals can now *operate* the machine.

We made the claim that to be competitive in software today, managers need to be fluent in PLG. We showed examples of where incumbent software players have been disrupted by newer PLG products that were easier to find, adopt, purchase, and expand.

We looked to the next thirty years, when software will likely be embedded in many physical goods, and we speculated that software will not only continue to eat the world, but it will be a Trojan horse for AI and further automation of the GTM function. Many physical goods will have accompanying service contracts, consumables, feature upgrades, monitoring, optimization, and other associated options that can be purchased via embedded software.

*Empathy* for the end user is at the heart of every PLG product. With this deep understanding of the user's situation and the job he wants to get done, PLG companies strive to help him make progress on that job and lead with *generosity*—often giving away the service for free. *Metrics* communicate to PLG product managers when the user is succeeding and when she is failing with the software. By iterating to make the experience smoother and better, product managers can build well-oiled machines for acquiring, activating, and monetizing customers without making it necessary to interact with salespeople.

With the mindset of empathy, generosity, and metrics in place, the framework and timeline for building PLG are well understood. Given the right talent, structured into Growth Teams, and the right intermediate objectives for Year 1, Year 2, and Years 3–4, companies should be able to follow established patterns and achieve success with PLG.

## Up Next

**PART TWO: PRODUCT-LED GROWTH IMPLEMENTATION AND TACTICS**

Read Part Two for a blueprint of how to build PLG from the ground up. Here we cover **how** and **why** PLG works, what the components are, and various tactics, strategies, and blueprints for how to make it work in your company.

# Product-Led Growth
# Implementation and Tactics

**FIVE**

# Creating and Managing Growth Teams

The Internal Politics and Realities of Launching PLG

*WITH BEN WILLIAMS*

> *"With product-led growth (PLG), the mindset of cross-functional collaboration and alignment is foundational. Everyone has to be working together."*
>
> —Sahir Azam, CPO MongoDB

In Chapter 4 we discussed the importance of executive-level alignment and commitment to three key decisions:

1. **Mindset**: We commit to placing the customer squarely in the center of product and go-to-market (GTM) decisions.

2. **Talent:** We dedicate 5–7 of our best and brightest people to this effort.

3. **Timeline**: Although we have leading indicators of success, we understand that significant revenue will take 1–3 years to develop in a PLG strategy.

In this chapter, we discuss how to organize a Growth Team to maximize your chance of PLG success.

## What Is a Growth Team, and Why Do We Need One?

*("Growth Team" and "PLG Team" can be used interchangeably, with Growth Team being the more common term. In this book, when we use "Growth Team" we are describing a team that includes product managers and engineers.)*

Pursuing a product-led GTM strategy requires integrated, cross-functional work that often goes deeper than mere cross-departmental collaboration. A Growth Team is a small, self-contained team that includes Product, Engineering, Marketing, Design, and Analytics. Growth Teams are charged with growth objectives, designed to work at speed, iterating quickly through experiments to find things that can—directly or indirectly—improve the velocity of the revenue engine.

Most companies don't have Growth Teams because of historical, siloed organizational structures. Typical companies are organized with a marketing team, a sales team, and a customer success team, all working on their portion of the revenue engine. These teams usually report up to separate executives, only intersecting at the C-level.

Product and engineering virtually always report up a separate management chain than the revenue functions.

But because PLG, by definition, uses the product to help deliver revenue and de-labor some of the traditional GTM functions, product-led growth strategies require product to be involved in revenue activities. With revenue "over here" and product "over there" in a typically organized company, it's unlikely that product would understand the revenue process, much less dig in to help make it better. This is why we organize Growth Teams. The point is to pull product, engineering, and marketing out of their silos to work side by side and focus singularly on growth objectives.

For this chapter, I partnered with my friend Ben Williams, who built his twenty-year career in product roles at Telelogic, IBM, and Temenos and most recently led product-led growth at CloudBees and then Snyk, a developer security

FIGURE 5.1.   Growth Team Structure

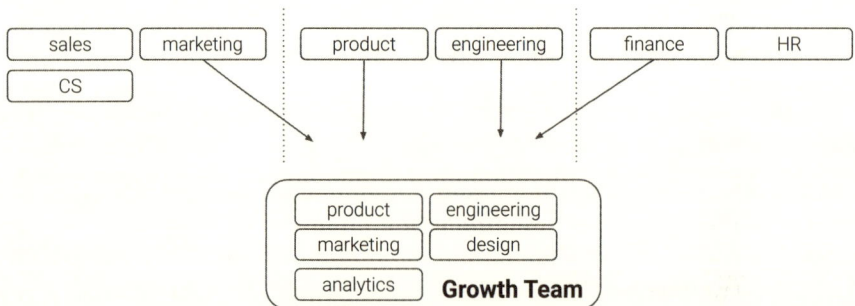

platform valued at $8B. In his two most recent roles, Ben ran multiple product and Growth Teams, scaled across the businesses.

Ben is now an active growth advisor to pre-breakout, post-Product-Market-Fit companies, maintains a popular PLG newsletter on Substack, and is a faculty member in Reforge's Academy.

To assemble the insights in this chapter, Ben and I drew on experiences from CloudBees, Snyk, HubSpot, Amplitude, Miro, Figma, MongoDB, and Unity Software.

## The Internal Politics of Assembling Growth Teams

If you are considering building PLG into an existing business, the issue most critical to your success is building executive alignment. Because PLG is a long-term commitment, it is difficult to make it succeed as a "side project." Not only will you not get attention and contribution from the right people, but you may run out of time before being able to succeed. Rather than treating this as a side project and then hoping the results will be compelling enough to convince upper management to support it going forward, we recommend having the alignment conversations up front (on how to secure alignment, see Chapter 4: Product-Led Growth Is a Long-Term Growth Strategy).

You need full support from each of the functional leaders who will dedicate resources to the effort. Assuming that the Growth Team structure presented above is in place, this means that you need support from the leaders of product, engineering, marketing, and finance. The larger your company, the more difficult it will be to align these functions. Sometimes they report to the same general manager (GM), but sometimes they report up more siloed, functional lines, making it difficult to align priorities. Ideally you would have the support of a GM or CEO to help get the alignment of objectives and expectations required to assemble a dedicated team with the appropriate talent, mindset, and timeline for success.

Even if you are yourself the GM or CEO, you may get pushback on the notion of creating a Growth Team.

- Your head of marketing may want to support the effort, and they may even be willing to loan their best performance marketer to work on it, but they may not want to "give up" that person and surrender them as a permanent member of their team.

- Your head of engineering may be skeptical that anyone can manage engineers as well as they can, and they may fight to retain control of any code or any engineers that work on code.

- Your head of sales may not like the idea of self-service sales in accounts within their territory without sales involvement. They may worry that their team will not get paid commissions if they don't work directly on a sale. And they may hate the idea that the product they sell for real money is now available for free, with the free tier readily visible on the website.

- Your head of customer success (CS) may be convinced that human-led onboarding and human-led training is the best way to serve customers and cannot be replaced by product-led motions.

When you suggest pulling people out of their former organizations and organizing them into a Growth Team, managers may at first resist the idea and try to "lend" people to the effort but not dedicate people. If you insist that people must be dedicated, you may be offered people you know are not the best talent available (expendable people).

You may be tempted to "just get started" with a small coalition of willing participants or to pursue a PLG effort as an "off-book" experiment. We have not seen these approaches succeed. Instead, when building PLG into an existing company, we have seen only one model work:

1. A dedicated Growth Team of high-caliber people . . .

2. That is sponsored by the CEO or GM.

Why does sponsorship have to go all the way up to the CEO? Why can't the project live in product or in marketing? The short answer is that it can "live" in product. But it must be *sponsored* and *protected* by the executive to whom both marketing and engineering report, and that is almost always the CEO.

This Growth Team, once commissioned, will have free rein to work on all aspects of growth for the product. Some of its growth ideas will be more marketing-dependent, and some will be more engineering-dependent. To help you get in the mindset of how this could play out internally, consider the following scenarios.

### Hypothetical Scenario 1: Acquisition Marketing

The Growth Team has been acquiring new customers via specific landing pages, but they want to see what would happen if they put a "Start Now" call to action (CTA) on the homepage of the main website. Right now the main CTA on the homepage is "Contact Us." The marketing team owns the homepage, and they are understandably protective of its content and design, as well as the conversion metrics for the "Contact Us" CTA. The marketer in charge of the website tells the Growth Team they will not be able to launch a new CTA on the homepage.

Faced with this dilemma, the growth product manager needs executive support to negotiate a solution whereby the Growth Team is allowed to run tests on the homepage. Let's assume the Growth Team reports to Product. Now the executive in charge of product needs to speak with the executive in charge of marketing. If they cannot work out a solution, they will need to escalate to their mutual boss—usually the CEO.

### Hypothetical Scenario 2: Back-End APIs

The Growth Team is working on keeping monthly active usership high. One of its ideas is to push out alerts via email with an invitation for the user to revisit the product. This alert might be triggered by a certain condition within the product, such as a pending approval, a new set of available data, or a state change. The idea here is to proactively alert the user to this new condition and pull her back into the product to address it.

To accomplish this, the growth engineer needs access to data in the core platform that is not currently available via application programming interface (API). The engineer can either get permission to directly access data in the core platform (usually forbidden for all except a small group of approved engineers), or access could be provided via a supported API, which would allow any engineer to access data without coding directly to the platform.

The engineering team tells the growth product manager that their API update request cannot be prioritized for at least the next two sprints, and it is unwilling to commit to ever updating it—especially since it hasn't heard this request from any other part of the business. "This is just an experiment," says the engineering team.

If this experiment is important to the Growth Team, the growth product manager now needs executive support to negotiate an agreement to update the API.

In both of these scenarios, if the Growth Team itself is viewed as a priority for the CEO, negotiated solutions are more likely to be found.

For this book, we interviewed executives from three companies who successfully added PLG after they had already established revenue of over $100M via a sales-led GTM: HubSpot, MongoDB, and Unity. In all three cases, a new cross-functional team was established (the "Growth Team"), and in all three cases that team had the explicit support of the CEO (you can find details on these cases in Chapter 16: Lessons from Building PLG Within Large, Established Companies). In addition to these examples of starting PLG from scratch after already being at scale, we also draw on experience with dozens of PLG companies that have managed Growth Teams at all stages of company growth, from startup to scaleup to grownup.

## The Product Growth Model: The True North for All Growth Efforts

A Growth Team is tasked with optimizing one or more aspects of growth related to its product. At the highest level, in any product growth model, there are four growth levers: Acquisition, Retention, Monetization, and Expansion.

Every business needs to be able to answer the following questions:

- How do we Acquire users/teams?
- How do we Retain users/teams?
- How do we Monetize users/teams?
- How do we Expand usage?

Put more simply, how do we grow?

With answers to these questions, a company can construct a set of planning assumptions and combine them into an overall picture of the company's trajectory. This results in what we refer to as a product growth model.

> The product growth model is the True North for all growth initiatives.

- Are Expansion initiatives delivering the expected results?
- Is the new customer Acquisition engine performing better or worse than the assumptions in the product growth model?
- Do we need to make adjustments in targeting—given that Renewals are underperforming expectations?

Within each of the domains above, a business will have primary (and sometimes secondary) growth motions, including:

- No-touch (product-led growth, or PLG)
- Low-touch (product-led sales, or PLS)

- Medium-touch (inbound marketing-led, or "Inbound")

- High-touch (outbound sales-led, or "Outbound")

- Dedicated-touch (account-based sales, or ABS)

When users realize impact from a product, it's unsurprising that most companies' primary motion for *retaining* users and teams is product-led. Many businesses also either have—or aspire to have—product-led motions for Acquisition, Monetization, and/or Expansion.

The product growth model ultimately describes and quantifies how a product grows. A founder or first growth hire might create the initial iteration, but over time, Growth Teams typically own the product growth model. They ensure that it is kept up to date with feedback that incorporates the observed performance of Growth Loops (see Chapter 12: Shifting from Marketing Funnels to Product Loops), learnings from the Growth Team, evolution of the product, and shifts in company strategy or the wider market.

The Growth Team uses the product growth model to plan and execute the strategic opportunities on which they focus. Ultimately, the product growth model should inform plans not only for the Growth Team but also for teams across the company: R&D, marketing, customer success, and beyond.

Without this dedicated team, there is often no ownership of the product growth model—or worse, the product growth model isn't created or quantified at all. This can lead to prioritization decisions being made without strategic input. Inevitably, competing priorities such as building feature X to help close the next big deal can mean that important product growth initiatives are inadequately funded, under-resourced, or passed over entirely.

> (Anti-pattern: You may find your organization defaulting to the belief
> that PLG is the sole responsibility of this single team. As a result,
> others in the organization might assume that PLG is not their concern.
> This is a red flag. For PLG to work, it must be a central concern for
> everyone—even those not directly assigned to a Growth Team.)

Standout PLG companies have growth built into their DNA. Product teams prioritize capability development based on whether the resulting motion supports the overall product growth model and whether it fuels or inhibits micro and macro Growth Loops (see Chapter 12: Shifting from Marketing Funnels to Product Loops). The criteria for judging the initial and ongoing success of new features can include relevant growth metrics at the feature level and at the product level. When that is the case, having a Growth Team can be an additional superpower, as the Growth Team can focus on:

- Core constraints within the product growth model;
- Finding and alleviating those constraints;
- Getting Growth Loops to spin faster;
- ... and, where and when appropriate, layering on new Growth Loops.

When growth is not programmed into the DNA of the whole company and the business effectively delegates PLG success to a single team, that team will not be set up for success (on executive sponsorship, see Chapter 4: Product-Led Growth Is a Long-Term Growth Strategy).

## How to Structure Growth Teams at Scale

> *"A Growth Team is a cross-functional team empowered to create, evolve, and optimize whole-product experiences to drive customer Acquisition, Retention, Monetization, and Expansion."*
>
> —Ben Williams, growth advisor

Growth Teams have primary responsibility for the growth that results from whole-product user experience. As such, the following are hallmarks of a Growth Team and its work:

- **Multiple connected outcomes:** Growth Teams may work on growth outcomes sequentially or in parallel. These objectives all connect in the product growth model, where assumptions and interconnectedness is documented.
- **Whole-product:** Growth Teams consider the end-to-end experience from the first time a user hears about the brand through their entire lifecycle as a customer. This may also include the product-supported portions of the journey that are Sales-assisted or Customer Success–assisted.
- **Cross-functional:** Growth Teams are staffed with an explicit intention of sourcing diversity in ideas, ability, and agency to execute across that entire product surface.

The product growth model and strategy determine where Growth Teams focus at any given time. Sometimes the focus is on driving improvements to Activation through onboarding as a means to driving improved long-term Retention and downstream Monetization. At other times, the focus may shift to drive new-user growth through, for example, content loops or viral loops. Monetization initiatives might cover a self-serve revenue channel and/or synergy with an enterprise GTM via a product-led sales process. Larger Growth Teams are able to execute on multiple focus areas concurrently.

Given the definition above, Growth Teams will typically be organized by outcome as opposed to by function or product architecture. It is common for the structure of a Growth Team to evolve over time to adapt to changes in the broader product growth model and market.

An outcome-oriented organization provides the freedom for Growth Teams to operate wherever opportunity lies. Here are some examples of outcomes-focused teams that are empowered to work outside the immediate domain of their particular outcome in an effort to improve that outcome.

### EXAMPLE 1: ACTIVATION TEAM WORKING ON ACQUISITION

A team driving improved Activation, for example, could undertake initiatives to unlock new Acquisition channels, with the hypothesis that these channels are able to reach ideal customer profile (ICP) users who are known to activate at consistently higher rates than average users.

### EXAMPLE 2: ACQUISITION TEAM WORKING ON ADOPTION

A team focused on new user Acquisition could work on initiatives like standing up a new Growth Loop via a sidecar product, building mechanisms that support virality, or optimizing the signup and login experience.

In this case, the surfaces worked on might include the company website, web apps, mobile apps, content in integrated third-party platforms, notifications (emails, Slack/Teams), and more.

**CASE STUDY**

#### How Snyk Growth Teams Work Across All Surfaces

When Ben Williams was running PLG at Snyk, the Growth Team pursued various strategies in the service of Acquisition alone:

- Conversion optimization on website landing pages and login flows;

- Building content-based search engine optimization (SEO) Growth Loops (company generated company distributed content loops using non-search distribution channels, i.e., SCMs such as GitHub, GitLab, and Bitbucket);
- Building and optimizing team invitation and referral mechanisms; and
- Free taster tools requiring no signup.

---

To be effective in growth execution across the entire user and customer lifecycle, Growth Teams need to be truly cross-functional.

Working across this variety of surfaces and mediums requires diverse, balanced teams. Product managers, developers, and designers tend to form the core of a product team. Growth Teams necessarily also include data/decision scientists and growth marketers. Not only does this kind of diversity bring a broader toolbox to new paths of innovation and experimentation, it also brings a wider palette of creative ideas.

A good rule of thumb is that each Growth Team in a PLG company would have:

- 1 product manager
- 1–3 engineers
- 1 designer
- 1 growth marketer
- 1 data analyst

At the company's option, the data analyst could be a shared resource and central function, with each analyst supporting two to three teams, helping join the dots with data across the customer lifecycle.

Growth marketers are often specialists and therefore part of teams where they have relevant expertise. For example, a team focused on Activation is best supported by a lifecycle marketer, whereas a team focused on Acquisition might benefit from influencer marketing, paid marketing, and SEO expertise.

On the engineering side, starting smaller and scaling out over time is generally preferred. Teams in smaller, earlier-stage organizations will likely have more hands-on engineering managers.

The number one distinguishing characteristic of a Growth Team as opposed to an Acquisition marketing team is that Growth Teams include engineers. It is impossible to leverage the product in growth objectives if the Growth Team can't

FIGURE 5.2.    Growth Team Roles

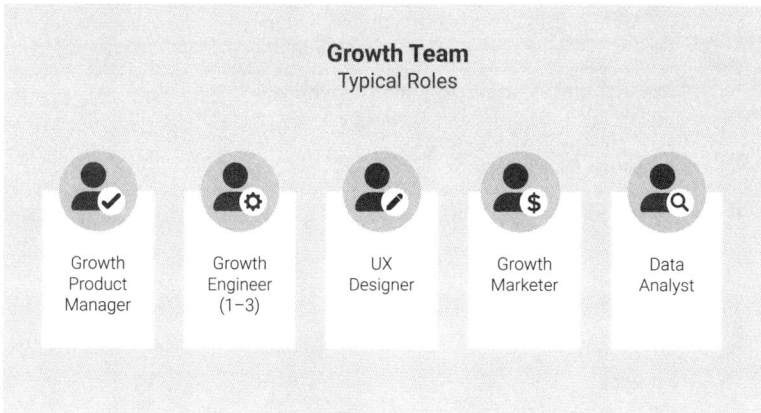

Growth Team
Typical Roles

| Growth Product Manager | Growth Engineer (1–3) | UX Designer | Growth Marketer | Data Analyst |

control the user experience in the product. Growth engineers tend to focus on user features, messaging, and workflows. Working together with their colleagues in Product, Marketing, and Design, they systematically release features and measure the impact those new features have on growth metrics.

## Experimentation Is the Core Work of Growth Teams

In pursuit of its objectives, a Growth Team maintains a backlog of proposed experiments and systematically cycles through them. Each week the team reviews the results of the experiments currently being run to determine if the targeted objectives are being met.

In a Growth Team environment, no feature, message, landing page, prompt, or experience is launched without first defining which metric it is designed to impact. Steve Blank calls this "stating your hypotheses," and he treats this practice as a major plank in the Lean Startup methodology.[1] With the hypothesis stated and the success metric selected, the team defines how the metric will be measured and tracked, and the experiment is fielded.

Growth Teams do not fall in love with their ideas—they launch them as experiments to see if they "work," i.e., if users respond in a way that will support growth objectives.

To better understand how a Growth Team operates, let's take a look at a weekly Growth Team meeting agenda.

## Weekly Growth Team Meeting Agenda (Example)[2]

- Review of Metrics and General Update (15 minutes)
  - Review the latest data for the key impact metric and other leading indicator growth metrics.
  - Discuss progress on short-term growth objectives in the team's focus area.
  - Highlight key positive factors and improvements in metrics resulting from experiments.
  - Review key negative factors and issues holding back growth.
- Review of Last Week's Testing Activity (10 minutes)
  - Assess the tempo of experiments launched in the previous week compared to the team's goal.
  - Discuss the tests that were not launched and explain the reasons for any delays.
  - Data analyst presents preliminary results from tests launched and conclusive results from analyzed experiments.
  - Answer questions, consider suggestions for further analysis, and evaluate the implications of the experiments.
- Selection of Growth Tests for Current Cycle (15 minutes)
  - Discuss nominations for the next set of tests to launch.
  - Each team member provides a brief overview of their nominated ideas.
  - Engage in a brief discussion about the merits of the experiments.
  - Aim for consensus, with the growth lead making the final call where there is disagreement.
  - Assign owners to each experiment based on expertise and responsibility for getting the test launched.
  - Identify experiments that will not be ready for the current cycle and schedule them for a future date.

- Check on Growth of Idea Pipeline (5 minutes)
  - Report on the number of ideas waiting for consideration or future launch.
  - Encourage the team to add more ideas if the ideation volume is low.
  - Recognize top contributors from the previous week to inspire the team to generate fresh ideas.
- Wrap-up and Next Steps (5 minutes)
  - Summarize key decisions made during the meeting.
  - Confirm action items, responsibilities, and deadlines.
  - Set the date and time for the next Growth Team meeting.
  - Conclude the meeting on a positive note, encouraging collaboration and innovation.

In weekly growth meetings, the team reviews results from ongoing experiments, ideates and prioritizes new experiments, and schedules the launch of the experiments that are up next.

As an experiment runs, it provides feedback, which is then used to tune future experiments, relaunch, and re-measure.

- If users are succeeding with the product, we want to know.
- If users are getting stuck, we want to know.
- If users are sharing, getting angry, rage-clicking, upgrading, defecting—we want to know all of it.

This feedback helps us know where to focus our experiments, what portions of the experience need attention, and how to tune up the growth engine by removing friction and providing avenues for growth.

For some product managers who are not used to this immediate and high-fidelity feedback, it can seem harsh at first, and we sometimes go into denial.

*Why can't the users understand that flow?*
*I can't believe this doesn't have more adoption—it's designed so well!*
*Give it time—they'll get it eventually. . . . If not, I'm worried about their intelligence.*

But eventually, we begin to fall in love with feedback. It's timely truth that serves better than blind love for our product. Feedback is life for a product-led growth practitioner. We crave it, seek it, architect for it, and pursue it with absurd precision.

Growth Teams are obsessed with learning.

### Impact and Learnings Reviews for Companies with Multiple Growth Teams

In larger companies with multiple Growth Teams, each team runs its own cadence of experimentation and weekly meetings (described above). But since learnings for one team can be useful for another team operating in an adjacent space, it is important to get the teams together to share relevant results of their work.

To this end, a second weekly meeting is established—this one across all Growth Teams. At Snyk, this meeting is called the Impact and Learnings Review (I&L), and each team is invited to answer five questions:

- **What did we do?**
  - This question gets everyone on the same page by sharing how we arrived at the learning.
  - Was this an experiment? Qualitative research? Quantitative exploration?
  - Here we describe what we did in enough detail to provide context for alignment.
- **What did we believe was going to happen?**
  - We provide detail on what we expected to see/observe/happen.
  - Why did we expect those things?
- **What actually happened?**
  - Given that we expect maybe 1 in 5 experiments to validate our hypotheses, it's typical that not all things we thought would play out as expected.
  - Insight comes from analysis and conversation around the observed outcome, including any delta from the hypothesized outcome.
- **What did we learn?**
  - Here we describe the learning itself.
  - Have we established causal relationships?
  - Do we understand why we've observed something?
  - What were the effects on secondary and health metrics, and what does that tell us?

- Where else could we apply what we learned? In what other contexts might these learnings be relevant?
- Have the learnings led to other hypotheses?

■ **What do we intend to do next?**

- As a result of our learnings, what do we intend to do next? Some examples (not an exhaustive or mutually exclusive list) are:
  - › Implement learnings at scale to create ⟨xyz⟩ impact.
  - › Experiment further to learn ⟨xyz⟩ or validate hypothesis ⟨xyz⟩.
  - › Analyze event data to understand ⟨xyz⟩ better.
  - › Conduct user interviews to understand ⟨xyz⟩ better.
  - › Conduct the same experiment in a similar area ⟨xyz⟩.
  - › Deprioritize: we've learned ⟨xyz⟩ and decided not to move forward in this direction.

I&L reviews foster an ongoing sense of curiosity and experimentation. As one Growth Team hears about successful experimentation in another team's domain, it may gain inspiration for its own pursuits. Sometimes findings in one area can directly impact another area. Overall, the culture of learning, the emphasis on empathy, generosity, and metrics, and the pursuit of growth results, as represented in the product growth model, can be effectively reinforced via effective weekly I&L reviews.

## Final Thoughts

Growth is a labor of love, pursued passionately by Growth Teams.

It runs on empathy, generosity, and metrics.

It depends on incessant iteration and experimentation to fine-tune every aspect of the experience for users.

Even at scale, the machine that produces product-led growth keeps running.

It doesn't rely on individual large deals. It doesn't depend on quarterly sales heroics. It runs on a steady rhythm of independent discovery by humans who are in the market for help with a problem, a try-before-you-buy experience, and a simple self-service user experience, leading to impact, Retention, and Expansion.

Seems logical, because it is.

Seems simple, because it is.

Competitors who didn't care enough to put in the work or who thought they could take shortcuts will look at well-run growth companies and believe they just got lucky. They didn't. They earned it by pursuing deliberate growth tactics.

Growth Teams are at the heart of all PLG efforts:

- PLG startups are Growth Teams by definition.
- Larger PLG companies carve out Growth Teams to attack specific aspects of growth within the larger structure.
- Established companies that add PLG to their existing GTM motions also carve out Growth Teams to get PLG working within their environment.

Growth product management and growth engineering are two of the most sought-after skill sets in the market today.

### Chapter 5 Summary

- Growth Teams are small, cross-functional teams focused on specific growth objectives.
- Growth Teams are organized by objective, not function.
- Growth Teams focus on learning in the pursuit of impact.
- Growth Teams measure themselves against a product growth model that contains the key assumptions around various growth levers.
- Growth Teams architect Growth Loops and iterate quickly through growth experiments to create the cumulative impact of improvements across growth levers.

## Manager Minute

Thinking about your own company, take time to reflect on the following questions:

1. What is our primary strategy across these five growth levers? (circle one)

| | | | |
|---|---|---|---|
| Acquisition | no touch (product-led) | low touch (marketing-led) | high touch (sales led) |
| Activation | no touch (product-led) | low touch (community-led) | high touch (CSM-led) |
| Monetization | no touch (product-led) | low touch (community-led) | high touch (CSM-led) |
| Retention | no touch (product-led) | low touch (community-led) | high touch (CSM-led) |
| Expansion | no touch (product-led) | low touch (opportunistic AMs) | high touch (territory AMs) |

2. If Growth Teams are defined as being inclusive of both marketing personnel and engineers who can work on product, how many Growth Teams do we have at our company? List as many as possible:

_____

_____

_____

3. If we were to spool up one additional Growth Team, on which area of the business would we want them to focus?

_____

_____

_____

## SIX

# Building a Minimum Viable Product
# for Freemium Adoption

> ### Stripping Down to a Single Use Case
> ### to Match Job To Be Done

Building a product for freemium adoption is different.

- It's different than the process described by Geoffrey Moore in *Crossing the Chasm.*[1]

- It goes beyond the process outlined by Marty Cagan in *Inspired.*[2]

- It cannot be done with a single anchor customer or joint development partner.

- It cannot be distributed via a partner.

- Salespeople are not your primary ears to the ground, collecting customer feedback.

- Amazing technology is not good enough.

- Engineers can rarely do this on their own.

- More features are rarely better.

- Bigger customers are not better.

No, building a product for freemium adoption is its own thing—an art closer to developing consumer apps and games than to developing legacy business-to-business (B2B) software.

I learned this lesson in 2010, when I moved our small crowdfunding software company from Westford, Massachusetts, to Palo Alto, California. The company was Fundly, and our aspiration was to make fundraising easy for any organization—formal or informal. The initial version of our product was used by large political campaigns on both sides of the aisle. These campaigns were staffed with very smart people who were quick to deploy our widgets and forms on their websites and highly adept at rallying their supporters. Political organizations also moved millions of dollars, which made it relatively easy for them to justify paying Fundly for the technology that powered those efforts.

As soon as we opened our sights to include nonprofit organizations and informal organizations like teams, classrooms, and individuals, we quickly learned our software was far too complex, far too technical, and far too expensive to serve the needs of these groups. Even if we could attract them to our website, the process we had for implementing the software reached well beyond the capabilities of most small organizations—even though we had people on our own staff ready and willing to help them.

We had to rethink everything. Suddenly it mattered much less that we could process millions of dollars in a single afternoon, and it mattered much more that a schoolteacher should be able to launch a fundraising page within five minutes. This was a whole different set of challenges.

### How to Identify the Single Problem Your Product Solves

If you want to build a freemium product, your challenge starts with identifying a real problem that real humans have, for which they would love to find a solution—their Job To Be Done. It is important to distinguish between building for an end user and building for an organization or a purchaser or an approver. We need to identify an end user with a JTBD they can solve by "hiring" a solution that we build.[3]

If our goal is to build a B2B application, we also need to understand how solving a single problem for a single user can grow into solving a scaled version of that problem across an entire organization.

Most aspiring product creators have ideas about how to answer these questions. You may even already have a product currently sold by salespeople, and you want to convert it into a freemium product. Either way—whether you are inventing a new product or adapting an existing product—you will need to think fundamentally about the end user.

### Defining Your Ideal Customer Profile

Most B2B business leaders work daily with the concept of an ideal customer profile (ICP). This customer can be described in terms of industry, company size, location, and other firmographic descriptors. When selling a B2B product, we want to make sure we understand the size of the total addressable market (TAM), serviceable addressable market (SAM), and serviceable obtainable market (SOM) constituted of our ICP customers. When speaking about the total size of the market we are going after, we often shorthand this as "TAM," expressed in dollars, e.g., "The TAM for our service is $60B."

None of this changes for a freemium product. We still need to know we are solving a problem that affects a large set of potential users. We want to know what those users look like, and in the case of B2B products, we want to know how to identify the companies where these individual people work. We also need to know how many of those types of companies exist, and how we might target potential users at those companies with marketing campaigns?

Understanding your target market at this level is "kind of" important. You should spend just enough time on it to convince yourself there is a large market and an unmet need—and no more. But since building and launching an MVP is difficult, you need to conserve most of your research time and energy to focus on the individual user and her needs.

### Getting to Know Your User, the Human

At the end of the day, the end user of your product will be a person. Understanding this person and how she approaches her life is much more important than understanding the organization in which this person works. Therefore, we will channel much of our energy and empathy into getting to know her (on empathy, see Chapter 3: First Principles of Product-Led Growth). In business-to-consumer (B2C) markets, this was our customer all along. In B2B markets, this requires a shift from focusing on the ICP Company that might buy our product to focusing on the human who might adopt our product to help them make progress on a specific JTBD. In this very real sense, key aspects of designing freemium products for B2B and B2C end users are quite similar.

How do you build empathy for someone you haven't met? Sometimes the easiest path is to build for someone like yourself. If you've experienced a certain pain or frustration, and you want to build a solution to solve that problem for yourself and for people like you, you have built-in empathy for the end user. But in the likely case that you are not the target user for the product you are building, you will need to meet that user. Spend time with her. Perhaps shadow her while she goes about the task(s) you hope to streamline. An effective way to get to know your target persona is to go onsite with her—in her natural environment—and conduct a JTBD interview.

## The Importance of Aiming Your Product at a Job To Be Done

A Jobs To Be Done interview is a qualitative research method used to understand the underlying motivations and needs of customers when they "hire" a product or service to accomplish a specific task or address a problem. Unlike traditional market research, which often focuses on demographics or preferences, JTBD interviews delve into the functional, social, and emotional dimensions of consumer behavior. By uncovering the core job or problem that customers are trying to solve, businesses can develop products and services that truly resonate with their target audience.

To conduct a JTBD interview effectively, it's crucial to start by identifying a diverse sample of customers who have recently purchased or used a product or service to address the issue at hand. Remember to keep the conversation free-flowing, allowing the participant to organically articulate their experiences and decision-making process. Use open-ended questions to probe deeper into the circumstances surrounding the purchase, the struggles the customer encountered, and the outcomes desired by the customer. The goal is to uncover patterns and insights that shed light on the customer's goals, challenges, and decision criteria.

Throughout the JTBD interview, it's essential to pay close attention to both verbal and nonverbal cues from the participant. Look for recurring themes, emotions, and unmet needs expressed by multiple interviewees. Additionally, listen for any contradictions or surprises that challenge your assumptions about customer behavior. It's also important to consider the context in which the job is being performed, including external factors such as time constraints or social influences. We are really trying to develop a sense for what lies at the center of the customer's heart and motivations when they consider the job they want to make progress on.

Key words and phrases are important here. The same words a customer uses to describe the pain they are experiencing may be key terms to use in marketing to attract potential customers' attention. The emphases they put on different aspects of their decision process can shed light on feature priorities. It's equally important to pay attention to things they do *not* bring up—this may include features or aspects of our product we thought would be important that we can now assume are not core to a customer's consideration.

Remember—we will not be in the room when a new customer encounters our product. We cannot "talk them into" anything, nor can we convince them they have a problem they don't already recognize. Thus, during this JTBD definition process, we are looking to *discover* what the customer already believes and tap into how she thinks and feels about potential approaches to making progress (for more on JTBD research, see *The Jobs To Be Done Handbook* by Chris Spiek and Bob Moesta).[4]

The words we put in front of a prospective customer need to match customer sentiment so perfectly that the prospect's reaction is, "Yes! Exactly that!"

And then when our prospect first encounters the product, they need to quickly find their way to First Impact, before they lose patience or run out of attention span. We are not looking to dazzle this customer with all the things our product *could do*. We do not want to confuse them or overwhelm them. We are looking for a *direct match* between job and solution. Marketing copy got them here with a certain expectation around a JTBD. Now we need to deliver on that JTBD as quickly and seamlessly as possible—with minimum friction and maximum ease.

This points us to a single value proposition per customer. No extra features, no extraneous options, no superfluous steps, no unnecessary configuration or setup. Just a single value proposition, and a straight line to achieve it (on self-service onboarding, see Chapter 8: Building Self-Service Onboarding into Your Freemium Product).

### "Just Enough and Not More"—How to Build a Minimum Viable Product

An MVP is the most basic version of a product that can be released to the market to start the process of learning from customers. It contains only the essential features needed to satisfy early adopters and gather feedback for future development.[5] When considering what goes into the MVP, we channel the empathy we developed for the end user, and we think like we imagine they would: "Why am I here, what am I looking to accomplish, and how much time and attention am I willing to spend figuring out how to get it?"

An honest assessment of these questions usually results in the following answer:

"Less, not more."

When considering how to position an existing product for self-service customer Acquisition, we often have to hide, disable, or eliminate most of the features that make our product flexible and robust for use in larger organizations. Our end user does not care about security. She doesn't care about reporting. She may not care about options B, C, or D. She cares only about "Option A"—her primary use case. She came to solve a specific problem, and we must clear everything else out of her way and accelerate her path to First Impact.

An MVP is designed to do just that. If we're building from scratch, we can be scrappy. We can even build a barely-functional prototype. At first, we are only looking to see if the combination of features we chose is appealing enough to a prospective customer to interest them in trying it.

For teams I work with that are building a brand-new product, I encourage them to present product designs to potential customers—before they have even built an actual product. You can go back to the same people you talked to during JTBD interviews and this time present a proposed "solution" for the JTBD you discussed. In these "reaction" interviews, we cannot fall into the trap of explaining the product or trying to sell it. We just "slide it across the table" (metaphorically) and see if the customer picks it up.

I like to have the customer narrate out loud what they are thinking as they encounter a new product (whether a design, a prototype, or a fully functioning MVP). During these sessions, you might hear a prospect say, "Well, I think the next thing I would do is click this button, and I would expect that to do <xyz>." If they are misinterpreting the desired action or flow, it is very difficult to stay quiet. Most product managers at this point want to say, "Wait. . . . Did you notice the blank field right above? Wouldn't you want to fill that in first?" As tempting as it is to direct the user at this point, it is better to stay as silent as possible and let them fumble through while narrating their own thoughts. Remaining silent, we learn much more.

When discussing MVPs, Steve Blank advocates, "Just enough and no more." He's referring to how robust and feature-rich we make our initial product. Just enough to learn, and no more. It does not have to be beautiful. It does not have to be secure (in most cases). It does not have to have advanced features. We can populate it with fake data. We can build in a time-lapse simulation. Some design tools like Figma make it easy to simulate a fully functional application without writing any code. All we are looking for is the customer's reaction. If we are not getting the uptake we want, we have not wasted too much time on this version, and we can quickly make adjustments and try again.

## The "First Impact Success Rate"—Quantifying Product-Market Fit with an MVP

At some point, the design becomes the prototype, and the prototype becomes the MVP. The MVP is the version of the product with the minimum amount of functionality we can introduce to new users unsupervised and with no instructions. The ultimate test of our MVP is to actually do that—introduce it to new users, and see what happens. To execute this phase, we need a source of new users we can tap for successive cohorts of usage.

Cohort one might fail abysmally. If we have a first cohort of fifty users, it would not be uncommon for all fifty to fail to achieve the desired outcome. Sometimes this is because of a bug in our product, and sometimes it is because of a non-intuitive design. Often, if we have slimmed down an enterprise product for self-service adoption, we still haven't simplified it enough. Whatever it is, that first cohort of users teaches us what needs to improve.

After making adjustments, we send through a second cohort. This one may do slightly better, but we need a way to measure that. In Chapter 8 we discuss how to define and measure First Impact, but here it is in a nutshell.

The goal of launching an MVP is to learn enough to iterate toward Product-Market Fit. PMF is achieved when X% of new users achieve First Impact within time $(t)$, with $t$ being our best estimate of the attention span of our users. We call this the First Impact success rate.

This metric is tracked cohort-by-cohort, with incremental improvements measured until X is somewhere in the range of 70%.

## Common Pitfalls with MVP Development, and How to Avoid Them

It is almost never the case that a team *underdevelops* an MVP. I have seen paper prototypes work perfectly well for testing customers' initial reactions. The common pitfalls we see fall into five categories:

1. **The MVP is designed or derailed by a HiPPO.** The HiPPO is the Highest Paid Person's Opinion (in the room). When the HiPPO offers an opinion, it can sometimes sound like an order. But their opinion is not the one that matters. The only thing that matters is how the customer will actually react when she encounters our product in the wild. Beware the HiPPO. Many experts, including Marty Cagan, principal at Silicon Valley Product Group and author of *Inspired*,[6] have advice on how to manage the HiPPO.

2. **The MVP has too many features.** This is most often the case when we are trying to slim down an enterprise product for self-service use. "This is a very cool feature—we don't want to cut that out." Well. . . . Most likely you *do* want to cut that out. The cooler the feature, the more likely it isn't part of the core set of features needed to accomplish the JTBD. Cut, cut, cut. Get all the way to the bare essentials. Anything that is optional has the potential to confuse and distract. Err on the side of eliminating features, and make every feature fight for inclusion.

3. **The First-Time User Experience (FTUX) is confusing.** We may have the feature set right, but we may have difficulty presenting those features in a way that is intuitive for a user who has never encountered our product before. Be flexible when this happens. Just because it makes sense to you doesn't mean it makes sense to an average user—pay attention to where she gets stuck, and think creatively about how you can adjust the FTUX to better help the user succeed.

4. **The FTUX has too many steps (it's too long).** Does your user really have to fill out a profile before getting on with the JTBD? Do we really need her to authenticate outside services? Does she need to input data? Could we have her do a "practice run" with dummy data instead? If a step is optional in any way during the FTUX, we should skip it during FTUX and circle back later.

5. **Testing is not objective.** Of course we are proud of our product. But to get an objective view of whether it will work "in the wild" with customers we have never met, we need to simulate that as closely as possible. Once our close circles of friends and colleagues have tried it, how about people outside of those circles? Instead of only putting it in front of technically-savvy people, what about inviting a broader cross-section of users that better represents the target market?

MVPs are a phenomenal opportunity to discover the magic combination of features and FTUX that will help users accomplish their JTBD within their attention span. If you don't overbuild, you prioritize customer actions over HiPPOs, you eliminate all optional features, you streamline the FTUX, and you commit to testing on a continued basis until you can reliably succeed with representative cross-sections of new users, you will be ready to move to the next phase: Customer Acquisition.

## Final Thoughts

The process of understanding and developing for the end user is critical to product-led growth (PLG). Getting this right is the essence of Product-Market Fit, and it greases the wheels of all subsequent PLG mechanics. If your end user naturally discovers, uses, and succeeds with your product, you have Product-Market Fit, and all downstream growth mechanics have a chance. If you do not have Product-Market Fit, it makes no sense to proceed. All the PLG tactics described in the rest of this book cannot and will not work without PMF.

In a nutshell, our objective in iterating toward PMF is to make things easier for the customer. We want it to feel so natural that our user progresses toward her own success on her own journey without confusion. Each step of her journey is deliberately designed and optimized to remove friction and increase success for the customer—without help from sales or customer success (CS). This means that all the possible ways to "mess up" in the customer Acquisition and onboarding journey have been discovered and eliminated.

This can take some time. Even with a good understanding of the user and a minimum viable product already in place, it can take twelve months or more to tune the initial product experience to where we would declare initial victory on PMF.

*"Always?"*
Yes, pretty much always.
*"What if I already have a product?"*
We are assuming there is already a product! And with that product
in place, instrumenting, testing, and tuning still take time.

We can't accelerate experiments beyond natural limits, and we can't parallelize them too much. This will take time, but the effort is worthwhile. We are working toward a reality where customers can discover, adopt, use, and succeed with our product, all without any assistance from marketing, sales, or customer success. Once the machine is built, it works for you. Customers are acquired, they onboard themselves, they achieve impact by themselves, and the whole thing runs like a flywheel, with very little additional energy requirements from your team. Your team is free to work other parts of the system.

Building this kind of machine can seem overwhelming, but in this book we break it down. In the following chapters we walk through this process one step at a time so you can follow along in the context of your own business. The

whole of Part Two is intended to lay out the blueprint, with more specific explanations of the underlying mechanics and measurements along the way.

## Chapter 6 Summary

- Building an MVP for freemium adoption requires an obsessive focus on the end user (not the buyer or approver).
- JTBD interviews are an effective way to develop understanding and empathy for the end user and her Job To Be Done.
- MVPs can and should be made as low-fidelity as possible at first—design, then prototype, then minimum viable set of features—just enough to test user sentiment and no more.
- Beware the HiPPO—the boss's opinion does not carry the day when it comes to MVP development. We are looking for data from experiments we run with target users.
- Testing how a potential user responds to the product is the only way to truly assess Product-Market Fit.
- Everything depends on Product-Market Fit.

## Manager Minute

Thinking about your own company, take time to reflect on the following questions:

1. How well do we know our end user? What direct experience do I have with her?

_____

_____

_____

2. For the PLG product we are considering, what is the customer's Job To Be Done?

_____

_____

_____

**3.** What alternative products or services could our customer "hire" to accomplish her Job To Be Done?

_____

_____

_____

**4.** How would we build and test an MVP to iterate toward PMF?

_____

_____

_____

# SEVEN

# Filling the Marketing Funnel: How to Acquire Self-Service Customers

Making Your Product Easy to Find and Adopt

In most business-to-business (B2B) environments, sales is king.

The chief revenue officer (CRO) is generally the highest-paid executive reporting to the chief executive officer (CEO)—sometimes even earning more than the CEO.

Each quarter Wall Street investors eagerly await quarterly earnings reports from public B2B companies, a key feature of which is the "bookings" number—the total amount of sales won (measured in dollars) during the period in question. As long as CROs can deliver against bookings forecasts, they can keep their job and maintain their position at the top of the company food chain. When the CRO misses enough bookings forecasts, they lose their job, investors lose confidence, and everyone looks for a more secure footing with a new CRO and a new set of bookings forecasts.

## Why "Bookings" Is No Longer the Primary Metric for Recurring-Revenue Businesses

This dynamic has changed somewhat with the increasing prevalence of recurring-revenue business models. Why? Because with recurring-revenue businesses of scale, the bulk of the revenue in any given period is not contributed by bookings from *new* customers but rather by renewing contracts with *existing* customers. New-customer bookings are important, but they are important as a *portion* of the revenue machine—a portion that will layer into the machine and contribute to the overall revenue stack for years to come as those customers renew and expand their contracts.

In recurring-revenue businesses, "bookings" has taken its rightful place as a *component* of revenue—not the sole focus—and investors have adjusted their approach accordingly. SaaS investors in particular have adopted an entirely new set of metrics that goes well beyond bookings. These metrics are designed to assess the health of the overall revenue factory, not just the output (revenue) and certainly not just a single input (bookings):

- The **Magic Number** is the ratio of the increase in recurring revenue in any given period to the amount spent on sales and marketing in the previous period.

- **LTV: CAC** is the ratio of average customer lifetime value (LTV) to the amount of sales and marketing expense required to acquire a new customer (customer acquisition cost, or CAC).

- **CAC Payback Period** measures the time (in months) required for customer-generated revenue to replenish the expenses incurred acquiring the customer.

- The **Rule of 40** measures the sum of the free cash flow percentage of revenue and the overall revenue growth rate.

- **Gross revenue retention (GRR)** measures the percentage of customer spend retained from one Renewal cycle to the next.

- **Net revenue retention (NRR)** measures not only the retained portion of existing contracts but also the Expansion of those same contracts (net retention can be greater than 100%).

These metrics and others like them attempt to extend beyond bookings and beyond the income statement and evaluate the true health of a SaaS company. They help compare one SaaS company to the next, and they help establish benchmarks for what "good" looks like. The evolution of SaaS metrics has been helpful, and it has given rise to an entire new discipline of revenue architecture—the study and articulation of the underlying models and principles of recurring revenue.[1] Benchmarks are also available that establish best-in-class results for the metrics above and many more.[2]

The best product-led growth (PLG) companies have the potential to exceed many of the best-in-class benchmarks established for the above metrics, because of the way PLG companies' revenue factories are built.

FIGURE 7.1.   Relative Performance of Product-Led and Sales-Led Companies.

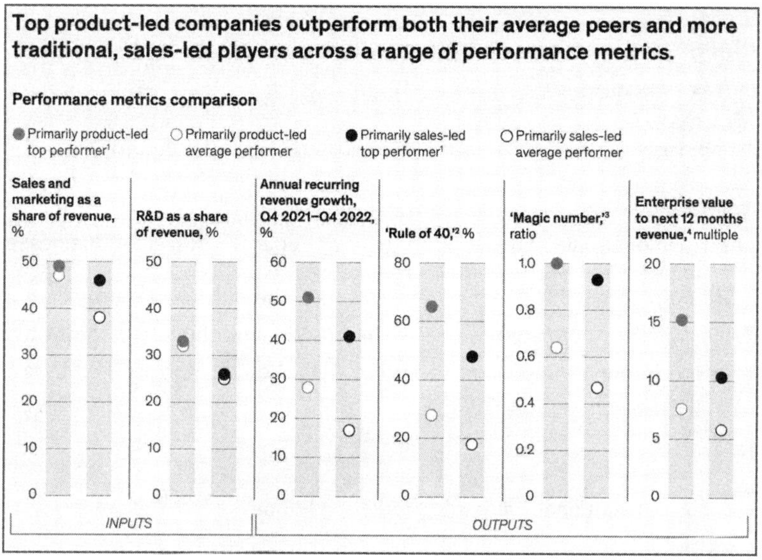

Notes: Primarily product-led top performers, n = 11; primarily product-led average performers, n = 21; primarily sales-led top performers, n = 14; primarily sales-led average performers, n = 62.

1. Twice the annual recurring revenue growth + free cash flow>80%.

2. This popular operating performance metric says that the combination of a software company's growth rate and free cash flow rate should be >40%.

3. A sales efficiency metric that measures the amount of annual revenue growth generated by every dollar spent on sales and marketing.

4. As of Jan 2, 2023.

Source: Exhibit from "From product-led growth to product-led sales: Beyond the PLG hype", August 2023, McKinsey & Company, www.mckinsey.com. Copyright (c) 2024 McKinsey & Company. All rights reserved. Reprinted by permission.

Since a PLG company's go-to-market (GTM) motions can at least in part be executed by the product itself, growth is less dependent on things that take time and cost money, like hiring and training humans to do tasks, when the product can accomplish these tasks automatically.

Not all PLG companies are better than sales-led companies, but the best-performing product-led companies outperform the best-performing sales-led companies on the major growth metrics (see Figure 7.1).[3]

Breakout PLG companies are in a class of their own. They defy gravity. Which begs the questions:

Why?

How?

The answers to these questions begin with new account Acquisition.

### How the Traditional Sales Funnel Shortchanges Recurring-Revenue Businesses

In traditional, sales-led GTM motions, the sales and marketing funnel is a mainstay. Leads are dropped into the "top of the funnel," and they work their way from awareness to interest to decision and ultimately the sale, represented here as the "bottom of funnel."

FIGURE 7.2.   **Traditional Sales and Marketing Funnel**

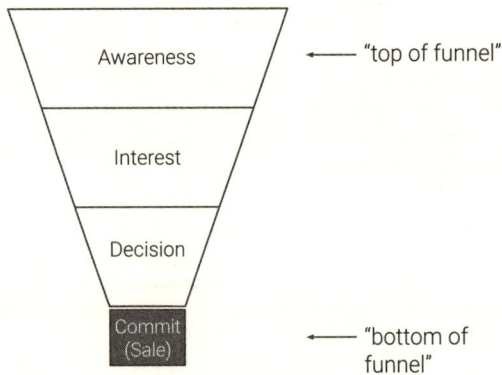

### The Recurring-Revenue Bowtie as a Modernization of the Sales and Marketing Funnel

The nature of recurring-revenue businesses requires that we rethink the finality of this "bottom-of-funnel" thinking. If a customer's decision to purchase is in fact a decision to *subscribe*, then that decision is the beginning—not the end—of the revenue process.

FIGURE 7.3.    The Recurring Revenue Bowtie

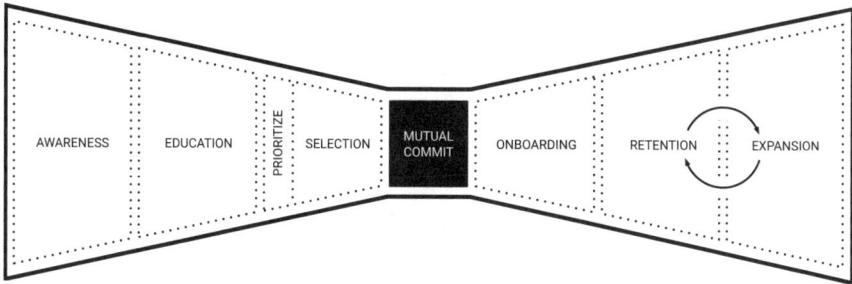

*Source:* Winning by Design

To this end, Winning by Design has made famous "The Bowtie," which turns the sales and marketing funnel on its side and extends it to include the post-initial-sale stages of the customer journey.

The Bowtie illustrates a customer's presale journey as well as their post-sale journey, which is where recurring revenue actually happens.

### In PLG, Customers Are Invited to Experience the Product Before Purchasing

In PLG we don't emphasize sales or contracts. We focus on Acquisition—*user* Acquisition. If we can acquire enough users, a subset of those users will go on to Monetize—at their own pace and of their own accord. PLG Monetization models are largely self-service, sometimes with assistance from Sales, but not dependent on sales.

PLG relies on a very wide top-of-funnel, filled with all types of users:

- Users who will not stick around.

- Users who will stick around but never Monetize (free users).

- Users who will Monetize but never expand to a team or an organization (pro users).

- Users whose usage will lead to adoption within their team or organization (team users).

- Users whose usage will spark eventual enterprise-wide adoption (enterprise users).

- Users who promote and advocate outside their organizations.

FIGURE 7.4.   In PLG, Customers Experience the Product Before Purchasing

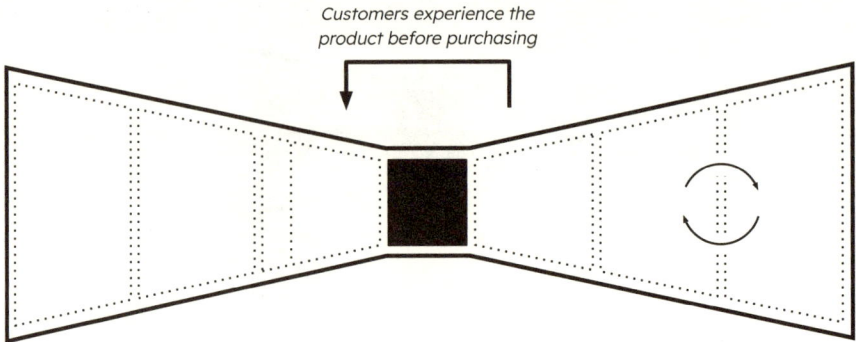

The indisputable focus in PLG is on users and usage—not contracts and contract value.

Usage, not bookings.

Whereas in sales-led GTM motions the sales and marketing goal can often be contract quantity and contract size, in PLG motions the analogous goal is end user Acquisition, Activation, and Monetization. In PLG motions we manage a funnel that is wide at the top, with no money involved when the user initially creates an account.

We encourage the user to experience the product before committing to pay for it. We are searching for customers who may pay us later, but who are willing to engage with the product now with no financial commitment whatsoever. We count the Acquisition of these non-paying customers as a "win," as we know it is the first step on their journey to future Monetization.

> PLG is a go-to-market strategy whereby users are allowed
> to experience the product before purchasing.

## The Updated PLG Bowtie Reorders and Reprioritizes Customer Actions

With the emphasis shifted from human-led to product-led marketing and sales activities, and with the focus squarely on helping a customer accomplish her Job To Be Done, PLG practitioners have renamed and reorganized the stages of the customer journey to reflect a product-led growth approach:

FIGURE 7.5.   The PLG Bowtie

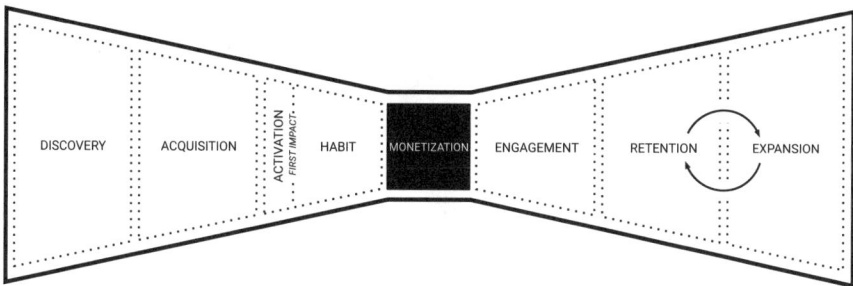

Discovery, Acquisition, Activation, First Impact, Habit. These are the phases that describe the PLG journey for a new customer on the left-hand side of the Bowtie. Notably, Activation—historically a post-sale stage—has now become a pre-sale stage in the customer journey.

Monetization happens only after the customer already has an account and has achieved impact using the product. Engagement, Retention, and Expansion are objectives on the right-hand side of the PLG Bowtie.

For existing, paying customers, the goal is to continue to be relevant in their lives—to maintain active engagement and to expand usage and revenue (Expansion). This Expansion includes usage from the original users, expanded usage within their team, and usage from additional users they might invite to experience the product.

### How to Think About Product-Led User Acquisition Conversion Metrics

For every one user account that eventually pays us money, we often need to create ten or more initial "free" user accounts.

Creating a free account is not as easy as it sounds. It might require one hundred or more unique website visitors to create a single new free account. Some of those visitors will create accounts, some of those new users will continue forever free, some (1 in 10 or so) will create a paid account, and still others will "churn" (stop using the service).

## FIGURE 7.6.   PLG Conversion Rates from Web Visit to Paid.

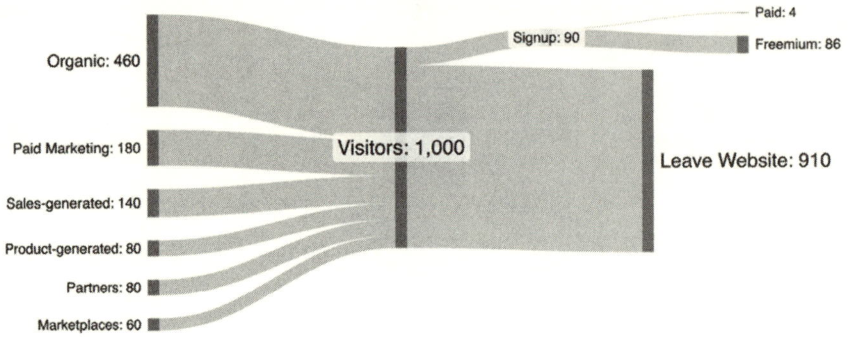

Organic: 460

Paid Marketing: 180

Sales-generated: 140

Product-generated: 80

Partners: 80

Marketplaces: 60

Visitors: 1,000

Signup: 90

Paid: 4

Freemium: 86

Leave Website: 910

*Source:* Kyle Poyar, "Your Guide to PLG Benchmarks," Kyle Poyar's Growth Unhinged, 2022. https://www.growthunhinged.com/p/your-guide-to-plg-benchmarks.

This process in PLG is called Acquisition, and entire teams are dedicated to designing the experiences and experiments that optimize user Acquisition, with an eye toward ongoing Monetization.

We know at some point in the future we will be asking for money. But in the beginning, we just want to demonstrate we have a product that can address the user's Job To Be Done.

So we throw the door wide open.

We invite customers to visit us, to come inside, to see if they like what they see. To try it out. To use it. To get value from it.

We know that if enough customers try our product and experience impact, a subset of those customers will continue to rely on the product, invite their colleagues, and eventually upgrade to a paid plan.

### Where Is Sales in Product-Led User Acquisition? Nowhere.

This worldview of attracting and serving the end user first has significant implications for Marketing and Sales.

1. **Marketing**'s job is not only to raise awareness of the product or to drive visits to a page but to drive actual sign-ups for a product. This means working hand in hand with Product to understand the target customer, what their specific needs are, and how to align end-user Acquisition with long-term Retention and Expansion.

**2. Sales** is not involved at this stage.

**3. Product** has taken responsibility for the education, initial success, and Monetization of the customer.

If Product and Marketing are both working to get customers started on the product, then they need to work together. Silos are not going to work here.

Imagine if Marketing were to say, "Page visits are up—the rest is on you!"

This is not a formula for success

So in PLG we have Acquisition teams. They often report to Marketing, but they work very closely with Product, and their sole focus is acquiring new users.

---

`CASE STUDY`

**How Figma's Acquisition Marketing and Product Teams Worked Together to Gain Four Million Users**

Figma is a design tool that allows users to create and collaborate on design for digital products' user interfaces. Consistent with Figma's product-led go-to-market (GTM) strategy, the company's growth marketing team worked closely with the product team during its first few years of existence to create a self-service Acquisition and onboarding process. Figma focused on making it easy for users to get started with the product and see the value of it, without the need for sales or customer success intervention.

The marketing team was responsible for creating awareness of Figma and driving traffic to the website through a variety of channels, including search engine optimization (SEO), social media, and content marketing.

The product team worked on making the product easy to use and understand. It also added features that would encourage users to continue using the product, such as collaboration tools and integrations with other popular apps.

By working together, the marketing and product teams were able to create a PLG motion that helped Figma grow rapidly. In its first ten years, the company grew to over 4 million users, including within large companies such as Dropbox, Rakuten, Slack, X, and Volvo.[4]

### Product's Role—Working with Marketing—in New User Acquisition

In the PLG Acquisition paradigm, Product assumes at least partial responsibility for:

- Educating the customer
- Onboarding the customer (more on that in Chapter 8: Building Self-Service Onboarding into Your Freemium Product)
- Monetizing the customer (more on that in Chapter 9: How to Convert Free Users into Large Paying Contracts)

Acquisition is thus a *collaboration* between Marketing and Product:

- **Marketing** owns the messaging and initial sign-up experience.
- **Product** is responsible for translating those sign-ups into onboarding that seamlessly guides the customer toward First Impact.

FIGURE 7.7.   **Product-Led User Journey to First Impact**

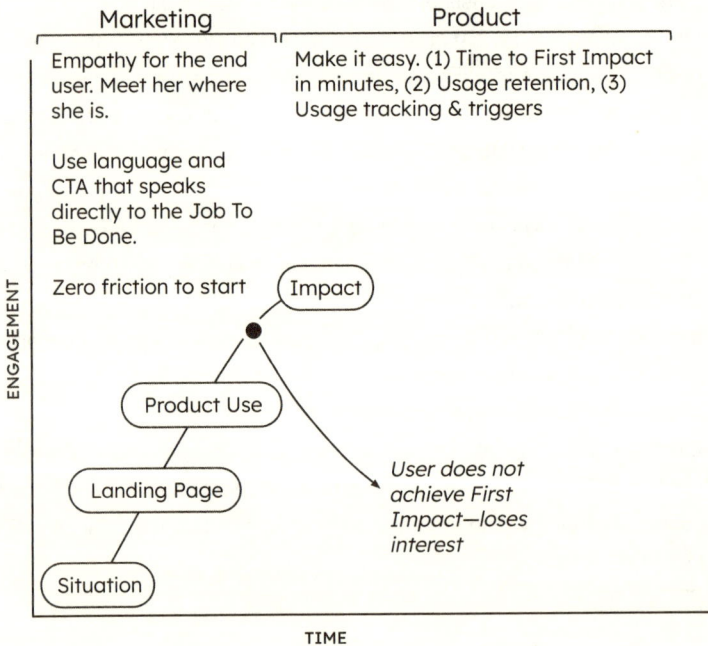

This partnership between Marketing and Product is a match made in heaven. Marketers are accustomed to running experiments to see what combination of copy/layout/placement delivers the desired campaign results—often measured in page views, click-throughs, or form fills. In the case of PLG, the objective is new user sign-ups, but the number one tactic to get there from a marketing perspective is the same:

experimentation.

Before PLG, B2B product managers had little to do with marketing (beyond product marketing). Now Product needs Acquisition marketing (also known as demand generation) to drive traffic to the product, and Marketing needs Product to convert that traffic. This is the type of mutual reinforcement that drives companies to create Growth Teams that are fully empowered to pursue growth objectives (on Growth Teams, see Chapter 5: Creating and Managing Growth Teams).

To determine what will maximize user signups, we must experiment.

Who is this user? What is her Job To Be Done? How does she typically research solutions to problems like this? Where does she get her information? From whom does she take recommendations?

Armed with this understanding of the target user, Marketing can then experiment with various channels, tactics, and messages, doubling down on what works and abandoning what does not. Typical channels include:

- **Organic:** direct traffic to the website; the user types in the URL directly.
- **SEO** (search engine optimization): optimization of terms on the website such that the product ranks high when potential customers are searching for solutions.
- **SEM** (search engine marketing): paid advertisements that key off of specific search terms.
- **Display advertising**: online display ads targeted to users with specific demographic characteristics.
- **Referrals**: programs that incentivize existing customers to refer new ones.
- **Loops**: flows that leverage existing users to invite new users in the natural course of collaboration or sharing (on Loops, see Chapter 12: Shifting from Marketing Funnels to Product Loops).
- **Email**: outbound email campaigns to targeted lists.
- **Partner marketing**: exposure to a large number of prospective customers via a partner on whom they already depend.

- **Community marketing**: creation of demand within existing communities of potential customers, usually by stoking and promoting word of mouth.

- **Content marketing**: publication of educational content related to the product that can show up in web searches

- **Marketplace**: availability as a tool or application within an existing marketplace or ecosystem, such as those provided by Snowflake, Salesforce, HubSpot, or Atlassian.

Study any product that has grown impressively from relatively unknown to thousands or millions of users, and you will likely see "Organic" as the top traffic referral source (sometimes combined with "SEO," as shown in Fig. 7.6). This is a good outcome, but it is hard to manufacture. Organic traffic is untraceable. Organic traffic represents people who already know about our product or company—they type in the URL directly and visit the website with no traceable source for their motivation. If we like organic traffic, wouldn't we want more? How would we double this traffic? Or triple it? Since it's difficult to trace the origins, it's similarly difficult to increase whatever is driving the traffic. Organic traffic is free, and we love it, but since we cannot directly impact it, we need to focus on tactics we can control and treat "Organic" as a happy outcome that will likely grow with our overall popularity.

Search engine optimization is a long-term strategy. Ranking high for search terms key to your industry may require years of content generation, optimized for certain keywords. SEO is "free" in the sense that we don't pay for each impression or click, but it requires ongoing investment that is also difficult to link directly to outcomes. Directionally, the more we publish on the topic, and the more our content is recognized as authoritative, the higher our website will rank for those specific terms. High-performing SEO remains one of the top strategies for driving top-of-funnel traffic.

Other channels like SEM or display advertising are easier to measure directly: Advertisement X produced Y clicks and Z new users. Loops (covered in detail in Chapter 12: Shifting from Marketing Funnels to Product Loops), email, and social media can be similarly traceable. The categories of community, partner, and marketplace marketing fall somewhere in between, with some traffic traceable and other traffic not.

In general, it's best to treat all Acquisition marketing as multi-modal. We know we need to be active in all channels—varying the channel mix and the targeting of certain customer segments—and we will adjust the specifics over time.

## Why Unit Economics for Acquisition Matter Less at Launch

The initial phases of a product launch involve tactics, schemes, awareness campaigns, influencer solicitation, power-user education, and almost anything the product and marketing teams can think of to get their product to the top of the consciousness of target customers. During this phase, we are less worried about how scalable or sustainable our process is—we just want to see people using the product. From a marketing standpoint, we are building buzz about the product and initiating word of mouth. Influencers can be highly effective in fueling initial excitement about our product. From a product standpoint we also want these initial users so that we can fine-tune the product experience (see Chapter 8: Building Self-Service Onboarding into Your Freemium Product).

## Why Unit Economics for Acquisition Are Everything During Scaling

As a product matures, we begin focusing explicitly on the economics of new customer Acquisition. We need to find scalable and sustainable sources of new users.

Not only do we need a large source of potential users, but we need to be able to acquire these new users at a reasonable cost. In general, we want the net revenue from a new customer to pay back all the expenses we incurred in acquiring that customer within twelve months. This measure is called CAC payback (customer acquisition cost payback), and it is measured in months (target CAC payback periods vary by segment).[5]

With a twelve-month CAC payback in mind, if we expect to net on average $1,000 per year from each paying customer, then we ideally want to spend no more than $1,000 on average to acquire each customer. This $1,000 budget includes all marketing and sales expenses.

If we achieve this CAC target, then all sales and marketing expenses are recouped by the end of year one. Any net revenue we achieve in years two and beyond is pure contribution margin. Contribution margin can be used to fund fixed expenses like engineering and overhead expenses like administrative costs. Anything left over is profit. The fact that SaaS can be optimized to recoup all variable expenses in year one, while maintaining a multi-year cashflow for years two and beyond is one of the most attractive aspects of this recurring-revenue business model.

How do we know an average customer will pay $1,000 per year when we first launch a product? We don't know it. We have to make an assumption. We can update this assumption as we go, but we need a working assumption to establish a budget for acquiring new customers.

Based on this assumption, we can afford to spend $1,000 all-in to acquire each new paying customer. If most new customers adopt the free plan and only 1:10 convert to a paying plan, then we can only afford to spend 1/10 of our budget to acquire a new *free user*. In this case, we can spend $100 per new free user and $1,000 total for 10 new users (one of whom, we assume, will convert to paid).

Organic and SEO traffic are always the least expensive source of new users, but since they are difficult to trace back to specific actions we take, we will focus most of our proactive efforts on measurable channels. Not each channel must perform independently on a CAC payback basis, but the blended results across all Acquisition channels must perform, or we are building a money-losing machine instead of the opposite.

To accomplish this, we run experiments in each channel, in the following manner:

**TABLE 7.1.**   PLG Experiment Pipeline (Example)

|  | Channel | Target | Test |
|---|---|---|---|
| Experiment 1 | *LinkedIn* | People who look like existing successful customers in the automotive reseller industry | Test ads that focus on "speed-to-value" messaging |
| Experiment 2 | *Google* | Adwords (focus on specific long-tail terms) | Increase SEM limit price and double budget for terms related to "save time organizing" |
| Experiment 3 | *Display ads* | Site visitors from the prior week | A/B test two variants:<br>• "Better than competitor"<br>• "Faster than competitor" |
| Experiment 4 | *Existing customers* | Activated customers whose usage dropped to zero within the last week | Email to the newly inactive customer that includes their lifetime stats and an invitation to share their last project for feedback |

We might queue up dozens of experiments each week, testing various targeting strategies, messages, and channels and looking for segments, messages, and channels that will result in an increase in our ability to acquire new customers within our CAC targets.

Achieving reliable CAC payback is the quantitative indicator of Go-To-Market Fit (GTMF). Our threshold for the CAC payback that signals GTMF will vary, depending on our product, price point, target market, and target user. Twelve months is a rough rule of thumb, but most business-to-consumer (B2C) products target shorter CAC paybacks, and some enterprise-focused SaaS products target CAC paybacks of two years or even longer.[6]

As Acquisition marketing teams work day to day and week to week, they look for a blended customer acquisition cost (CAC) of less than their target—in this example $100:

- Each experiment is tracked.
- Each target segment is tracked.
- Each channel is tracked.
- Each value message is tracked.

Acquisition marketers prioritize digital channels because of their closed-loop measurability, but all channels are viable, as long as approximations can be made regarding efficacy in generating profitable user Acquisition at scale. In the end, we are looking for a "blended acquisition cost" that hits our CAC threshold.

Marketing is not the only way to acquire new users, and Acquisition teams are not limited to marketing only—their focus on outcomes drives them to look for new users any way they can get them.

## The Holy Grail of "Acquisition Loops": Getting One User to Invite Another User

The Holy Grail of Acquisition in PLG is finding new users via Acquisition Loops. If we can get one user to invite another user into the product, we have a self-distributing system. And that is more efficient than any one-at-a-time, marketing-fueled Acquisition model.

## Acquisition Loops and Virality

Loops can also be referred to as "viral loops," and rapid growth in the use of a product has also been called "viral"—a reference to how viruses spread in populations. Sometimes when a product experiences explosive growth, we say it has "gone viral."

This analogy is accurate, as the word "viral" does indeed describe the mechanics of how a product's use might spread from one user to the next.

In epidemiological terms, viruses that spread from one host to another can be "self-sustaining" (the virus will survive and grow in the population indefinitely) or "self-limiting" (the virus will not grow and may die out entirely).

The formula that formally describes getting to self-sustaining "viral" growth is easy to understand.

In epidemiology, scientists use the reproduction factor (R-Factor, or $R_0$) to describe a virus's reproduction rate within a population.

- $R_0$ indicates the number of susceptible individuals that will on average be infected by a single host before the host becomes non-infectious.
- If $R_0$ is greater than 1, the virus will continue its propagation (if no environmental changes or external influences intervene). An $R_0$ value lower than 1 means that the virus is doomed to extinction.[7]

Or in plain speak, if a virus-infected host can infect more than one person before its infection dies, the virus will grow in the population.

In growth, this mechanism is described in terms of "Growth Loops." Loops are invitations from a current product user to a future product user. When this invitation succeeds, a new product user is acquired. If a single user can successfully invite more than 1 new user in her lifetime, $R_0$ is > 1, and the product is said to be "viral."

> Virality is not a requirement of PLG, even though viral mechanics
> are an important component of any PLG strategy.

Although virality is not a requirement of PLG, Loops are an important Acquisition tactic. PLG uses Loops when and where possible, and because users who arrive at the invitation of other users are "free" to acquire, Loops can greatly reduce the average CAC. We cover Loops in detail in Chapter 12: Shifting from Marketing Funnels to Product Loops.

## Chapter 7 Summary

- PLG focuses on "user Acquisition" (vs. sales contract size or quantity).
- Users are invited to experience the product prior to purchase.
- Unit economics are used to measure efficacy of Acquisition—specifically, the CAC payback period.
- Expect a wide top of funnel, with many happy users never becoming paid users but still an important segment of the ecosystem, driving referrals and other opportunities for paid growth with users.

## Manager Minute

Thinking about your own company, take time to reflect on the following questions:

1. In what ways could we allow our customers to experience our product before purchase?

2. How do we currently measure our customer acquisition cost (CAC)?

3. How do we currently measure our CAC payback period?

# EIGHT

# Building Self-Service Onboarding into Your Freemium Product

How to Make Your Product Easy to Start Using

> *"When you're product-led, you have to be very focused on user experience and customer value."*
>
> —Kipp Bodnar, CMO of HubSpot

We live in an attention economy.

Companies vie for our attention.

They try to hold on to attention.

They leverage attention to get more attention.

In freemium models—where it's easy to start using a product and just as easy to stop—maintaining a user's attention is critical.

Once we have acquired a customer (he's created an account), the next thing we want is for him to achieve impact.

Immediately.

If our prospective customer is not convinced within seconds or minutes he's in the right place, he may move on to another option from his Google search results and see if he can make that option work.[1]

But if we can keep his attention long enough to create an account and achieve First Impact, we have a shot at turning him into a long-term, paying customer. Product-led growth (PLG) practitioners use the term *Activation* to describe this process of getting from account creation through to First Impact.

FIGURE 8.1.    **Product-Led User Journey to Recurring Impact**

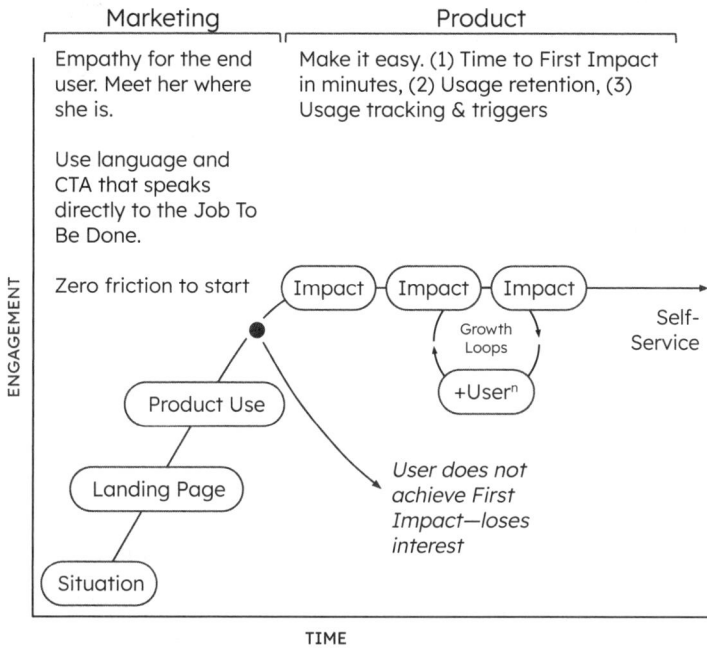

### How Product (Not Sales) Takes the Handoff from Marketing

Marketing's job is to get the customer to visit a landing page and select a call to action (CTA) that lands the customer in the product. Product and Marketing work together to help the user seamlessly progress to a point where he experiences the first substantial milestone toward accomplishing his Job To Be Done (JTBD). We call this milestone First Impact.

### The Number One Critical Event That Drives All Compound Growth: First Impact

Defining First Impact is a core decision for Growth Teams. We need to define it in a way that signals real impact for the user (as opposed to something more banal, like a signup step). Growth Teams debate what specifically in its product experience constitutes First Impact. This is a healthy debate—we encourage it. In fact, we think this is one of the most important decisions to be made when building a PLG go-to-market (GTM) motion. The core question is: What is the impact our customer is trying to achieve with our product, and what is the first experience that convinces her she's in the right place?

Because the decision of what to designate as First Impact is so critical, we believe it is useful to have product, engineering, and marketing executives debate the question and settle on an answer. Note that our initial definition of First Impact for our product does not have to be the final answer. We can make a decision, run with it for a while, see if it serves us well, and then make a change if warranted.

It does not have to be the final answer, but it does have to be defined, measurable, and informed by an understanding of user needs from both qualitative research and initial testing.

Why do we need to define the First Impact event for our company and product specifically?

Because we are going to use First Impact—this defined and measurable event—to set the state of the user to "Activated."

Before a user has performed this action and experienced First Impact, he is considered "Not Activated," and after he has performed this action, he is "Activated." Experiencing First Impact is what updates the user state to Active.

> *(We do not consider a user activated if they have merely created an account. This is a user, but it is not an active user. Our definition of "Activated" ties to the First Impact, and as you will read in the next chapter, recurrence of this same impact comes into play when assessing the ongoing state of a user.)*

A well-defined First Impact has a few key requirements:

1. First Impact must deliver value to the user.

2. First Impact must reasonably correlate with long-term usage Retention. "What is the moment when we believe this customer is here to stay?"

3. First Impact must be achievable with little friction. We will be optimizing to shorten "time to First Impact," so we want the customer journey to be as easy as possible.

The fact that (1) and (3) are pulling in opposite directions helps fuel the debate:

FIGURE 8.1A.   We Want Real Impact; We Want it Fast and Easy

"We want real Impact"   ⬌   "We want it fast and easy"

This is a healthy tension, and teams should discuss the pros and cons of defining First Impact too strictly (e.g., "The *real* impact isn't felt until the first month of results shows up in a report that is emailed to the user") or too loosely (e.g., signup or profile creation).

### "I Understand What an Acquisition Team Does. What Is an *Activation* Team?"

Now that First Impact is defined, the Activation Team can get to work.

The primary objective of an Activation Team is to get a new user to First Impact as quickly and reliably as possible.

To do this, we must be single-minded about making the first-time user experience (FTUX) easy and seamless.

In his book *Product-Led Growth*,[2] Wes Bush talks about a bowling lane, where a first-time bowler might put up bumpers to keep his ball from going into the gutters. These bumpers all but assure that the ball will hit the bowling pins.

> *"As easy as bowling with bumpers up?"*
> *"Yes. That easy."*

We want it to be nearly impossible for our user to fail at accomplishing what she wants to accomplish.

If she's getting "stuck," our product will tell us where she is getting stuck, via the instrumentation we installed (see Chapter 3: First Principles of Product-Led Growth). As soon as we know there is a portion of the onboarding flow that causes users frustration or confusion, we can iterate to make that portion of the user experience easier.

- *"What if we eliminated the requirement to connect a LinkedIn account?"*
- *"What if we pre-populated fields?"*
- *"What if we eliminated choices?"*

FIGURE 8.2.   **Bowling with Bumpers Analogy for New User Onboarding**

*Source:* Wes Bush, *Product-Led Growth: How to Build a Product That Sells Itself* (Product-Led Institute, 2019).

We want new users to reach First Impact within minutes or hours, not weeks or months. And we want that to happen reliably—i.e., "70% of new users achieve First Impact within 24 hours."

You know the work of a good Activation Team when you see it. Think of the products you have used that were so intuitive you could not fail, right from the start:

- Netflix
- Instagram
- Uber

    Now think of products that frustrate you:

- IKEA
- Comcast
- Wireless printer

These are all personal products (business-to-consumer, or B2C), but consider that business-to-business (B2B) products are also being made to be easy to use "out of the box":

- Zoom
- Slack
- DocuSign

This level of tuning is not by accident. For a PLG company, Activation and First Impact must happen seamlessly and without human assistance. It must happen so seamlessly that before a user runs out of patience, he is already seeing impact from the product.

> Our promise is that within a user's attention
> span, we will deliver First Impact.

It's as simple as that—but also quite difficult to achieve. The skills required to iterate toward hitting this goal include: product, user experience (UX) design, engineering, and analytics. These skills are present on all Growth Teams (see Chapter 5: Creating and Managing Growth Teams).

> "Okay, easy-to-use = good, difficult = bad. Got it.
> But how do we get from here to there?
> Especially in a way that can support self-service?"

---

**CASE STUDY**

### Miro Onboarding: Fail Once, Twice, Three Times? No Problem![3]

Three years after launching her professional UX/user interface (UI) design career, Kate Syuma joined RealtimeBoard (later rebranded Miro) in 2017 as its third designer.

#### ATTEMPT NO. 1

The primary issue for RealtimeBoard at that time was onboarding. Week-one retention showed significant usage dropoff, so Kate and her team went to work redesigning the experience, creating a guided, step-by-step experience for each anticipated role held by new users. Channeling its design expertise, the team built beautiful workflows that earned high marks from industry observers. Even small details like the cursor "hover state" were considered. Based on user feedback and reviews, Kate expected the results of this redesign to be ground-breaking.

They were not ground-breaking.

In fact, the actual impact of these new onboarding flows on first-week retention was *negative*.

In Kate's own words: *"We quickly learned that the interactive beautifications of the flow distracted users from completing the main tasks. As a designer, I was awakened from my traditional UX/UI-oriented perspective."*

Kate's product manager colleague at the time offered the following advice: *"Every time you run an experiment, you need to run user interviews also. Data says what is happening, but only users can tell you why this is happening. You cannot succeed the first time. It is best to learn from users why it doesn't work and run 1, 2, or even 3 iterations so that you can get the most out of your hypothesis. Launch, learn from users, iterate—these three steps are critical for achieving business impact."*

As the product team continued to improve the first-time user experience, the company made two pivotal decisions. First, it decided to rebrand the company as Miro. In conjunction with that decision, the company also decided to lean into a freemium business strategy. Since the market for online collaboration tools was so competitive, Miro believed it could carve out a unique space if it lowered the barrier for entry and allowed teams and individual users to experience the core features of the platform without any initial cost. If it succeeded, Miro believed it could harness network effects and word-of-mouth marketing, where satisfied free users would advocate for the tool within their organizations, leading to broader adoption.

In a confluence of luck and preparation, 2020's global pandemic lockdown and forced remote-work environment created an opportunity to test Miro's freemium model. With workers all over the globe working from home and needing to collaborate remotely, ease of use became a critical consideration in choosing a platform. Many of these new users were less tech-savvy than their predecessors, and the team therefore determined they needed to further simplify the onboarding experience.

**ATTEMPT NO. 2**

Confronted with escalating volume, Miro got deliberate about its growth efforts. First, it ran a massive correlation analysis, to determine which activities (Miro calls them "moments") during the onboarding phase correlate with long-term retention. Miro defined the "setup moment," the "aha moment" (First Impact), and the "Habit moment," using data from their study. It combined this quantitative analysis with end-user interviews, to better understand the Jobs To Be Done for their target personas. One of the key insights gained from their qualitative research was that even though Miro was positioned as a "team-centric" product, new users didn't know what their teams could do with Miro.

*(The First Impact defined by Miro was the moment a user receives feedback on one of their pieces of created content. Receiving feedback from a teammate correlated strongly with long-term retention.)*

Miro's product and Growth Teams invested a full calendar quarter of time and attention in this research, which then led to an overhaul of the entire onboarding experience, including the introduction of an artificial intelligence (AI) avatar to help guide new users through a tutorial.

The results of this overhaul were controversial:

- Only 25% of new users took advantage of the tutorial.

- The overall experience led to more content creation during the onboarding experience.

- But there was still no uplift in the percentage of new users reaching the "aha moment" (First Impact).

**ATTEMPT NO. 3**

A second iteration on this experience improved the take rate for the tutorial by a factor of 2, but this still had no effect on First Impact.

**ATTEMPT NO. 4**

Kate and team continued to delve into usage patterns to uncover deeper insights. Her team ran "diary studies"[4] to better understand the first twenty-eight days of free-trial user behavior, looking for impediments to Activation and long-term Retention. It analyzed anonymized user experiences during the initial phases of usage, including collaboration experiences, looking for correlations with long-term health.

Eventually, the team discovered two archetypes that proved useful in designing toward First Impact: "creators" and "joiners." Creators were project initiators, while joiners were team members who were merely asked to collaborate on a project. These two archetypes played very different roles in getting to a First Impact moment, and designing specifically for those roles proved to be the first strategy to move the needle on achieving First Impact.

During Kate's six-year tenure at Miro, the company grew from *1M users* to over *50M users.* Kate's top lesson learned was this:

> *"Don't give up after the first iteration, always ask why, and keep listening to your users."*
>
> —Kate Syuma, former head of growth design, Miro, and founder, Growthmates

**Final Thoughts:**

By this point in Part Two of the book (Product-Led Growth Implementation and Tactics), we have discussed how to set up the team, how to design and launch a minimum viable product (MVP), and how to architect Acquisition and self-service onboarding into the product itself.

When working my way through this part of a product's lifecycle, I like to think about designing for my dad or my grandma. If I were designing for them, the point would not be to impress them with lots of features. I would want it to be so easy to find and use my product that they couldn't fail. Confusion would be my enemy. Too many features or options would be my enemy. For my dad or my grandma, the experience would need to speak directly to them, guiding them through the process in a way that makes it almost impossible not to succeed.

But even the best, most intuitive, and most empathetic product designers get things wrong. That's why we have instrumentation and metrics. They will tell us where we need to tune up, and as long as we follow the data and keep iterating, we will be good.

### Chapter 8 Summary

- User attention is the currency of PLG.
- Activation is PLG's term for capturing a user's attention and delivering First Impact.
- To effectively Activate and Retain a user, we must deliver First Impact within minutes or hours.
- The UX objective during Activation is to make things so easy that the user cannot fail to reach her objective .

### Manager Minute

Thinking about your own company, take time to reflect on the following questions:

1. When was the last time I personally went through our product's onboarding flow? What was my experience?

_____

_____

**2.** How long does it take for a new customer to achieve First Impact on our product?

_____

_____

_____

**3.** I would rate our ease of Activation as follows (circle one)

| 5 | 4 | 3 | 2 | 1 |
|---|---|---|---|---|
| The clunkiest enterprise competitor in our space | | | | The easiest-to-activate-and-use competitor in our space |

## NINE

# How to Convert Free Users into Large Paying Contracts

The Four Major Types of PLG Monetization

*Seek first to create value, then to extract value.*

When I moved from Boston to Silicon Valley in 2010, it felt like I had entered a warped dimension. Houses cost twice as much, every fifth car was a Tesla, no one cared that I had a Harvard MBA (in fact, it was a detriment), and entrepreneurs were building business-to-business (B2B) software they gave away for free.

Only a few years earlier, in 2005, we had sold our SaaS company, Profit-Logic, to Oracle. At the time, ProfitLogic's customers paid on average $1.2M per year to use our software. This was the *average*, so some customers paid less, and some paid much more. At ProfitLogic, we had no free trials and no small up-front contracts. If you wanted to use our software, you committed (on average) $1.2M just to get started. To help customers make this financial commitment, we invested heavily in the selling process, working with customers to develop the business case in detail for how and when this investment would pay for itself. We called this "value selling," and ProfitLogic was among the best in the world at it.

In Silicon Valley in 2010, value selling was *passé*. The "cool kids" had figured out how to build software they could give away for free. B2B startups like Dropbox, Skype, Twilio, Mixpanel, and Yammer all provided critical business functionality via software that was free to use. If you liked it, you kept using it as long as you wanted—for free—until reaching a point where paying for additional volume or features made sense.

Seeking first to create value, before extracting value, is a core tenet of product-led growth. It feels generous, because it is generous. It felt good to build my 2010 startup using software I wasn't paying for. I felt in control when I upgraded to paid plans, based on having succeeded with some of those platforms. I felt like I was partnering with like-minded companies that were empathetic and generous. And I didn't want to go back to buying from salespeople if I could help it.

## How to Tell a PLG Company from a Sales-Led Company

Since product-led growth (PLG) revolves around creating value and giving it away before charging money, it's relatively easy to tell if a company is pursuing a product-led go-to-market (GTM) model vs. a sales-led model. The easiest way to distinguish a PLG company is by its main call to action (CTA), featured prominently on its home page. If the CTA is . . .

- Schedule a demo

- Speak to a representative

- Register to receive more information

... it is not PLG.

Instead, these are tactics to get a salesperson engaged in the process. If the CTA is . . .

- Get started

- Use for free

- Try it now

... that points toward self-service. That might be a PLG company.

Click on the CTA to see if you can get all the way into the product without human assistance. If so, then it is a PLG model.

You are now in a version of the product designed to capture and maintain your attention, guiding you to achieve your goals as quickly as possible. This version may expire (free trial) or be feature-limited (freemium), but take notice of one important and essential thing—it does not stop short of allowing you to achieve real impact without payment.

Seek first to create value,
then to extract value.

## Why PLG Companies Are Not Afraid of "Free"

Many PLG companies are perfectly happy having thousands of non-paying customers. These companies may have little to no marginal cost of keeping a free user, so they welcome them. In some cases, these companies can leverage the free user base for visibility—more positive reviews, more downloads, a higher profile in app marketplaces, and so on. They may also be able to leverage free users for distribution—free users can invite others onto the platform, after all. Whatever the rationale, PLG companies must become comfortable with Free.[1]

As mentioned in Chapter 1, free users also provide a large base for experimentation and testing. Many companies use this base of low-demand customers to launch new features, refine processes, and learn about usage patterns before introducing the features to the rest of the user base.

Free is not new. Media companies have been giving away free for decades—in exchange for advertising dollars. Cell phone companies give away free hardware. Coffee shops give away free internet. Gyms give away free membership months. Digital products are easier to give away because of their zero marginal cost. And here is where we can get creative. With zero-marginal-cost but high-value giveaways, we can build entire brands, loyalty bases, even movements.

Once we mentally commit to the idea of Free, we can get very enterprising about how we deploy our solutions into the world, seeking out solvable problems and providing solutions that meet customers where they are. Monetization becomes one *outcome* of value creation, not the primary objective.

## How PLG Companies Make Money: The Four PLG Monetization Models

Having built a product or service that delivers impact to customers, it becomes incumbent on us to determine how and when we will Monetize the solution. Infinite variations exist, but most Monetization models can be categorized into one of four archetypes:

### 1. Freemium

Freemium products feature a forever-free version of the product, with an option at some point to upgrade to a paid version that includes enhanced capabilities.

### 2. Free Trial

A free trial provides access to all necessary features to experience impact from the product. The trial has an expiration, after which the user is encouraged to enter into a paid contract to continue accessing the service.

### 3. Reverse Trial

A reverse trial starts with a full-featured version of the product with an expiration date (a free trial), but instead of losing access to the product at the end of the trial, the user either pays for continued access or reverts to a forever-free version, with some capabilities limited until they decide to upgrade to a paid version.

### 4. Product-Led Sales (PLS)

Free product usage drives pipeline for sales to convert to paying contracts (see Chapter 14: Crossing the Chasm from Pure PLG to PLG-Plus-Sales).

### Freemium Monetization for PLG Products

Perhaps the most notable PLG model is freemium.

In a freemium model, users of the service are able to achieve their Job To Be Done (JTBD) easily, without paying for the privilege. In this model the core service is free forever—no expiration date and no requirement to ever upgrade.

Consider the following:

- Zoom allows users unlimited video meetings lasting up to 40 minutes each.
- Slack allows free use of its features, with messages archived for 90 days.
- Lucid allows users to create unlimited diagrams of up to 60 objects per diagram.
- Calendly allows unlimited 1:1 meeting scheduling for a single calendar.
- Dropbox allows up to 2GB storage for free.

Freemium product developers lean on generosity as a core principle (see Chapter 3: First Principles of Product-Led Growth). Generosity is the principle behind creating value before extracting value. We want our users to benefit from our product, develop habits with our product, and feel grateful for our product before we ask them for money.

But freemium products have their limits. Some features or volume levels sit behind a paywall. At some point users reach a stage where they need access to additional capabilities, and we ask them to pay for that access.

When we get to that point, we want the general emotional response to be:

> *"Oh! I knew this day was coming. I'm happy to upgrade at this point. I've gotten so much value from this product, and I trust the next tier of service will be similarly amazing."*

Freemium (also known as "Free Forever") has the lowest friction of all Acquisition methods. In 2023, the average signup rate from website visit to freemium product was 9%.[2] This is an extremely high conversion rate for any CTA. Highly targeted marketing emails typically get a click-through rate of less than 5%. The relatively high 9% signup rate for freemium PLG products reflects the relentless focus those companies put into getting the value proposition, wording, design, and CTA right.

A freemium GTM strategy is well suited in the following circumstances:

1. **Single-user value proposition.** If our user is also the decision-maker and the person who will benefit directly by using your product, then why not get her into the product right away? If we can demonstrate impact with no delay and no friction, we will maximize our chances of convincing a new user she is in the right place.

2. **New concept offering.** If users didn't know they needed a service before this concept was introduced, they may need a little time to become familiar with the solution and incorporate it into their routines before considering a paid upgrade.

3. **Zero or near-zero marginal cost of service.** If it costs nothing to deliver a version of our service to prospective paying customers, why not do it? It maximizes our chance of increasing exposure in the target market and building a positive reputation via direct product experience.

4. **Clear paid upgrade path.** An essential element of the freemium strategy is the upgrade path to the paid version. Is it clear that you can deliver impact with the free product and also deliver *additional* impact via a paid upgrade? If yes, then your product is a candidate for freemium.

Not every product is well suited for freemium for reasons articulated in the following section on free trial. But if our product is suited to freemium, it is a low-friction way to scale quickly across a user base.

### Free Trial: The Most Popular PLG Monetization Model

A free trial is the most straightforward of all Monetization models. Customers get free access to the product (usually a rich or full-featured version of it), but only for a limited time. Once the trial has expired, the customers must purchase ongoing access.

Free trials have the built-in feature of a compelling event. Rather than happily proceeding on the free product forever, users are forced to make a choice—do I want to continue with this service or not? If yes, I will need to pay. With trial expirations, there's no chance a customer will "forget" to upgrade—the decision point is fixed.

Being upfront that the free trial has an expiration date filters out buyers who are not serious about paying for a solution, assuming the solution works for them. Intent clearly exists to "try" the product, so conversion-to-paid rates are typically higher for free trials than for freemium.

The risk of a free trial, of course, is that the customer gets offended—feeling like she is required to make a decision before she is ready. A forced decision can be frustrating if the customer is enjoying the product but just not yet sure if it's a full solution to her problem. If the customer needs more time to test it out but the trial has expired, it can leave her with no options.

Free trials are well suited in a few specific circumstances:

1. **Nonzero marginal cost of service**. Free trials are a good choice for services that have a nonzero marginal cost of delivery. Twilio, for instance, has a "start for free" CTA, which kicks off a free trial. But it can't be free forever, because Twilio offers telephony services (phone and SMS) for which it has to pay telecom carriers. Since Twilio is on the hook for ongoing costs, it's logical that its trial would expire and the customer would have to pay thereafter.

2. **No individual user value proposition**. Free trials are also good for solutions that do not deliver value for an individual user but rather require Activation across multiple users or a team. In this case, we want to minimize friction for getting multiple users set up on the trial account. With multiple users in place, we can facilitate a true test of whether the solution will work in a team environment. Here a free trial allows multiple people to get access to the full-featured product for an evaluation period, maximizing the potential that the group or team will find value and decide to commit.

3. **High Annual Contract Value (ACV)**. In our experience, free trial is the right CTA for enterprise-type solutions with higher ACV. In this case, return on investment (ROI) justification is generally required for a purchase. Achieving ROI will likely require a full-featured version of the product, which is best delivered in a time-boxed free trial. Free trial licenses are more easily distributable to multiple users who can help act as influencers or advocates for a high-ACV solution. Furthermore, the higher the expectation around ACV, the more generous a free trial seems, increasing the likelihood a potential buyer would enter the trial.

In 2023, 19% of SaaS companies used free trial as their primary CTA, and 29% offered a free trial as one of multiple CTAs.[3] Some of these companies self-identified as Sales-Led, and some as Product-Led. We consider free trial a product-led strategy, even when it is combined with sales motions.

### Reverse Trial: Combining the Best of Freemium and Free Trial

Some products are suited for a combination of the free trial and freemium strategies into what is known as a reverse trial.

The reverse trial begins with a free trial of the full-featured product. Just like in the standalone free trial strategy, the trial period is time-boxed, and at the end

FIGURE 9.1. TRIAL VS. FREEMIUM VS. REVERSE TRIAL

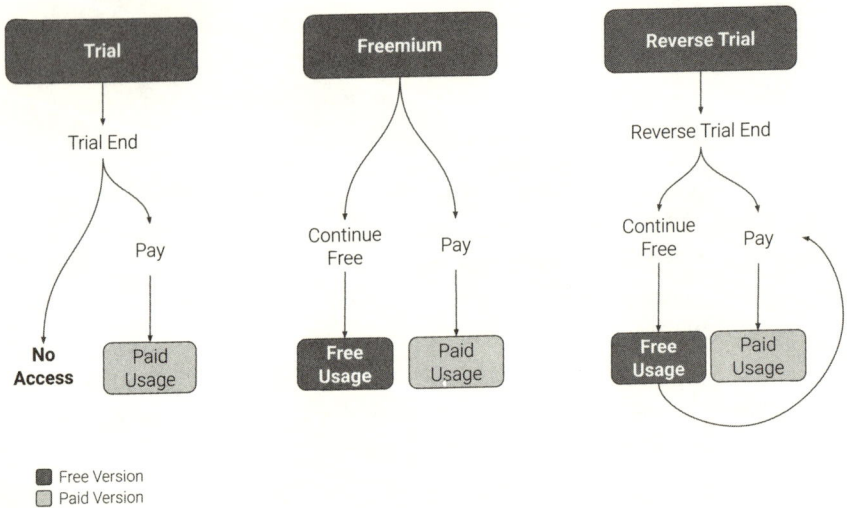

of the trial the customer is faced with an option to begin paying or lose access to the full-featured product.

In this case, however, the alternative to paying is not to lose access altogether—rather, the user is reverted to a free version of the product, which has limited features or capability.

The reverse trial avoids the abrupt shutoff at the end of the trial period, and it generally leaves the user's account and any work in progress intact. The user is then presented with an option of continuing for as long as they like on the free product, or—on their own timeline—upgrading to the paid version.

An additional advantage of the reverse trial is that it gives users exposure to the full-featured product up front. This allows users to experience (not just hear about) the additional features, and, where appropriate, make a formal or informal case for why it would be important to have continued access to those features.

Reverse trials are well suited wherever a free trial is well suited (see above), with some notable exceptions.

1. **Ongoing cost of service.** If the product continues to cost money to deliver, and there is no ongoing value proposition once the money-costing portion is disabled, there may be no option to revert to a free product that is valuable to the user.

2. **No clear value tiers.** If there is only one thing the customer values, and it's tied to the paid version, then, again, there may be no option to revert to a free product the customer values.

3. **Freemium is better.** For some products, in some markets, freemium is just better. Some examples of this include when there is a large horizontal market, when Acquisition is low friction, when ACV is small, etc. This is something that can be reasoned through, but ultimately we may want to experiment our way to confidence on this decision.

### Product-Led Sales: PLG Monetization for Enterprise Contracts

The final Monetization prototype is product-led sales. In PLS, product usage builds pipeline and identifies opportunities for salespeople.

Imagine a scenario where multiple end users who work at the same company independently find their way into a PLG funnel and adopt and use the same solution. These individuals may work in different departments or geographies, and their adoption may have spread to other members of their individual teams.

**Q:**   *How easy would it be in the above scenario for a salesperson to learn about the existing product usage and the success being achieved, create a narrative around those use cases, and then go find and speak with a decision-maker who may want to standardize on the solution across entire teams?*

**A:**   *Way easier than cold calling.*

The strategy of leveraging product usage to develop opportunities for sales is called product-led sales (PLS), and many industry observers believe PLS is the future. PLS leans heavily into PLG tactics in the arena where they are best suited—Discovery, Acquisition, Activation, and Retention—and sales where it is best suited: large-scale adoption of enterprise solution (for more on PLS, see Chapter 14: Crossing the Chasm from Pure PLG to PLG-Plus-Sales).

## How to Choose Your GTM Motion

PLG and sales are not mutually exclusive. The companies mentioned at the beginning of this chapter—Dropbox, Skype, Twilio, Mixpanel, and Yammer—all developed sales motions to complement their freemium models. The key is to match the appropriate GTM motion with the expected ACV.

For a customer contract lower than $5K per year, customers may expect a self-service buying experience. Product-led GTM motions make sense for

FIGURE 9.2.   **Matching GTM Motion to ACV Aligns Processes and Economics**

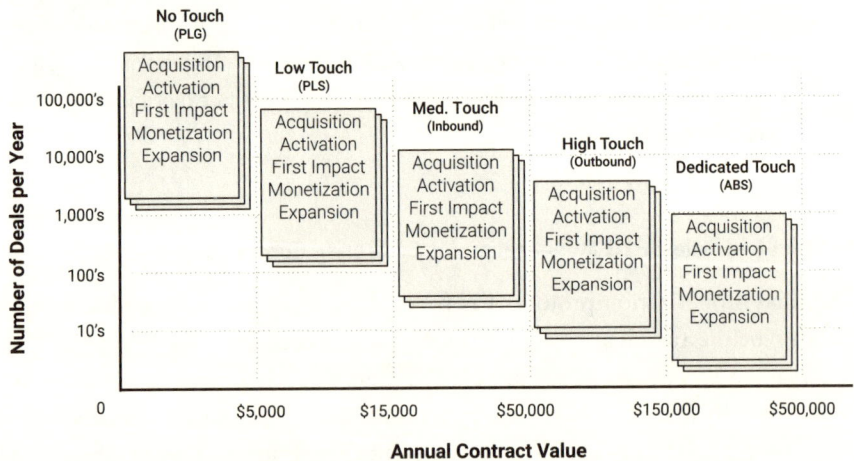

serving this segment of the market. But what if the customer is paying more than $5K per year? What about a customer paying $50K per year? Or $500K per year? Different market segments require different GTM motions, which are not mutually exclusive.

In Chapter 13 we discuss when it is appropriate to add another GTM motion on top of an initial PLG motion, and in Chapter 14 we discuss how to add sales effectively.

### Final Thoughts

Product-led motions have the benefit of being anchored directly and securely to the end user. This is their strength. In many cases, end user allegiance is used to refine the product itself. But we are also building a business, and we know that when the time is right, users will want to upgrade into higher tiers. Having covered the primary Monetization model archetypes of free trial, freemium, reverse trial, and PLS, the next consideration in Monetization is pricing.

### Chapter 9 Summary

- PLG Monetization happens after the customer experiences value, not before.

- Monetization models are built to meet the customer where she is and make it easy and painless for her to do business.

- Monetization models fall roughly into four categories: freemium, free trial, reverse trial, and PLS.

- Each model is suited for specific circumstances—there is no "one size fits all."

## Manager Minute

Thinking about your own company, take time to reflect on the following questions:

1. What could we reasonably give away for free to begin building a relationship with prospective customers (ideally something with low marginal cost and high engagement)?

   _____

   _____

   _____

2. Based on the criteria outlined in the chapter, what Monetization model makes most sense for us?
   - Freemium
   - Free Trial
   - Reverse Trial
   - Product-Led Sales

3. What changes would need to be made to our product to ensure a free or free-trial experience leads to First Impact and therefore sets up a Monetization opportunity?

   _____

   _____

   _____

**TEN**

# Pricing Strategy for Enterprise-Level PLG

> Charging for What the Customer
> Cares About: Impact

**For Products with Product-Market Fit, Pricing Is the Highest-Leverage Decision**

Entire books, consulting practices, and even technology companies have been created to facilitate good SaaS pricing. Pricing is simultaneously one of the most *vexing* and *financially impactful* business decisions you will make as you build, launch, and manage product-led growth (PLG) products.

If you were to crack open any guide to SaaS pricing, the first thing you might read is something like:

> Price according to a metric your customer values.

**How to Choose a Pricing Metric**

We won't spend long on this, since it's so obvious by now, but it's surprising how many companies get this wrong. Consider the following examples:

1. If the customer is looking to publish work schedules, charge according to work schedules.

2. If the customer wants to screen résumés, charge by the résumé.

3. If the customer wants to scan for software vulnerabilities, charge by the "project" uploaded and scanned.

What would be some plausible and mistaken alternatives in the situations listed above?

- ✖ Instead of charging by the work schedule, charge by the employee. Now the customer can't have a flexible workforce with lots of employees on call, because just to keep an employee in the system costs them money, whether they are being scheduled or not.

- ✖ Instead of charging by the screened résumé, charge by the hire. Now you're focused on something over which you have no control. After all, your solution is not directly responsible for whether or not someone is hired.

- ✖ Instead of charging by the project, charge by the number of vulnerabilities for which your solution scans. This sets up a perverse pricing incentive to scan for fewer types of vulnerabilities, which helps no one.

Sometimes we talk ourselves into a metric we think will make us more money: "Recruiters charge 30% of first-year base salary, why couldn't we charge just 5% for each employee hired using our resume screening software?"

Those types of ideas sound good in a conference room, but they don't appeal to customers, and in a world where we need to earn and keep a customer's trust by delivering ongoing impact, I agree with the pundits—"Price according to a metric your customer values."

Tiering is another hot topic in pricing, i.e., which features should go in the "Silver, Gold, Platinum" versions?

In PLG it's a little different . . . .usually the versions are more like:

- Free
- Pro (individual paid account)
- Team (multi-user account)
- Enterprise

Still, the question remains: what goes in which tier? How do we meaningfully differentiate in a way that allows us to charge little enough for the Pro and Teams accounts, so as not to slow down the speed of Acquisition, and enough for the Enterprise edition to be able to fund the costly sales function we will need to sell Enterprise contracts. This often requires product teams to think hard about differentiation features and messaging.

---

**CASE STUDY**

**Lucid's Prices Range from $7.95/Month to $1M-Plus/Year**

Consider the following scenario:

- Lucid's entry-level account is free.
- Its Individual (Pro) account is $7.95 per month.
- Its Team account is $9 per user per month.
- And its Enterprise contracts can be up to $1M per year.

How does that work? $1M for 12 months divided by $9 per user would be over 9K users. Surely Lucid's enterprise accounts don't have 9K users?

Some do, but that's not how pricing works at the enterprise level. Enterprise editions have features not needed at the lower tiers, such as multi-level reporting, team member onboarding and offboarding, enterprise-grade security, General Data Protection Regulation (GDPR)–compliant collaboration, enterprise-grade integration with core systems such as Workday/Salesforce/Salesloft, etc. The inclusion of these enterprise-grade features is what resets the pricing paradigm and allows Lucid to charge an enterprise price that pencils out to much more than $9 per user per month.

---

Enterprise reps used to get bent out of shape about pricing like the above ($9 per user) being visible on the pricing page. "How do we build a case for $1M annual contract value (ACV) when our 'low, low pricing' is just out there on the website for all to see?" At this point, most of the world knows that Individual and Team pricing are different from Enterprise, and they expect enterprise editions to be "enterprise grade," handling greater complexity and scale (such as GDPR compliance, increased integrations, etc.). The main challenge is to ensure the differential impact delivered justifies the difference in price. If we can get that right, we will be okay.

### Pricing Simplicity—the Single-Metric Rule

Once we have determined the aspect of our product that customers value, we need to capture that concept into a single metric, such as:

- Work schedules published
- Résumés screened
- Software projects uploaded and scanned

When setting up pricing tiers, this single metric should be the basis of differentiation between tiers, as follows:

- Free: Up to 3 résumés screened per month
- Pro: Up to 10 résumés screened per month
- Team: Up 100 résumés screened per month, across 5 seat holders
- Enterprise: Unlimited seat holders; up to 300 résumé screens per seat holder per month

In this example, the primary pricing metric is résumé screens. There would be, of course, additional parameters involved in owning a Team or Enterprise license, but those are not highlighted as the primary differentiation. The more we can minimize distraction and put all the focus on the primary pricing metric, the easier it will be for customers to opt in to the appropriate tier.

Alternatively, the differential value might be access to certain features by tier:

- Free: All design features; artificial intelligence (AI) assistant; designs saved for 180 days.
- Pro: All features above plus templates available; designs saved indefinitely; designs publishable to marketplace.
- Team: All features above plus collaborative workspaces; basic project planning; team dashboards.
- Enterprise: All features above plus team member onboarding and offboarding; enterprise security; multi-layer permissioning.

It may be tempting to combine metrics—in this case, volume metrics and features. Do not do this. It becomes far too confusing for customers, and it can slow down adoption. For an example of this gone badly wrong, see the "Pricing Transparency" section below.

## PLG Pricing Tiers—Get This Right and Unlock Tremendous Value

The very definition of the term *freemium* includes a concept of pricing tiers:

> *Freemium is a way of charging*
> *for a product or service in which*
> *the basic product or service is free,*
> *but the customer pays for extra features.*
>
> —Cambridge Dictionary

## FREE TIER

For Monetization strategies that include a free tier (on Monetization options, see Chapter 9: How to Convert Free Users into Large Paying Contracts), it is imperative that the free tier solves actual problems for actual users without leaving them frustrated or unable to accomplish their Job To Be Done (JTBD). In this sense, the free tier demonstrates true generosity. If users get the sense we are trying to trick them, they will revolt. No one likes the situation where they begin down a path to solving a problem, only to realize partway through that in order to *really* accomplish their JTBD, they will have to pay money. This is the "uncanny valley" of PLG, and it does not work over the long term. When users feel tricked, they may pay money one time to get their problem solved, but the trust is broken, and long-term loyalty is unlikely.

On the other hand, when users get true value from the free tier, trust is built. Free products that solve problems on an ongoing basis engender loyalty. In this situation, when the time comes to upgrade to a paid version, users tend to trust the provider and welcome the opportunity to pay for the next tier of service.

## PRO TIER

Most PLG products have a paid version of an individual account—sometimes called the Pro tier or the Premium tier. This version unlocks certain advanced capabilities that benefit an individual user. These advantages could include additional volume beyond what is allowed in the basic tier. They could also represent features not available in the lower tier that are useful to accomplish more complicated or advanced versions of the JTBD.

Deciding what to include in the Free vs. Pro tier can be a delicate balance. We recommend erring on the side of generosity. For all but the most "consumer" type products—most business-to-business (B2B) PLG products will not make their money on Pro conversions—the real revenue opportunities are with Team and Enterprise licenses. Unless your business model revolves solely around free-to-paid conversion for individual users, you may consider the Pro tier as just another waypoint to Team or Enterprise usage.

## TEAM EDITION

The Team edition is a critical leverage point in any B2B PLG go-to-market (GTM) motion. This is the point where individual usage translates into multi-user adoption, which unlocks features that benefit the organization more broadly.

Team editions can be Monetized via self-service flows or sales-assisted flows (product-led sales), and as such, they are an effective middle-ground between pure PLG and enterprise sales. (For more on product-led sales, see Chapter 14: Crossing the Chasm from Pure PLG to PLG-Plus-Sales.)

Team editions typically include collaboration features, basic reporting, and basic license provisioning (ability to transfer licenses, etc.). Team editions do not typically include enterprise-level security or support. Those features are reserved for the highest, Enterprise-tier product.

### Enterprise Pricing: How to Charge Millions of Dollars for a "Free" Product

What are some sources of differential value for the Enterprise version of the product versus the Free or Pro or Team versions?

## TABLE STAKES

In the early days of open-source software, the main difference between the Free version and the Enterprise version was that the Enterprise version was "managed." The managed version usually came with professional support and maintenance services. These services included bug fixes, security updates, technical support, training, and consulting services.

PLG has adopted this paradigm, and enterprise tiers of PLG software are expected to include enhanced security and technical support and maintenance at the Enterprise level. In addition, Enterprise subscriptions generally include centralized license management (provisioning/deprovisioning), data privacy management, usage reporting, and enterprise-grade security.

These features have come to be expected of Enterprise software versions, and they tend to justify most but not all of the price premium.

## ADVANCED ENTERPRISE FEATURES

In addition to the foundational enterprise capabilities described above, customers have come to expect feature-level advantages in an Enterprise edition of PLG software. These are features not available in any other tier—they are unlocked only by subscribing to the highest tier. Opportunities to design these features into your solution will vary, depending on the specific JTBD you are facilitating, but here are some some conceptual examples:

- **Collaboration:** What additional collaboration opportunities exist within an enterprise that could be explicitly facilitated in your product?

- **Approvals:** What approval workflows exist in an enterprise for your specific JTBD? Can you build approvals into the product?

- **Reporting:** Basic reporting may be part of the Teams package, but how far could you go? Usage reporting, yes.... How about reporting on specific metrics beyond usage, like volume processed, yield, or total savings?

- **Integrations:** Many applications have both basic and more advanced integration opportunities. Don't hold back integrations required to effectively use the product, but there may be value-added connections with other platforms or services that could be offered only for enterprise customers.

- **Advanced features:** You may have differentiated end-user features you hold in reserve for the highest tier subscription. These should not be "must-have" features whose absence would cripple a lower tier but rather advanced features that would render the highest-tier version of your product extraordinary.

### Above All, Keep Pricing Simple and Transparent

In PLG and self-service GTM models, the goal is to make it as easy as possible for a customer to advance from one tier to the next without assistance. Confusion, in this case, is your enemy. When a customer gets confused, they hesitate, second-guess, and stall. If we want a customer to confidently adopt each successive tier of pricing, we must be as clear and transparent as possible about *all* tiers of pricing up front.

You may have been in a situation where something was being given away for free, yet you still were hesitant to take it. Why? Maybe you were worried about what comes next—the big ask. Maybe if you accepted something for free, you'd be obligated to pay an unacceptable amount to continue. To avoid confusing our customer or causing her to be skeptical or worried, it's best to show all of the pricing up front and make the pricing as easy to understand as possible.

Some companies make it an art form to be obtuse about their pricing. You've seen pricing pages where each tier incorporates a jumble of features, access provisions, and volume limitations. For some products, just deciphering the pricing page to determine the appropriate tier for your use case could require some dedicated research or, even worse, a scheduled call with a sales representative to

**FIGURE 10.1.   Fictitious Example of Confusing Pricing**

| Free Edition | Pro Edition | Team Edition | Enterprise Edition |
|---|---|---|---|
| **$0** | **$50** | **$25** | **$100K** |
| | *per user per month* | *per user per month, for a minimum team size of 5 users* | *unlimited users* |
| • Up to 3 resume screens per month<br>• Includes work history verification<br>• Optional background check available for $25 per candidate | • Up to 10 resume screens per month<br>• Includes work history verification<br>• Optional background check available for $15 per candidate | • Up to 100 team-wide resume screens per month<br>• Includes work history verification<br>• Optional background check available for $15 per candidate<br>• Customized, anonymous reference checks available for $1K setup fee per position and $100 per interview | • Up to 3 resume screens per month<br>• Includes work history verification<br>• Up to 15 background checks per user included; additional checks @ $10 per candidate<br>• Up to 3 customized, anonymous reference checks available per position ($1K setup fee applies)<br>• Enterprise security<br>• Advanced reporting |

explain it to you. Scheduling a live call may be the intention of obtuse pricers, but it is antithetical to PLG.

Consider the fictitious pricing page in figure 10.1.

If you read through this example, I am sorry. It was deliberately built to confuse and obfuscate. Although it looks like you get "more" in the Enterprise edition and "less" in the Free edition, the devil is in the details. And the details are confusing.

Don't do this.

Every aspect of the pricing example above may be rooted in an operational or cost reality of operating the business. It may make perfect sense to the chief financial officer (CFO), who is managing fixed and variable costs. But it does not make sense to a customer, and depending on whether the customer needs seat holders or résumé screen volume or reporting or reference checks, it would be nearly impossible to choose a tier without first having a detailed conversation with a sales representative.

When it comes to pricing, simple and transparent is better. If we want to establish a "self-service happy path" for our customers to adopt so that they can seamlessly move up within our pricing scheme, we need it to be as simple as possible for them to say yes to the next tier.

## Final Thoughts

We ended on Enterprise pricing, which may make some business people happy and comfortable. With a strong enterprise offering and GTM, Enterprise is likely to be the lion's share of revenue. But remember, in any PLG business, the lion's share of our "customers" are not paying any money at all.

PLG funnels are wide at the top, capturing all the free users and then funneling them into paid plans.

The good news is that the work at the top of the funnel to acquire and activate customers is performed by the product itself. Because we have "hired" our product to do this work rather than humans, we incur very little expense to maintain a wide top of funnel.

The major limiting concern becomes not cost but availability of a sufficiently large market to support a funnel that wide.

Just like the rest of PLG, Monetization is about meeting the customer where she is.

If a free trial is the easiest way for a prospect to engage with your product, then we should offer her a free trial.

If freemium is best for the customer, then we should choose a freemium strategy.

As we figure out which features and capabilities to bundle into which tiers of our product, we need to keep this in mind—what is best for the customer? What does she value? What will she be happy to pay for?

It is not our goal to confuse, frustrate, or block our customer. . . . We want to do the opposite. We want to bring our customer along a Monetization journey that feels natural, respectful, generous, and frictionless.

If our customer is not ready to pay, we do not want to force the issue. If she needs to downgrade to a free version for a time, we want to allow the downgrade, no questions asked. If our customer needs flexibility to move between tiers or to add or subtract users, we want to make that as easy as possible.

The First Principles of PLG apply to pricing as well:

1. Empathy

2. Generosity

3. Instrumentation

Stick to that, and your pricing will work for the customer and for you.

## Chapter 10 Summary

- Pricing is a high-focus/high-leverage area for any SaaS company.

- As with any good pricing strategy, price according to what the customer values.

- PLG packaging tends to follow the following format:
  - Free
  - Pro (individual account)
  - Team (multi-user account)
  - Enterprise

- Each tier needs to provide unique value commensurate with the price. These differences can be volume- or feature-based.

- Enterprise pricing for PLG products should include table stakes differentiators (security, support, and administration) as well as feature-level differentiators for enterprise use cases.

## Manager Minute

Thinking about your own company, take time to reflect on the following questions:

1. What pricing tiers exist in our product(s) today?

_____

_____

_____

2. For each tier, what is the primary differentiating factor that justifies the additional price?

_____

_____

_____

**3.** How transparent is our pricing? If I were to show our pricing page to an uninitiated customer, what is the likelihood they would be able to interpret the page and choose the appropriate plan?

_____

_____

_____

# ELEVEN

# Customer Success Without a Customer Success Department

> How a Well-Designed Product Keeps
> Usage and Retention Rates High

### Why Usage Retention Is More Important than Dollar Retention

Once we have acquired a user and helped her achieve First Impact within her attention span, it is incumbent on us to ensure she finds her way back for Second Impact, and Third, and Fourth. . . .

We may or may not be not charging money today, but we certainly will be in the future, and it behooves us to remember the following:

> *"Recurring revenue is a result of recurring impact."*
>
> —Jacco van der Kooij

Growth managers often refer to recurring impact as "Habit." We are looking to create an experience so compelling and impactful that users will come back, and back again, and back again: Habit.

Our First Impact moment was defined so that we could measure when, how often, and in what circumstances users achieve it (see Chapter 8: Building Self-Service Onboarding into Your Freemium Product). We chose this definition of First Impact carefully as something we believe reasonably correlates with long-term usage Retention:

> *"If she reaches this impact moment in the product,*
> *she's likely to stay for good."*

### How to Measure Usage Retention: Daily, Weekly, and Monthly Active Users (DAU, WAU, MAU)

Now we need to test that assumption. Do our users really come back? How often? How often do they achieve what we hope they will achieve in the product?

We refer to this repeated use as usage Retention (as opposed to dollar Retention), and it is generally measured in terms of:

- DAU (daily active users)

- WAU (weekly active users)

- MAU (monthly active users)

Remember, the product is doing as much Retention work as possible. We have "hired" the product to do some of the onboarding work that people used to do. Similarly, we want to "hire" the product to keep users engaged and succeeding beyond the onboarding period. This is typically the domain of customer success teams, but we can offload some of those team members' work by programming it directly into the product.

> *"Human-centric mechanisms via customer success and support teams have an important supporting role to play, but they are too high-cost to rely on as the primary means to retain. And no matter how good our people are, they'll struggle if the product isn't sticky (both intrinsically and through manufactured means). This is why every software company must become product-led in at least the growth lever of Retention or risk eventual disruption from competitors who are."*
>
> —Ben Williams, growth advisor

### Inviting the User to Return Again and Again

At any point in the customer journey, from onboarding until Habit is firmly established, the product can be used to programmatically invite the user back into the product to perform an action. Consider these possibilities:

- Weekly dashboard summary gets emailed, with invitation to click into the product to explore.

- Reminders are sent for important tasks.

- Browser alerts appear when someone interacts with your content.

- Invitations arrive from team members to collaborate/review.

One of the most effective ways to invite a user back into the product is if he has an app installed on his phone. Consider the lengths to which phone-based apps go to keep users engaged.

---

**CASE STUDY**

### How Duolingo Doubled, and Then Doubled Again

Today Duolingo is a public company with over 500M registered users, 100M MAUs and 34M DAUs.[1] It is widely recognized as the leading brand in both language learning and online education generally.

In 2018, however, Duolingo's growth had stalled. It had been stuck at 3M DAUs for over a year.[2]

One year earlier, Jorge Mazal was recruited by Duolingo to be a product director. Jorge's experience at Zynga (online games) and MyFitnessPal had the potential to bring an interesting perspective to Duolingo. Jorge was quickly promoted to VP and then to chief product officer.

Jorge's initial challenge was clear: get Duolingo back to growth.

He and his team launched successive attempts to do this—the first two of which were utter failures:

1. Copy the Gardenscapes progress bar (from Jorge's online gaming background)—designed to increase Engagement.

2. Copy Uber's referral program—designed to increase Acquisition.

Neither of these experiments moved DAUs more than 3%, because people didn't care about in-app progress in learning in the same way they did in gaming (the dynamics and incentives were different), and people didn't care about a "free premium month" for referring new users when the Duolingo app they were already using was mostly free.

If users didn't care about these things, what did they care about?

Jorge and team went back to the drawing board to model out how growth works at Duolingo (on the product growth model, see Chapter 5: Creating and Managing Growth Teams).

Duolingo mapped out every user who had ever used the product, representing these users in blocks, according to their current state. Via careful modeling, it ensured

**FIGURE 11.1.    Duolingo Daily Active Users Model**

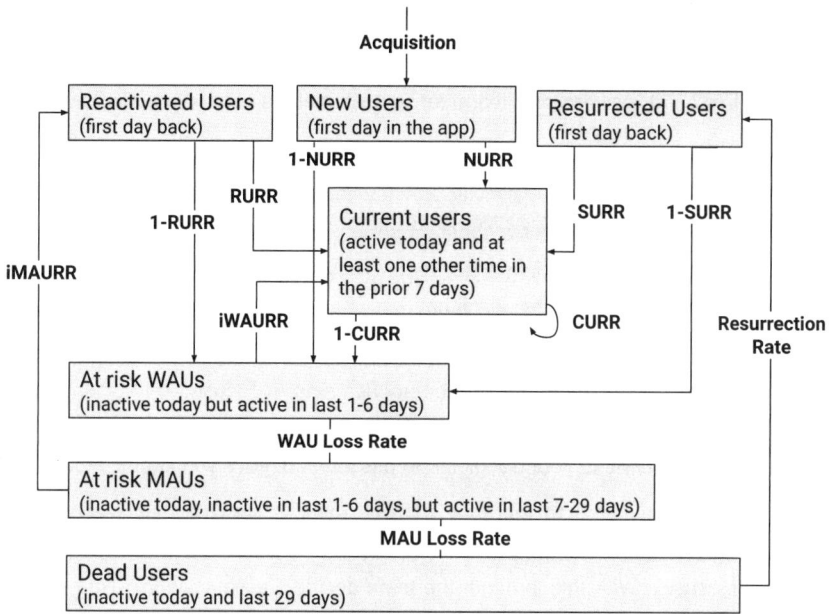

*Source:* Mazal, Jorge. "How Duolingo Reignited User Growth," 2023. https://www.lennysnewsletter.com/p/how-duolingo-reignited-user-growth.

that each user was in one and only one block on any given day. The arrows show how users move between states, and the combination of blocks and arrows constitutes a nearly closed system, with the only break being new users. The top four blocks combine to represent DAUs. For Duolingo, this was its product growth model (see Chapter 5: Creating and Managing Growth Teams).

With the product growth model in place, Jorge and his team ran simulations, adjusting the conversion rates represented by each of the arrows by 2% each quarter and simulating twelve quarters' worth of compound effects. Mathematically, they determined that one single metric—current user retention rate (CURR)—if it could be incremented by 2% each quarter for 12 quarters, had five times the impact on DAUs than the next closest competitor. Not to say that CURR would be easy to impact, but the math said *if* the team could improve CURR, the results would outweigh anything else they could do.

At this point, the team took a huge gamble. They reassigned people from other teams and formed a brand-new team focused solely on CURR.

> *"Only focus on metrics that, if you win, will actually have a big impact."*
>
> —Jorge Mazal, former CPO, Duolingo

From this point forward, this team concentrated all its efforts on CURR:

1. Leaderboards: **designed to increase CURR**. Jorge and team borrowed a leaderboard concept from Farmville 2. They compared learners to "similar strangers." This gave learners a constant set of "competitors" to compare progress with (similar to a heat in a larger race). They also built "leagues" learners could advance through, further designating smaller domains a learner could "win."

2. Push Notifications: **designed to increase CURR.** The team set out to launch not more notifications but better notifications. It focused on social notifications (versus app notifications). These social notifications included alerts when someone in your social circle passed you, gave you kudos, etc.

3. Streaks: **designed to increase CURR**. Analysis showed that a user with a streak of completing a lesson each day for at least 10 days cared a lot and was sticky. With this in mind, the team decided learners with 10-day streaks would appreciate streak-based notifications at any time. The team decided to enable push notifications to these users even late at night, on weekends, and on holidays to prevent learners from losing streaks in progress.[3]

Duolingo's main objective was to increase daily active users from 3M, where it had been stalled for over a year. Since Jorge and team had determined that CURR would mathematically have the largest impact on DAUs, they focused their attention on things that would move CURR. Unlike prior efforts that went after DAUs *directly* (e.g., the referral program for new users), these bets were designed to impact DAUs *indirectly*—by way of CURR. The math played out. These three optimizations not only boosted CRR, they also combined to increase daily active users from 2.9M to 13.2M over a period of 3.5 years—exactly as the model had predicted.[4]

Once leaderboards, push notifications, and streaks were doing their job of creating compound growth within the closed system, Duolingo reinitiated efforts to boost new user Acquisition. With the system designed to retain and grow, Duolingo knew that each new user would be well taken care of, creating new, productive nodes for growth.

Once Retention was where they wanted it, Duolingo began seeing the cumulative effects of ongoing Acquisition. This Acquisition-Retention engine boosted Duolingo's DAUs from 13.2M in 2022 to 21.4M in 2023.

**ADVICE FROM JORGE:**

> *"If you have a win ... that's a goose with golden eggs. Keep coming back to the same thing and get more of those golden eggs, as opposed to trying to find a different goose."*
>
> —Jorge Mazal, Former CPO, Duolingo

1. Define user states and flows.
2. Build this into a defined product growth model, including flows and conversion rates.
3. Let math rule. The math doesn't lie. Trust it.
4. Everything is an experiment. Know what metric you are trying to move and ditch anything that isn't working and move on.
5. Don't be afraid to copy.
6. Double down on what is working.

---

## Using Cohort Analysis to Optimize Retention over Time via Experimental Product Enhancements

Reminders and prompts to revisit the product are good, but the product must also be designed to hold the attention of the user naturally. Are we solving a recurring problem? Do we add value to the user's life on an ongoing basis? Does the user have reasons to come back? Can we deliver impact every time they are in the product?

For a recurring-revenue business, we must achieve recurring impact. And for recurring impact, we must engage the users consistently. Or, more accurately, they must engage our product consistently.

One of the most powerful tools in a growth manager's tool kit for measuring and optimizing usage Retention is cohort analysis. Cohorts group customers who share common characteristics in order to identify behavior patterns and correlations. For instance, we could group a hundred customers who came in from Campaign A and compare their success with customers who came in through Campaign B. Cohorts are used everywhere in Growth, but let's examine their use in usage Retention specifically.

For this example, we will define our cohorts by start date:

- Cohort 1: All users who started in January.
- Cohort 2: All users who started in February.
- Etc.

Now let's follow Cohort 1, tracking MAUs for the first year. If a user who starts in January also activates in January, they would be considered "active" in Month 1. Each month that user shows meaningful activity ("meaningful activity" is a defined event in the product growth model), they would count as "Active," and if we see no activity, they would be considered "Inactive."

We can see that in Month 1 we were able to activate 71% of users, but usage fell off precipitously until only 11% of our January cohort were still MAUs in Month 12.

Of course, we are not standing still. During the month of January we were already making upgrades to the product, designed to create a "stickier" experience for future cohorts in the hopes of retaining them better.

In this example, whatever experiments we ran to get the usage Habit to stick worked a little better for the February cohort—especially in the later months. For instance, in their eighth month as customers, 21% of the February cohort were still active, while only 17% of the January cohort were active in their eighth month.

FIGURE 11.2.  **Monthly Active Users as a Percentage of Accounts Created by Cohort**

| | 1 | 2 | 3 | 4 | 5 | 6 | 7 | 8 | 9 | 10 | 11 | 12 |
|---|---|---|---|---|---|---|---|---|---|---|---|---|
| Jan | 71% | 56% | 42% | 35% | 29% | 21% | 19% | 17% | 16% | 15% | 11% | 11% |
| Feb | 72% | 56% | 42% | 31% | 25% | 24% | 22% | 21% | 18% | 16% | 15% | |
| Mar | 69% | 60% | 51% | 47% | 39% | 35% | 30% | 28% | 23% | 19% | | |
| Apr | 74% | 61% | 55% | 46% | 38% | 36% | 36% | 31% | 27% | | | |
| May | 77% | 63% | 57% | 45% | 42% | 42% | 41% | 39% | | | | |
| Jun | 78% | 65% | 60% | 51% | 45% | 49% | 44% | | | | | |
| Jul | 82% | 66% | 59% | 54% | 49% | 48% | | | | | | |
| Aug | 81% | 68% | 65% | 56% | 51% | | | | | | | |
| Sep | 84% | 72% | 71% | 70% | | | | | | | | |
| Oct | 86% | 77% | 75% | | | | | | | | | |
| Nov | 85% | 80% | | | | | | | | | | |
| Dec | 84% | | | | | | | | | | | |

FIGURE 11.3.    **Product Retention Curve**

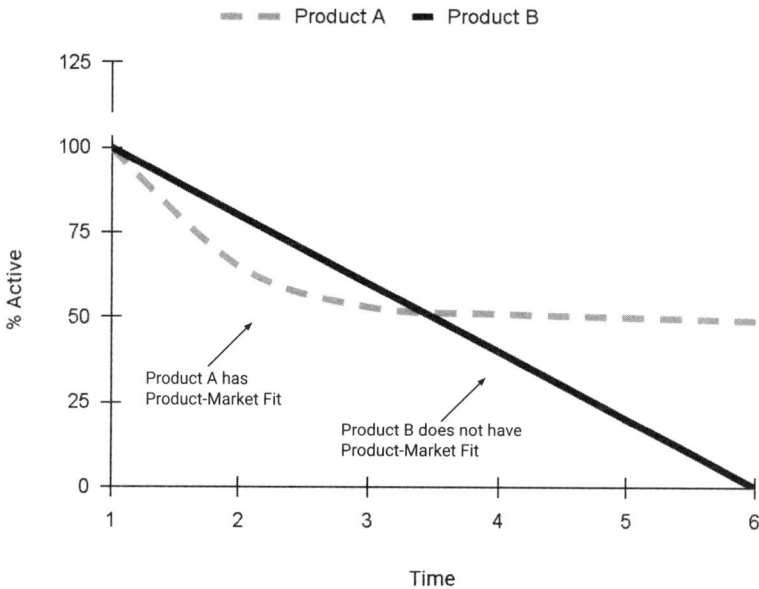

Each month we continue running more experiments. Some will work and some will not. When something works, we incorporate it into our permanent product; when something doesn't work, we deprecate it. This process of constant tuning, based on how users take to the product, is the process of Growth.

In this example, twelve months' worth of constant experimentation resulted in a better Activation rate (Month 1 MAUs went from 71% to 84%) and much better MAU Retention in Month 6 (48% for the July cohort vs. 21% for the January cohort).

Growth managers talk about the Retention curve "flattening out." By this they mean that usage churn reduces to near zero at a certain point in a customer's life (flattens), indicating that a base percentage of users are finding sustained value in the product over time.

The flattening Retention curve demonstrates Product-Market Fit. Working to get that curve to level off earlier and higher is the ongoing work of a Retention Growth Team.

`CASE STUDY`

**How Snyk Increased Usage Retention 15x**

In 2023, Snyk was a $100M revenue cybersecurity platform based in Boston, valued at over $3B due to its extremely high growth rate. Snyk's tools help software developers identify and fix vulnerabilities in their code. Snyk goes to market via a combination of product-led growth (PLG) and sales, but its roots were always in a self-service free trial.

When Ben Williams joined Snyk in 2021 as the head of product-led growth, there were myriad things to work on, including Acquisition, Activation, and Retention. At the time, the company had neither defined the customer journey in those terms nor instrumented or measured those specific milestones.

Job number one for Ben was to create a measurement framework so it could organize the work and the teams in such a way that it could monitor progress.

The team at Snyk collaboratively developed the following framework to describe the user journey in measurable terms. It called this its "User State Model."

This simple way of viewing the customer journey helped the team at Snyk visualize which sets of customers were having which experience and conceptualize what it could do to help.

For new customers, the job was to help them Activate.

For activated customers, the job was to engage them and keep them engaged (Habit).

For dormant customers, the job was to re-engage them or, as Snyk called it, "resurrect" them.

**FIGURE 11.4.   Snyk User State Model**

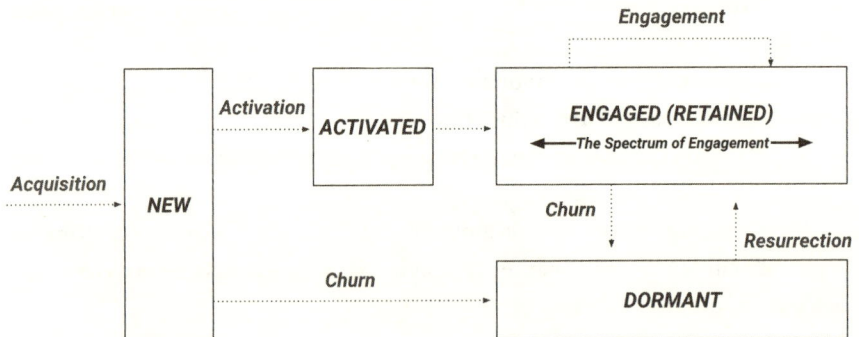

*Source:* Ben Williams

FIGURE 11.5.    **Snyk Activation Process**

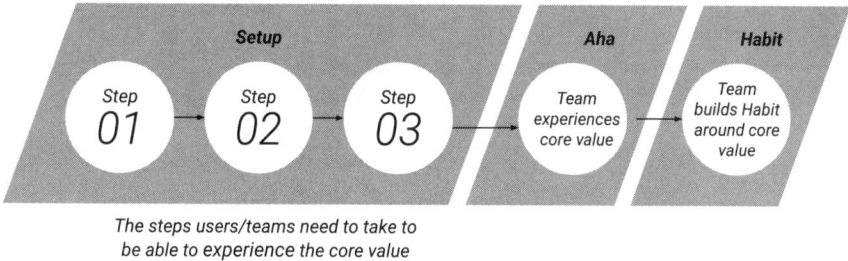

The steps users/teams need to take to
be able to experience the core value

*Source:* Ben Williams

This model could be helpful for any company in a recurring-revenue business, as all companies have customers in these various states at any given time.

At a more detailed level, Ben and team defined the specific steps within the model its users needed to take to Activate, experience First Impact (aha), and develop a Habit.

The specifics of Snyk's process are less important than the fact that they defined each step in this process, measured it, and tracked it religiously. Your steps will be different, but if we are to improve the customer journey and ultimately get to Habit, we must define the steps we believe will get us there, then iterate, iterate, iterate until we see the desired results.

For Snyk, it was all about Activation. If it could get users to complete step 1, step 2, and step 3 (in this case, completing one or more integrations, importing one or more projects, and creating a non-empty project list), it considered that user "activated."

These were not the first Activation steps Snyk designed—they iterated toward these specific steps. They wanted to know what correlated with long-term Retention. But once they identified the correct leading indicators, they tracked and optimized for them.

The result?

Teams that had completed steps 1, 2, and 3 (activated teams) were still achieving impact fifteen weeks after signup (Habit) at a rate of 48%.

Any guess what percentage of teams that didn't complete these steps were still fixing issues fifteen weeks later?

Three percent.

To state the obvious, 48% usage Retention is better than 3%.

Having identified the key drivers of long-term Habit creation, Snyk was able to optimize the user experience to ensure those drivers were prioritized and streamlined into the experience. Like the bowling-alley bumpers we saw in Chapter 8 (Building

Self-Service Onboarding into Your Freemium Product), Snyk implemented an on-boarding process so simple and so directed that it became nearly impossible not to complete the three Activation steps they had defined.

What if a user does activate but then goes dormant (see Fig. 11.4). What about the 52% of teams that completed all the steps but fifteen weeks later were not actively fixing issues? Do we write them off as lost? Try to replace them with new users who will be more committed?

Sometimes these dormant users just need a reminder, a prompt or nudge to get back to the job they initially wanted to accomplish using your product.

For these users, we can look into possible causes of the decline in activity and see what can be done to prevent them from churning permanently.

Sometimes we can identify accounts at risk even before they go dormant. Snyk calls these "Product-Qualified Accounts at Risk of Churn" (PQARC).[5]

It may come as no surprise that the approach to figuring out how to solve this problem is also experimentation.

---

### How to Use Correlation to Target Retention Experiments

Snyk's Activation process, depicted above, shows how setup metrics correlate with long-term Retention. What else correlates with long-term Retention? If we have instrumented the product (see Chapter 3: First Principles of Product-Led Growth), we will have metrics on what features are used, how often, and by whom. Simple machine learning models can help correlate this user behavior with churn, resulting in a scoring model that helps identify PQARCs.

Remember how we said Growth Teams often include both Marketing and Product? They also include data science. So if you have a Growth Team focused on Retention (Habit), the data scientist on that team will be tracking everything and correlating everything they can get their hands on with the outcomes you want or are trying to avoid.

Machine learning is just another tool in your analyst's tool kit to help correlate inputs (user behavior) with outcomes (predicted churn, Expansion, etc.).

The key is to measure everything. In a product-led world, our employees are not holding customers' hands during sales, onboarding them, or engaging them to ensure usage. So we rely on instrumentation and metrics to tell us what is happening at each stage. Those measurements become inputs to an overall decision framework that can help with each step of the customer journey. At this point we are talking about Habit.

FIGURE 11.6.   Data Feedback Loops

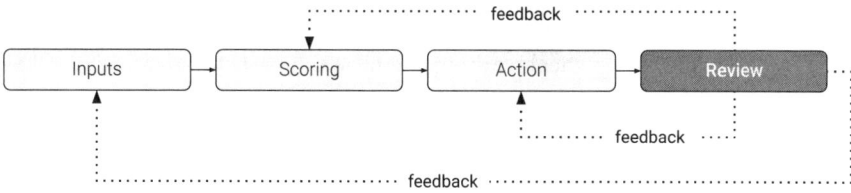

*Source:* Ben Williams

Consider the above diagram. Inputs are the data we get from product usage, and scoring is a way of interpreting that data, informed by experimentation.

Let's say we measure something called [completed_full_name] during the signup process, and we also measure something called [imported_first_project]. Which of these things correlates best with long-term Retention? For a customer who made it all the way through the signup process, we can forget the [completed_full_name] metric, because of course they did—they completed the entire process. Clearly, [completed_full_name] would have a 100% correlation with long-term Retention and would be completely un-useful in a scoring model designed to predict long-term Habit development.

But [imported_first_project] might factor in. Is it more important than [>_2_logins_per_user_per_week]? What about [has_invited_at_least_one_co-worker]? All these things might correlate with long-term Retention, but we won't know for sure which is most predictive until our analyst runs the data. Once we know where our strongest correlations are, we can create a scoring model that narrows down to the actions most relevant for long-term Habit creation.

Based on the output of our scoring model, we may now have a set of accounts at high risk of churn and another set of accounts at lower risk. This is where we develop action plans and begin experimenting with what might help a customer get back on track with the Habits we want to see them embracing. An action might be a reminder email, an in-app prompt, or a summary status report . . . we will want to test all of those and more. And of course, each of those experiments can be tested with A/B variations until we find out what works best.

As long as we have our reporting framework set up properly, we will be able to see which actions tend to result in which outcomes. This will then give us an opportunity to review and refine our system.

Earning users' attention vs. any number of highly entertaining and distracting alternatives also competing for their time is a challenge—even if we are not charging money. Once we have a user's attention, we want to do everything we can to prove our value in the first moments (First Impact) and then to keep her coming back over and over (Habit).

If we can get this flywheel working, we have the basis for an amazing PLG product.

With this foundation, Monetization and Expansion are natural outcomes, even though we have to work for those too (more on Expansion in the next chapter).

## Chapter 11 Summary

- First Impact is important, but recurring impact is the goal for long-term Retention and Monetization.
- Growth Teams aspire to cement their product into the habits of their end users.
- Instrumentation and metrics are required to monitor and optimize for long-term Habit creation.

## Manager Minute

Thinking about your own company, take time to reflect on the following questions:

1. Have we explicitly outlined our customer's journey, from initial signup through Habit formation? Can I remember it and outline it here?

 

 

2. Do we have measurements associated with each of the steps above? Do we know which key actions correlate most strongly with long-term Habit creation? What are those key actions, and how do we measure them?

**3.** When did I last see a cohort-based analysis of our Retention? Are we improving Activation and Retention rates with each cohort? Do our Retention curves flatten? What hypotheses do I have regarding our long-term Habit formation and Retention?

_____

_____

_____

# TWELVE

# Shifting from Marketing Funnels to Product Loops

> The More Customers Use the Product, the More Sales Will Grow

Traditional new-customer Acquisition relies on the sales and marketing funnel to move customers from left to right or from top to bottom through a customer journey toward purchase.

We have previously established that purchase is not the ultimate destination—that product-led growth (PLG) customers are allowed to experience the product prior to purchase, and that we hope to keep them for a long time through Renewal and Expansion cycles. To this end, the Bowtie is a better representation of the journey than the funnel (on the shift from funnel to Bowtie, see Chapter 7: How to Acquire Self-Service Customers).

### How to Use Growth Loops to Pull More Users into the Product More Often

PLG journeys are just not that linear and single-threaded. PLG practitioners think beyond the funnel to the Loop. And we are not satisfied with just "a single" Loop—we want as many Loops as we can get working.

*"What's a Loop?"*

> *"Loops are closed systems where the inputs into a process generate output that can be reinvested as input."*
>
> —Brian Balfour, Reforge CEO

In this context, Loops help us visualize the customer journey where increased product usage leads to more Acquisition, Retention, and Expansion.

- Once a customer is part of our system, how can she bring more customers in? This is an Acquisition Loop.

- As our user begins creating content, how can we use that content to drive collaboration and Engagement with other users? This is a Retention Loop.

- Can the potential value of collaboration encourage a user to invite a new colleague from within her own team to activate on the solution so she can get their input? This is an Expansion Loop.

> Growth Loops are tactics that leverage current users' product
> usage to drive more Acquisition, Engagement, and Expansion.

Consider the user of Zoom. She schedules a video meeting. She sends a link to the person with whom she would like to meet. That person installs Zoom so he can participate in the meeting.

This is a Loop.

Consider the user of Dropbox who wants to expand their "free" storage from 2GB. If they can invite a friend, they will get 500MB additional storage for free.

This is a Loop.

**FIGURE 12.1.   PLG Loops**

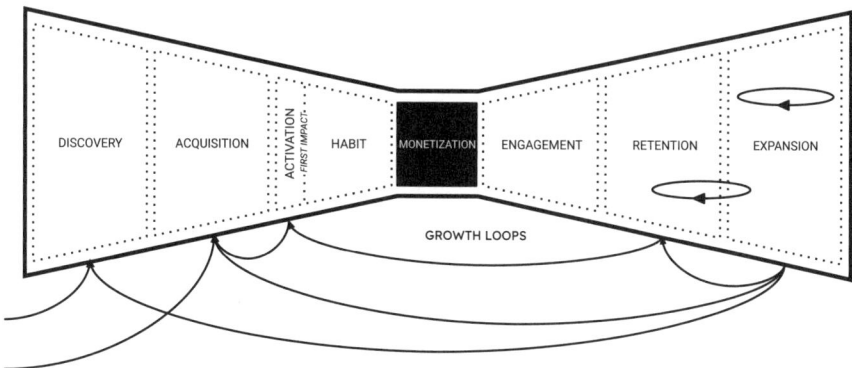

- Miro and Canva and Figma are design platforms. They leverage **collaboration** to build Loops.

- Calendly is a scheduling platform. It leverages the **multi-sided task** of scheduling as a Loop.

- Slack is a communication platform. It leverages the **multi-sided task** of communication as a Loop.

Marketers have managed referral programs for as long as we can track marketing; these are Loops too. The only difference is that in PLG we instrument and measure our Loops within the product, and we make it an explicit domain on which a Growth Team can focus.

Loops are a way of leveraging our existing base of customers to attract more usage and more customers.

- Loops can be built to bring users back into the product.

- Loops can be built to encourage the use of additional features within the product.

- Loops can be built to attract new customers into the product.

Let's take a look at Loops in real life.

---

**CASE STUDY**

### How Pledge.to Leverages Charitable Giving to Create Growth Loops

Pledge.to is a nonprofit digital giving platform. With Pledge you can create a giving page or campaign that channels funds to a nonprofit organization of your choice.

Pledge is used by:

- Nonprofit organizations that want to set up donation pages.

- Corporations that want to integrate giving into their business model.

- News organizations that want to support donations in response to world events.

- Celebrities who want to leverage their platform for good.

Pledge uses many Loops in its business to drive Acquisition, Retention, and Expansion:

- Upon completing a donation on a Pledge giving page, the donor is presented with a "share the love" option to post to social media platforms or to invite someone individually via email or text.

- Donors are invited to stay in touch with the nonprofit organization by allowing them to follow up (including future opportunities to give).

- Each giving page contains an invitation to launch your own campaign.

- Donor receipts include an invitation to launch a campaign of your own.

- News organizations publish generic pages that "split" the donations among non-profits serving the current need. If these nonprofits are not already Pledge customers, they receive the donation anyway, along with a solicitation to leverage Pledge in its own fundraising.

---

Once you start seeing Loops, you will not be able to stop seeing them.

As we highlighted in Chapter 7 (How to Acquire Self-Service Customers), recurring revenue models have built-in Expansion assumptions on the right side of the Bowtie, and this is where all the magic of compound growth happens.

Since we have automated most of the go-to-market (GTM) functions along the Bowtie, we can theoretically use a Loop to send users to any point in the Bowtie and have them engage on a self-service basis to accomplish the desired task. This allows us to Acquire new users, Activate users, increase Engagement, and expand usage via recursive Loops.

### How to Architect Loops into a PLG Product for Marginal Gains That Drive Compound Growth

Each time we improve any portion of this growth cycle, even the smallest of marginal gains contributes to compound growth.

> The law of marginal gains comes from the idea that if you break down a big goal into small parts and improve on each small part, you can achieve a huge improvement when you put them back together. Or in other words, the whole will be greater than the sum of the parts.

In the case of Expansion with PLG (Loops, not funnels), these marginal gains accrue in two areas:

1. Cohort Expansion (net revenue retention, or NRR)

2. Net new customer Acquisition

We covered the concept of time-based cohorts in Chapter 6 (Building a Minimum Viable Product for Freemium Adoption), where we measured the percentage of new users achieving First Impact, and in Chapter 11 (Customer Success Without a Customer Success Department), where we measured monthly active users by cohort.

To illustrate the power of Loops, let us use time-based cohorts to measure something else: total recurring revenue.

### Mathematical Explanation of How Nonlinear Growth Is Built Via Incremental Improvements

Consider a cohort of new accounts (companies). For the purposes of this analysis, let us consider an entire company to belong to a single cohort, based on the Activation date of the first user from that company.

#### 1. COHORT EXPANSION VIA LOOPS (NET REVENUE RETENTION OR NRR)

For this example, assume that a new user cohort includes ten users, each working at a different company, and each paying $1 per year to use the service.

One year later, two of these users have canceled their service, and eight have renewed. Importantly, each of the eight remaining users has recruited one additional user *from within their own companies* to join them—each at $1 per year.

In this simple example, the cohort was paying $10 total annual recurring revenue (ARR) at the beginning of Year 1 and $16 total ARR at the beginning of Year 2. Even though we lost two users, we gained eight new users, for a net gain of six.

Expansion of revenue from accounts within a single cohort is called net revenue retention (NRR), and it is an important component of compound growth.

Growth leaders do everything they can to get cohorts to grow. Loops, funnels, prompts, incentives, guides—whatever.

Cohort-based NRR of 160% (as in the example above) is best-in-class for the first few years of a cohort, but this rate of Expansion will inevitably taper off as the cohort matures and approaches its theoretical maximum adoption.

#### 2. NET NEW CUSTOMER ACQUISITION VIA LOOPS

Another feeder of compound growth is new-customer Loops.

Since we counted new users *within* the same account as members of the same cohort, the next avenue of growth is to look for users *outside* of the

FIGURE 12.2.    **Within-Cohort Expansion**

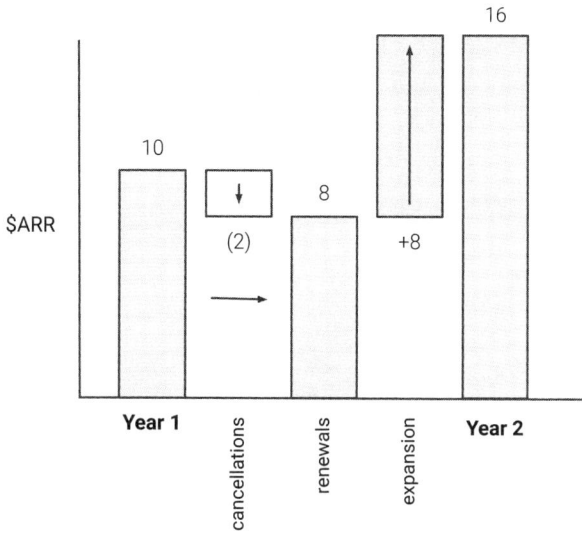

original accounts. Can we leverage usage in our current accounts to recruit new users from new accounts? Perhaps we can build in opportunities for current users to invite new users from new accounts to collaborate on their work. Or perhaps we can provide the opportunity for users from new accounts to review or approve work. Or maybe we just flat-out ask for referrals? Whatever the tactic, to the extent we can leverage existing usage to recruit new users from *new* accounts, we are now leveraging our existing account base to gain more accounts.

These new-user Acquisition tactics help grow the starting size of a new cohort by complementing the work of the Acquisition team. New users acquired via Loops have a lower customer acquisition cost (CAC) than those acquired via most other marketing channels.

With these two Expansion techniques in place—NRR and (Loop-based) new-customer Acquisition, we can put together the dream situation for any product-led growth team.

Consider each cohort represented in the chart above. The cohort with the earliest start date (the cohort on the bottom) has been growing gradually but

FIGURE 12.3.   **Cohort-Based Compound Growth**

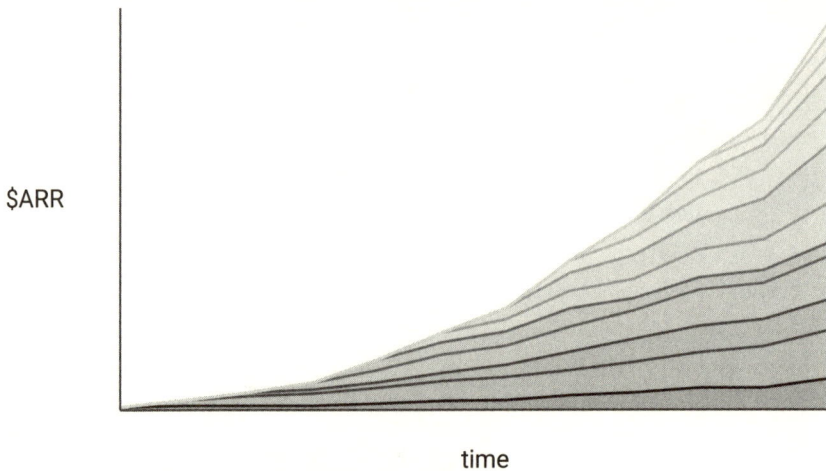

$ARR

time

steadily from the beginning. If we were to look at that cohort in isolation, the growth would not be impressive.

But when considering the mathematics of growth, it turns out any NRR over 100% is a tremendous tailwind. As long as cohorts are holding steady or growing *ever so slightly*, the next cohort will be a net add, as well as the next and the next. As long as these cohorts can stack on top of each other without having to fill in divots left by attrition in prior periods, growth will accumulate.

And if, as in this example, each cohort's NRR grows—even ever so slightly— that compounding growth results in an upwardly-convex growth curve, the kind that would hang on the walls of SaaS museums (there are no SaaS museums).

### Chapter 12 Summary

- Loops are tactics to leverage current users' product usage to drive more Acquisition, Engagement, and Expansion.

- Loops are explicitly designed and measured by growth managers as part of ongoing, iterative tuning.

- Small improvements in self-service metrics triggered by Loops can contribute to both growth within existing customers (cohort Expansion) and new customer Acquisition.

- Lots of small improvements in a self-service PLG machine can combine to create compound growth.

## Manager Minute

Thinking about your own company, take time to reflect on the following questions:

1. Where within our business do we currently have Loops (explicitly designed and measured or not)?

 

 

 

2. How many additional cohort Expansion Loops can I brainstorm for our business?

 

 

 

3. How many additional new-customer Acquisition Loops can I brainstorm for our business?

 

 

 

**4.** What other Growth Loops can I brainstorm for our business?

_____

_____

_____

_____

_____

_____

_____

_____

## Product-Led Implementation and Tactics

In Part Two we dove into *how* and *why* PLG works and the mechanics for building it into your company.

We demystified the term *Growth Team* and learned that Growth Teams are small, cross-functional groups focused on specific growth objectives. Growth Teams measure themselves against a product growth model that contains the key assumptions around various growth levers. Growth Teams include product engineers, which allows them to experiment with product features, messaging, Loops, etc. They iterate toward growth objectives, carefully measuring the results of each experiment and doubling down on tactics that work.

We learned that instead of placing a focus on sales, PLG companies focus on end-user Acquisition and Activation. Users are invited to experience the product before purchasing. If we can help users achieve impact, we can charge them money over time—after they have fallen in love with the product.

We looked at how explicitly PLG depends on a wide top-of-funnel: the more users in the front end of the funnel, the more opportunities we have to Activate, Monetize, Retain, and expand those customers. Once a new user is acquired, we must help her achieve First Impact within the limits of her attention span. We call this Activation, and we measure and optimize it.

We considered the order of operations for delivering value vs. extracting value. Delivering value comes first. Users and teams that are experiencing impact with the product are eventually invited to transition into a paid version of the product. This may happen at the end of a free trial or when they reach the limits of the free product. Free trials, freemium, reverse trials, and PLS are Monetization strategies often used by Growth Teams.

We learned why PLG companies focus so intensely on usage Retention, measuring daily-active, weekly-active, and monthly-active usership. Since usage Retention is a leading indicator of dollar Retention, and since Growth Teams can do something about usage Retention directly, this is where they focus.

We dove into Growth Loops and virality and learned that Expansion in PLG is achieved via Loops. Loops are used to invite new users into the product, existing users back to the product, and colleagues from other companies to join in using the product.

**Up Next**

Part Three: Product-Led Growth Within Large Enterprises
Read Part Three for a view into how PLG and Sales work together within large enterprises to produce multi-GTM revenue factories, according to sound principles of revenue architecture.

# Product-Led Growth Within Large Enterprises

# THIRTEEN

# The Enterprise Sales Inflection Point

When and How to Add Sales to
Product-Led GTM Motions

For any successful company that was built from the ground up as product-led growth (PLG), there comes a time when the siren song of enterprise sales is hard to ignore. Selling to enterprise-scale customers can be alluring. Board members make compelling arguments based on historical experiences in sales-led companies: "The contracts are larger, Retention and Expansion rates are higher, enterprise customers' brands are recognizable, and market leadership depends on owning relationships with the largest customers in any given space."

While these things may be true, there are better and worse ways to expand from PLG into sales. In my consulting work with Winning by Design, we have worked with dozens of companies that have managed through this inflection point, including Dropbox, DocuSign, GitLab, Snyk, Asana, Calendly, Figma, and Slack. Each case is unique, but patterns of success have emerged. In this chapter we lay out first principles for when and how to add sales to a successful PLG motion.

### Why all Recurring-Revenue Growth Follows an S-Curve

For foundational reasons outlined famously by Jacco van der Kooij,[1] recurring-revenue growth follows an S-curve, with each stage of growth governed by a combination of underlying dynamics.

**FIGURE 13.1.   Recurring-Revenue Growth Follows an S-Curve**

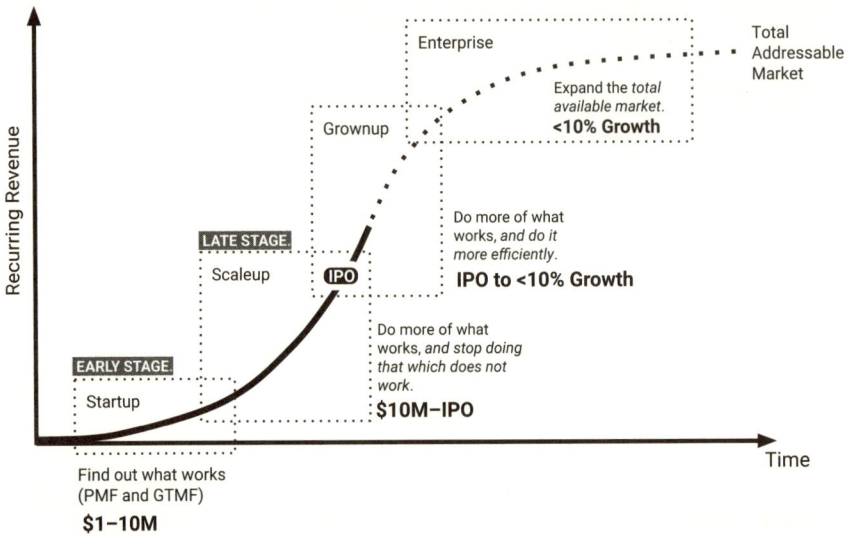

*Source:* Winning by Design

## STARTUP PHASE

During the initial stages of growth, the goal is to establish Product-Market Fit (PMF) and Go-To-Market Fit (GTMF). In this chapter we will explore some of the activities involved in establishing GTMF. From a growth-drivers perspective, new customer Acquisition is the largest driver of revenue growth during this phase from $0 to approximately $10M in annual recurring revenue (ARR).

## SCALEUP PHASE

Assuming reasonable Retention rates in a recurring-revenue model, the compounding effects of recurring revenue take over after about $10M in ARR, and Retention becomes the primary driver of revenue growth. As the base of recurring revenue increases, the ability to renew recurring revenue begins to outpace the ability to win new customers.

## GROWNUP PHASE

Depending on the GTM motion, Expansion begins to feature prominently somewhere in the scaleup-to-grownup phase. For GTM motions that depend on landing small initial deals within larger accounts with the intent to expand from there ("land and expand"), Expansion can be a significant growth driver at this stage.

## SATURATION

Under ideal circumstances, these growth dynamics compound to produce non-linear growth that follows a logistic curve. At first the growth looks exponential; however, growth rates in any given market inevitably begin to decay as these ideal circumstances become more elusive. As we monitor the saturation point for ideal customer profile (ICP) customers, we must of necessity move on to the next set of customers whose fit with our solution is less than ideal. At some point approaching saturation, each new set of customers produces conversion, Retention, and Expansion rates that are slightly worse than the last. When this starts to happen, we can of course attempt to shore up key metrics via optimization, but if the underlying cause is saturation within our core set of ICP customers, growth-rate attenuation is inevitable.

The only way to continue high growth rates through a saturation plateau is to add another growth engine on top of the one that got us to this point. This could be a new product or a new geography or, as we will explore here, a new GTM motion.

For successful PLG companies, these saturation dynamics can present at different ARR levels, depending on the size and accessibility of the target market. The right time to consider adding a new GTM on top of PLG is *after* we have established scalable and sustainable growth with our PLG motion (GTMF) and *before* we begin suffering from a decline in growth rate due to saturation. Since it is easy to measure GTMF (see Chapter 4: Product-Led Growth Is a Long-Term Growth Strategy), we can reliably avoid adding a second GTM too early. Saturation, however, is a more difficult signal to recognize. It is driven by demand and competition factors that are specific to your market and beyond the scope of this book.

### The Most Common Mistake Scaleup CEOs Make in the Name of Growth

As it turns out, missing saturation signals is not the most common revenue architecture mistake made by CEOs. No, the most common revenue architecture mistake made by CEOs is succumbing to the temptation to add additional GTM motions too early—before we have established GTMF with the current GTM motion.

**FIGURE 13.2.   Iterating Toward Go-To-Market Fit**

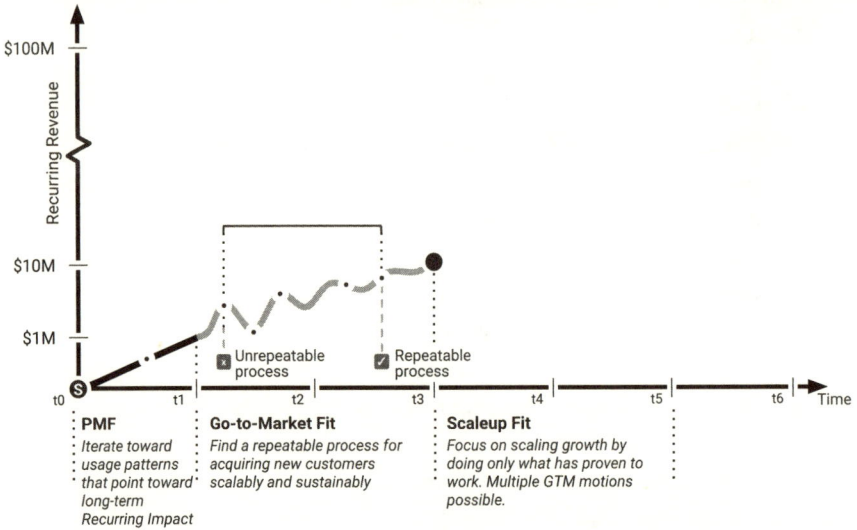

*Source:* Winning by Design

Consider the activities covered in Chapter 4 and the associated timeline of iterating our way to GTMF.

Some of what we try works, but it is not repeatable. Some experiments don't work at all. The goal of experimentation during the GTMF phase is to find successful actions that are repeatable. Remember we said we were looking for a source of new customers that is scalable and sustainable? This means we need a means of accessing these new customers that is not only economic (sustainable) but also repeatable (scalable). At some point, the variability in techniques we pursue begins to narrow, the predictability of our tactics solidifies, and the squiggly line of experimentation shown above converges into a smooth, predictable line. This is the point at which we enter scale mode and we accelerate investments in growth (see Chapter 4: Product-Led Growth Is a Long-Term Growth Strategy).

The mistake most commonly made by revenue leaders during the early stages of a product's life is to add another GTM motion too early. Fig. 13.2 helps illustrate the folly of that idea. If your first GTM is still in "chaos" mode—meaning we are still throwing things against the wall to see if they stick, and we are still working to get the squiggly line to converge—why and when would it make sense to spool up another GTM?

Answer: it would not make sense.

And yet, many leaders, desperate to meet the expectations of investors and disappointed with their early revenue results, prematurely add a second GTM, effectively stacking chaos on top of chaos.

For the PLG company, this could look like a young-but-promising product that has now advanced from being a minimum viable product (MVP) to being a production-ready product, showing good data around PMF, as indicated by First Impact attainment and ongoing usage Retention. At this point we believe in the product, and we are searching for a source of customers that is scalable and sustainable so we can establish GTMF. Since this takes time and our investors are impatient, we may feel pressure to *also* add a sales motion, feeling it could "accelerate" revenue growth.

At this stage, our Growth Team is working hard on new-customer Acquisition, Activation, and/or Monetization experiments, seeking to validate our assumptions around unit economics and to establish a repeatable process.

Now for the chaos move—an example of the most common revenue architecture mistake made by early-stage CEOs:

In the midst of these ongoing experiments with PLG Acquisition/Activation/Monetization, we hire a sales team, train it, and spin up a motion for sales to pick up inbound leads from the website to see if sales can convert this inbound demand better than product does. The idea is to send some leads to the product and some leads to Sales. Maybe we segment in a way that avoids channel conflict, but even if we do, the sales team will inevitably need support from the product team. It is, after all, running its own set of experiments and iterating toward its own GTMF. So now our product team, finance team, and marketing team are all trying to support two GTM motions simultaneously, each of which is still in "chaos" mode, looking for GTMF.

Don't do this.

Instead, stabilize each GTM motion before adding the next one.

## Run Your Multi-GTM Business Like a Lean Revenue Factory

In an ideal, multi-GTM-motion business, each GTM motion functions like a production line in a factory.

In a factory that produces physical goods, each production line has inputs, throughputs, and outputs, and each line functions according to a specific set of processes. Similarly, this principle also holds for revenue production via GTM

**FIGURE 13.3.** The Revenue Factory

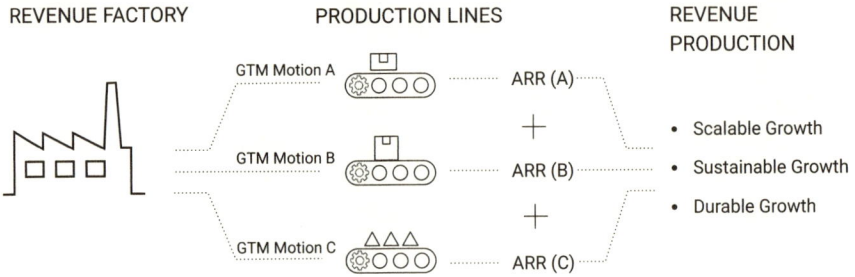

*Source:* Winning by Design

motions, with each GTM motion analogous to its own production line (in this book we explore the processes associated with the PLG GTM motion in detail).

The processes associated with PLG are different from those associated with inbound sales (where marketing creates leads and sales converts leads to paying customers), which are yet again different from processes associated with outbound sales (where salespeople create their own leads via outbound prospecting). Because each GTM motion operates according to specific processes, it does not serve us to manage the entire business by averages (e.g., "what is the customer acquisition cost payback for our entire business?"). Rather, we need to design, measure, and manage each GTM motion as its own independent production line.

## When to Add Sales to PLG

If a company has a single PLG GTM motion, and we want to explore adding a sales motion for all the good reasons mentioned above (access to additional customers, larger deal sizes, better Retention, etc.), the soonest we should consider adding sales is after our PLG GTM motion has reached GTMF—usually around $10M in ARR. At this point, we should have settled nicely into scalable and sustainable growth, having identified repeatable processes that produce predictable revenue outputs. If we reach repeatable processes with good unit economics at a scale smaller than $10M total ARR, we can consider adding sales at that point. And if we are over $10M in ARR but still not achieving good unit economics via repeatable processes, we should continue working toward repeatability before adding sales.

**FIGURE 13.4.   Adding Sales as a Second GTM Motion**

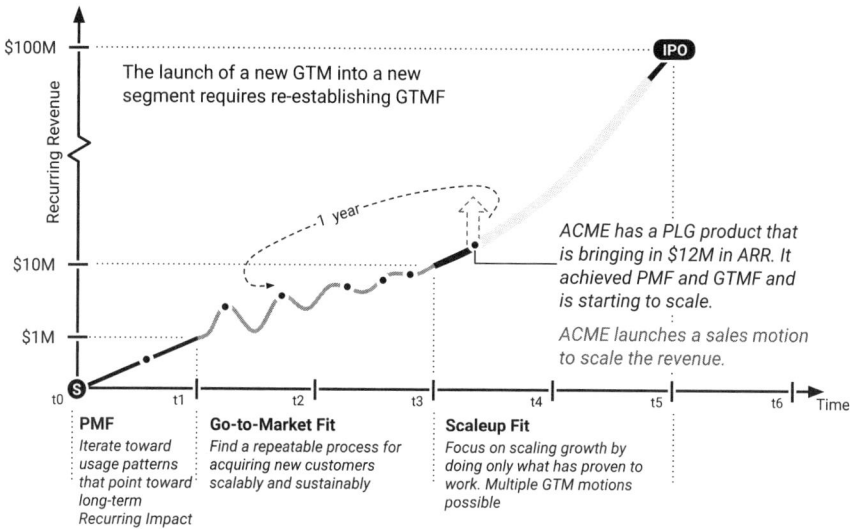

The launch of a new GTM into a new segment requires re-establishing GTMF

ACME has a PLG product that is bringing in $12M in ARR. It achieved PMF and GTMF and is starting to scale.

ACME launches a sales motion to scale the revenue.

**PMF**
*Iterate toward usage patterns that point toward long-term Recurring Impact*

**Go-to-Market Fit**
*Find a repeatable process for acquiring new customers scalably and sustainably*

**Scaleup Fit**
*Focus on scaling growth by doing only what has proven to work. Multiple GTM motions possible*

*Source:* Winning by Designt

Following this guideline, we can afford to put our creative attention on the inevitable iteration required to get the new sales motion to reach its own GTMF.

New GTM motion, new GTM fit—it's only logical.

From a leadership perspective, we already put significant time and creative energy into optimizing our first GTMF: PLG. That work resulted in repeatable processes, producing predictable results. If we took the time to program those into our product and our supporting human processes, they will continue to run well even without our constant attention. We can now turn our attention to the new GTM motion: sales.

### What Is the Best Next GTM After PLG? Or, the Second Most Common Growth Mistake

When the motivation to add sales is desperation or fear, we tend to make mistakes. The second largest mistake, after adding GTM motions too soon, is to add a second GTM motion that has nothing to do with the first.

Because the call of "enterprise sales" is so enticing, we can be lured into believing we can achieve all the goodness of enterprise sales in one big move.

FIGURE 13.5.  **Building GTM Motions Far Apart from Each Other Yields Limited Synergy**

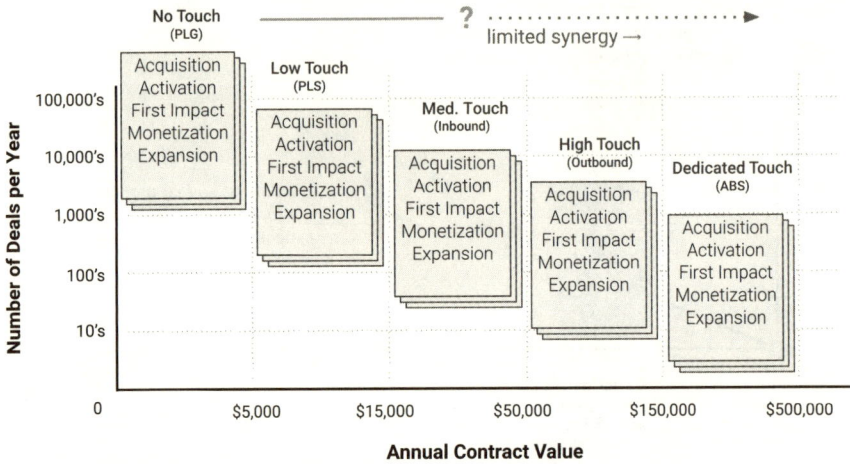

If you are a product-oriented founder or CEO and the conversations you are having with potential sales leaders are frustrating, you are in good company. Some sales leaders who grew up in sales-led environments truly believe—based on their experience—that sales is more of an art than a science. They rely on good hiring, skills training, and solid pipeline management to call and hit their number each month/quarter. These are good things, but if we want to build out an entire structure to support a sales-led approach to go after the largest enterprises, we may be in for a surprise, and the surprise is this: building an enterprise GTM motion is more difficult, is more expensive, and takes longer than anyone is willing to tell you.

Building a second (after PLG) sales motion to go after the largest customers would essentially mean PLG is "over here" and sales is "over there." Yes, it avoids channel conflict, but that's about the only good thing to say about this strategy. Everything else about this bifurcated strategy is expensive and disconnected. If we build out enterprise sales as our first sales-led motion to follow PLG (on the far right of Fig. 13.5), we will need entirely different marketing, targeting entirely different customers, feeding an entirely different sales process, supported by an entirely different onboarding process. We may as well be building a new company.

FIGURE 13.6.   **Building PLS Adjacent to PLG Yields Synergy**

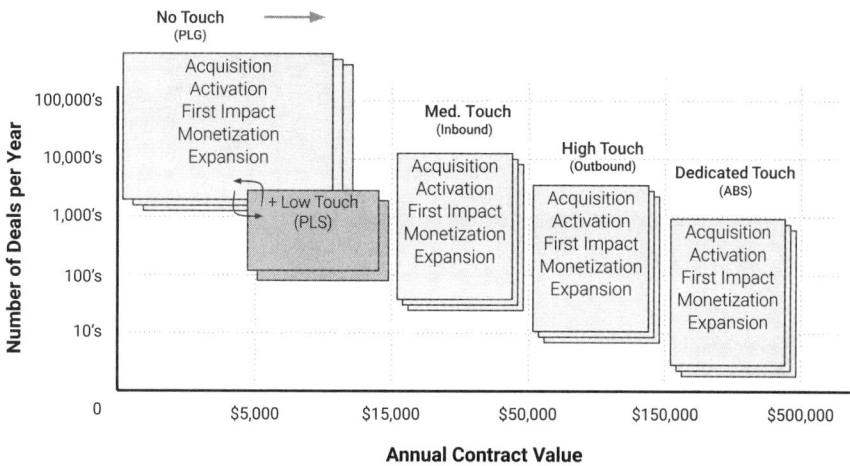

There is a better way.

What if we could build our next sales motion right next to the product-led motion? What if the capabilities we developed as part of our PLG launch (e.g., self-service Acquisition, Activation, First Impact) could be *of benefit to* our new sales motion? What if the adjacency of those two motions were an *advantage*?

When we build the second GTM motion immediately adjacent to PLG, we are able to leverage the power of our self-service Acquisition, Activation, and First Impact to tee up opportunities for sales involvement.

Imagine a world where the product itself acquires new users who happen to work at a company with Expansion potential. Imagine these users are able to Activate and achieve First Impact with no assistance, and then, via Loops, they are able to bring on colleagues who also begin succeeding on their own?

If this situation were then surfaced to a salesperson, imagine how that salesperson could help the company in question achieve *more impact* by helping them leverage advanced features, learn from best practices, and expand usage across the company?

This approach to layering on sales in a way that *benefits from* rather than *competing with* PLG is called product-led sales, and it is the topic of the next chapter.

## Chapter 13 Summary

- All recurring revenue growth follows an S-curve. Initial high growth results from adding new sales to the compounding effects of recurring revenue.

- To achieve high growth, companies must find both Product-Market Fit and Go-To-Market Fit and then invest in more of what works.

- Saturation occurs when market conditions begin to throttle your ability to continue achieving the same growth results in the same market with the same repeatable process.

- Adding a second GTM makes sense after achieving GTMF and before experiencing an attenuating growth rate.

- The best GTM motion to add to PLG is product-led sales, because PLS can benefit from much of the work required to get PLG working in the first place.

## Manager Minute

Thinking about your own company, take time to reflect on the following questions:

1. Have we achieved PMF? What evidence do we have?

 

 

 

2. Have we achieved GTMF? What evidence do we have?

 

 

 

**3.** Do we have more GTM motions running right now than we can reasonably manage at our scale?

_____

_____

_____

**4.** If we were to launch a PLS motion, when would we do so?

_____

_____

_____

# FOURTEEN

# Crossing the Chasm from Pure PLG to PLG-Plus-Sales

## How to Use Product-Led Sales to Reach Large Enterprise Customers

> *"Product-led sales (PLS) is a GTM strategy where end-user product usage is the basis for pipeline creation."*
>
> —Elena Verna, head of growth, Dropbox

*"Every successful SaaS company has a sales team."*
Yes, and?
*"So PLG isn't all you say it is."*
Really?
*"It's just a channel to market, and so is sales. PLG can't reach the big customers, the complex customers. . . . Sales is best for larger deals. Also for more complex deals. Also for platforms."*
Go on. . . .
*"So PLG isn't all that."*
Hmmm. . . .

It's true. Sales is important.

And all successful SaaS companies that reach scale have sales.

And most successful companies in the world have sales.

But this is not an either-or. Just because sales works doesn't mean that product-led growth (PLG) doesn't work. And just because PLG works doesn't mean that sales doesn't work.

### Why Every Successful PLG Company Also Has a Sales Team

The most successful of all SaaS companies—including those still growing 30% year over year, even at $500M or $1B in revenue—leverage PLG/self-service motions as well as sales motions.

Of the 722 PLG companies tracked in PeerSignal's 2023 PLG Index, 405 were actively hiring for sales roles.[1] That's 56% of PLG companies actively hiring for sales positions.

PLG companies indeed employ salespeople, but they employ them to sell differently.

> *"PLS is selling to people who already use your product."*
>
> —Alex Bilmes, CEO, Endgame

The industry has come to call this motion product-led sales, and it works very much as we described with Atlassian in Chapter 2.

For this chapter, I drew on experiences from Miro, Dropbox, DocuSign, Atlassian, Calendly, Lucid, Asana, MongoDB, HubSpot, Snyk, Hex, and Figma. Many companies have combined PLG with sales—some more successfully than others. Here we identify the patterns of success, designed to help more companies execute deliberate PLS strategies.

Instead of working with leads generated by marketing (marketing-qualified leads, or MQLs), PLS salespeople work with leads generated by the product (PQLs, or product-qualified leads and PQAs, or product-qualified accounts).

---

**CASE STUDY**

### How Lucid Went from Freemium to $30K Deals in One Phone Call

When Dan Cook joined LucidChart as its first head of sales, he was amazed at his first sales call. The prospect was Uber. Dan was introduced to Uber's director of information technology (IT) by a user of Lucid.

> **Dan:** *"Hi, I'm Dan. I noticed you have 121 employees regularly using the LucidChart product to build flowcharts and diagrams—some using free accounts and some using paid accounts. We've seen some companies consolidate users into a single instance to manage as a company."*

**Uber IT Dir.**   *"How much could we get for $30K?"*

Dan had to mute the call and do some quick math with a colleague.

**Dan:** *"Would 500 licenses work for you?"*

The IT director agreed and provided his credit card to close the deal on the call.

After they hung up, Dan's colleague looked at him and said, *"Dude. They are now our second largest account!"*

**Dan:** *"Do we have any more of these?"*

It turns out they did—a whole stack of them. LucidChart had been going to market via PLG for years, with no salespeople whatsoever. This phone call kicked off its sales-assisted motion.

---

## What's The Difference Between a Marketing-Qualified Lead (MQL) and a Product-Qualified Account (PQA)?

In traditional models, MQLs are created as potential customers engage with marketing materials or events. Marketing teams configure systems to score these prospects, based on activities that demonstrate interest in the product or service. Some examples include:

- Participated in a live event.
- Asked for more information on the product (e.g., a demo).
- Read product pages on the website.
- Downloaded a white paper.

In addition to tracking Engagement, MQL scoring pays close attention to ideal customer profile (ICP) and title level/persona. Marketing works to engage interested parties from target companies that also control the purchase decision at their company—the executive decision-maker (DM).

When the lead score reaches a certain level, the prospect is designated an MQL and it is handed off to sales for further qualification and selling.

PQAs work similarly, but they are created by way of a customer actually using the product. As long as we allow prospective customers to use the product prior to purchase, they are by definition:

1. Demonstrating their interest via action in the product.

2. Still not paying customers.

Data consistently shows that PQAs convert at extremely high rates—often at rates 4–7 times higher than MQLs.[2] But there is little reason to pit PQAs against MQLs. In both cases we are looking for purchase intent. In both cases we are looking for an ICP account,[3] and in both cases we are looking for an executive decision-maker.

FIGURE 14.1.   **Traditional Sales vs. Product-Led Sales**

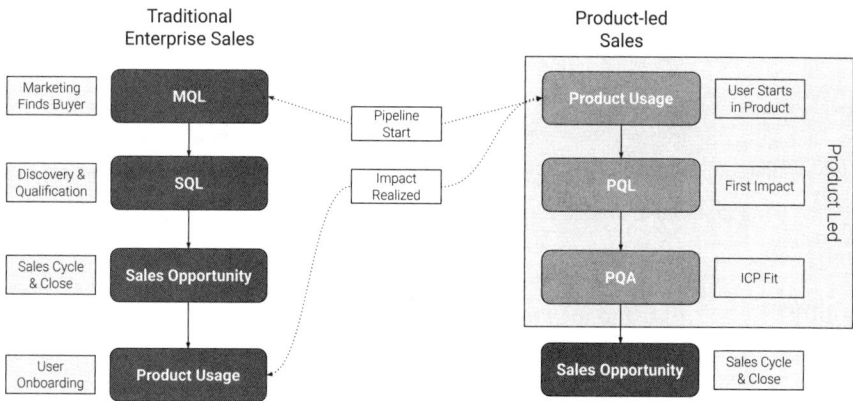

## PQA SCORING

At the top of the funnel for a freemium or free trial product will be many, many users. Only a subset of those users are relevant for sales, generally measured along two dimensions: fitness and readiness.

A fit score indicates the degree to which an account matches our ICP. Fit scores aggregate information about industry, size, growth, and other characteristics of a company associated with high-value customers. If we have users at non-ICP accounts—paying or not—we want to leave them right where they are: on the "self-service happy path." Investing human time and energy in these non-ICP accounts would be a waste, since non-ICP accounts are not expected to Monetize, renew, or Expand at attractive rates.

On the other hand, if we have users at a target ICP account, we want to consider engagement from sales.

> **Fit Score Example**
>
> Imagine we have a software solution that manages the administration involved in hiring and paying independent contractors. The solution has been built from the ground up as fully self-service, and many employers use the service to help streamline the administrative and tax implications of having temporary employees. Employers achieving impact with our solution range from individual households to small businesses to human resources (HR) managers within large corporations.
>
> We have determined it makes sense for our sales team to engage with accounts over $500M in annual revenue. At this size and above, we believe we have the potential to sell licenses for ten seat holders or more, which is an attractive prospect for sellers to add value while simultaneously retiring sales quota.
>
> Now assume ten new customers create accounts on our service during a given week. Which of those accounts are "sales eligible"? Answer: only the accounts associated with companies larger than $500M in revenue. If seven of those accounts fail to meet that criterion, that's fine—they won't speak to a salesperson, and instead they will remain on the "self-service happy path," still achieving impact with our easy-to-use solution.

**FIGURE 14.2. PLS and the "Self-Service Happy Path"**

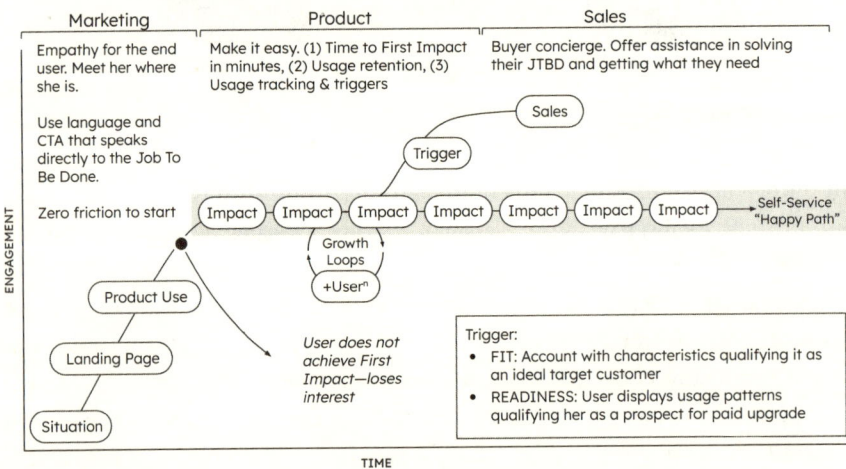

### Effective Product-Led Sales Depends on the "Self-Service Happy Path"

For accounts that don't meet our criteria for eligibility to engage Sales, the "self-service happy path" will do just fine (see the horizontal line in the figure above). Assuming the self-service happy path is well built, users from these accounts will be perfectly able to self-serve into First Impact and recurring impact. Some of them will upgrade to paid plans, and everyone will be happy.

**FIGURE 14.3. Fitness and Readiness Scores for PLS**

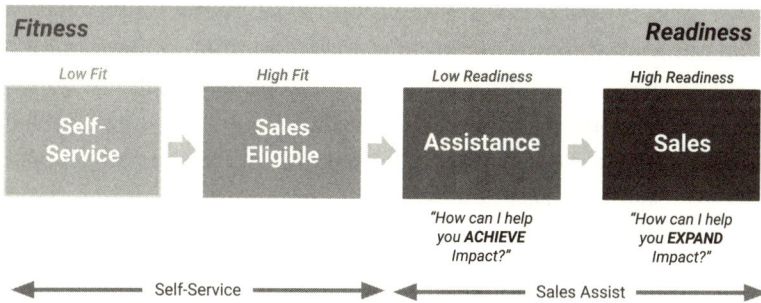

For accounts whose fit score makes them eligible for sales engagement, we look further to determine if they are indeed ready to engage with sales.

Depending on the solution, readiness could be based on elapsed time, patterns of usage, patterns of Expansion, or some combination thereof. Imagine a situation where a user from Delta Airlines (an ICP account) creates an account and gets a phone call from a sales rep a few minutes later—before they are even able to activate and begin using the service. This would be too early. If, on the other hand, a call from a sales rep arrives after the user has achieved First Impact and is looking to scale usage across the company, that would be a well-timed sales engagement. Readiness scores help determine the optimal time to engage an ICP customer and what type of engagement is appropriate.

> "Product-led sales is a powerful strategy, whereby sales teams no longer rely on high-volume, spray-and-pray tactics. Instead of using their best guess, reps access buying signals based on customer fit, product usage, and other forms of intent."
>
> —Alexa Grabell, CEO, Pocus

## Product-Led Sales Is Driven by Signal-Based Plays

Once a new account is determined via fit score to be an ICP prospect and via readiness score to be ready for engagement with Sales, this activates what is known as a signal-based play. We can establish any number of signal-based plays, depending on how detailed our metrics are and how granular we want our response to be. Generally these plays fall into two categories:

1. **Assistance**. If users (Free, Pro, or Teams; on PLG Monetization, see Chapter 9: How to Convert Free Users into Large Paying Contracts) have low Activation rates or otherwise have concerning usage data that indicates a need for help, the right play will be to deploy additional assistance: *"How can I help you achieve impact?"* Many PLS companies hire "product advocates" to do this job. They do not carry a sales quota but rather carry a "product usage" quota. Their job is to help accounts improve usage of the product, period. The idea is that further Monetization and upsell will follow once users are enjoying success with the product.

2. **Sales**. If usage patterns indicate that a sales motion could be well timed, it makes sense to deploy salespeople. And when these salespeople show up, they are also there to help: *"How can I help you expand impact?"* Sales plays can have multiple goals, including conversion, upsell, cross-sell, seat Expansion, etc.

## In Product-Led Sales, Never Confuse the User with the Buyer

The path described above assumes that Sales knows who to engage with. But as with traditional MQLs, we still need to locate an executive decision-maker. That decision-maker is highly unlikely to be a current user of the product. It is much more likely that the executive DM is somewhere up the reporting chain from the end user.

> *"Never confuse the user with the buyer."*
>
> —Kate Aherling, CRO, Calendly

At this point, the salesperson needs to identify who at this PQA is likely to make team-wide or company-wide decisions about standardizing on a specific piece of software: the executive DM.

If this is a target ICP account, Marketing—via its data enrichment efforts—may have already identified potential DMs in this account. If contact information for potential DMs is not known, Sales may need to do some sleuthing.

Sales's job is now to do what it does best: figure out how to engage the executive DM in a conversation. But in the case where users are already active on the product, this salesperson has an added advantage. She knows something the DM does not know—she knows where and how the product is already being used at the company.

---

**A Note on When PLS Makes Sense:** Not all PLG companies can or should add sales to their motions. Studies have shown that conversion rates can increase by up to 2x by adding sales to a PLG motion,[4] but that doesn't mean it makes sense in all cases.

**Product Positioning:** All PLG products by definition address a Job To Be Done (JTBD) for an end user. But if you cannot translate this end-user benefit into a business-level return on investment (ROI) narrative, you may struggle moving upmarket from PLG.

**Unit Economics:** Adding a sales touch is expensive, and it can increase PLG customer acquisition cost (CAC) significantly. We generally want CAC payback to be less than twelve months (see Chapter 7: How to Acquire Self-Service Customers), and if adding sales touch breaks this equation—even after the 2x increase in conversions—we can't afford to do it.

Usually our definition of ICP can handle the unit economics issue. By defining ICP to include only companies above a certain size, we can ensure that Sales only engages when the potential deal sizes are large enough to warrant the additional CAC.

---

### How to Use JTBD Effectively in Product-Led Sales

Product-led pipeline creation is the most effective way to qualify accounts for JTBD fit (also called use-case fit). With a good JTBD fit, renewals and Expansions are much more likely. In fact, if our cohorts are full of customers whose JTBD is the one for which our product is designed and who therefore are achieving impact, then renewals become non-events.

**TABLE 14.1.**   JTBD Fit for MQLs and PQAs

| MQL | PQA |
| --- | --- |
| Has engaged with marketing content | Has engaged with the product |
| Has heard about potential impact | Has experienced impact |
| Has learned about possible use cases | Has tested their JTBD within the product |

Now consider the likelihood of JTBD fit for an MQL vs. a PQA.

If each prospect that entered our sales funnel came in by way of PQA, imagine the stability that would introduce to the revenue stack. Because all PLG users who opt in to paying for the solution are doing so based on hands-on experience with the product, the likelihood of them being satisfied with the results is high. Accordingly, each cohort would have a high likelihood of attractive net revenue retention (NRR) (on cohort Expansion and NRR, see Chapter 12: Shifting from Marketing Funnels to Product Loops), and compound growth would therefore be architected into the system.

In a PLS GTM motion, two things are true:

1. PLG is the purest filter to ensure that only good-JTBD-fit customers enter the system. Why? Because they try before they buy, and they make their financial decision only after determining for themselves that the JTBD fit is good.

2. Sales is an activity best pursued as a consultant/concierge. We want to help customers make the best decision regarding whether our solution can help them make progress on their JTBD. We are wary of force fits, and we never want to pressure a fit. . . . We want natural fits that can move quickly and smoothly to First Impact, recurring impact, and recurring revenue.

When the product is effectively used to qualify accounts for JTBD fit, the pipeline fills with happy customers who are already experiencing impact. If these customers have additional needs that can be achieved via expanding the use of our product, they can be perfect candidates for sales engagement—to help *expand* their impact.

### Don't Add Sales Capacity Too Early—It Messes Everything Up

At least nine out of ten customers who use a PLG product will never need to speak to a salesperson. That means for every one PQA we need to create ten new customers overall—nine of whom are self-service.

And since one in five PQAs turns into a closed deal for sales, we need five times that—fifty new self-service customers—for every one customer that signs a contract with sales assistance:

**TABLE 14.2.**   Calculating PLS Conversion Rates for One New Sale

| 50 | * | 10% | * | 20% | = | 1 |
|---|---|---|---|---|---|---|
| New self-service customers | | Conversion rate to PQA | | Sales close rate | | New sales contract |

This dynamic puts a natural limit on how fast and how large we can grow a PLS motion—everything is constrained by how fast we can grow the top of the funnel. If we add account executives (AEs) faster than Product can produce PQAs, reps will need to augment their PLS motion with outbound prospecting—a completely different GTM motion.

When sales capacity is added too fast, it may look good in a spreadsheet, but it causes myriad downstream disasters. The general rule of thumb should be to add sales capacity only at a rate where salespeople can be sufficiently supplied with MQLs or PQLs (depending on the motion) such that they can reliably hit quota. In this scenario, where high-ICP opportunities are fed to sales in sufficient quantity, we can focus on sales skill as the overriding determinant of whether a sales rep achieves quota. If he is not receiving enough opportunities, he will likely not achieve quota, even if he is highly skilled.

### Premature Scaling Example

Imagine a hypothetical scenario where PLG has generated a healthy, $10M annual recurring revenue (ARR) business, and we determine it would be good to introduce a PLS motion to assist with accounts with high fit and readiness scores.

Our experiment is successful! Our first three reps are able to close PQA accounts at a high rate, and at ACVs that easily justify their compensation. In fact, estimated CAC payback for the PLS motion is <10 months. Each rep is achieving 100% of quota with seeming ease.

Given the success of this experiment, the recommendation is made to double down: "Let's hire three more reps!"

Good candidates are identified, hired, and onboarded. Soon all six reps are closing business, but each is achieving only 50% of quota. An investigation reveals that this is because the volume of PQAs has not yet increased to support the additional reps. Plans are made to invest in increasing PQAs to support additional sales capacity.

Rather than firing the extra reps while waiting for the increase in PQAs, management decides to task reps with finding 50% of their own pipeline. The reps ask Marketing for lists of prospects they can call on. Many of these prospects are not aware of the product, so reps ask for better marketing materials to help educate prospects. Even with marketing trying to support a new type of sales cycle, pursuits are slow and often unfruitful. Conversion rates for pipeline generated in this way are low, and the time required to close customers is 5x or even 10x what was required to convert highly qualified PQAs.

Reps then get creative and begin fishing in the pool of current product users who have not yet achieved PQA status. Maybe they have lower fit scores (not quite an ICP account). Or perhaps they have lower readiness scores (not quite ready to engage in a sales conversation). These accounts are easier to work than cold outbound attempts. The ACVs are only 20%–30% of historical ACVs, but these accounts close easier than those surfaced via cold outbounding, and reps are now hitting 75% of quota.

At this point, we have made a number of compromises, all of which show up directly or indirectly in our financials:

- We pay six reps a full base salary plus 75% of their variable pay.
- Marketing is distracted, trying to support an unanticipated additional channel (outbound).
- Salespeople and sales management feel pressure to perform, so they continue running all three motions (PLS, outbound, and "non-ICP PLS"), with high frustration levels.
- Many of the accounts we are now engaging are non-ICP, meaning:
  - CAC payback is > 12 months.
  - Renewal rates are anticipated to be lower.
  - Expansion rates are anticipated to be lower.

- Accounts that could have Monetized just fine on the "self-service happy path" are now being picked off by sales, and commissions are paid where they otherwise wouldn't have been necessary.

Scaling the sales team for PLS faster than necessary to support the volume of highly qualified PQAs is a bad idea—even if it looks good in a spreadsheet. If you feel pressure to grow the top line faster, the better investment would be in PQA generation, with the number of quota-carrying salespeople being determined only by the availability of highly qualified PQAs.

### When and How to Run Multiple GTM Motions in Parallel

In Chapter 13 (The Enterprise Sales Inflection Point) we discussed the theory behind when to add an additional GTM motion. We invoked the metaphor of the revenue factory, and we suggested that each GTM motion be built and optimized as if it were its own independent production line. It takes time to optimize a GTM motion, and we do not recommend launching an additional GTM motion if you are still busy optimizing one or more existing motions toward attractive unit economics.

In an ideal world, one would build the PLG business first, followed by a PLS business, and finally an account-based sales business—only for the largest customers.

Why?

As we saw earlier in this chapter and also in Chapter 6 (Building a Minimum Viable Product for Freemium Adoption) on building a minimum viable product (MVP), PLG is an ideal motion for fine-tuning a feature set toward a defined JTBD. As discoveries about JTBD are made, and as fine-tuning proceeds, adjustments can be programmed directly into the product. Because customers self-select in or out based on hands-on experience with the product, this is a perfect laboratory for getting JTBD fit right. Furthermore, as we optimize Go-To-Market Fit (GTMF) (also covered in Chapter 6), our GTM motion and unit economics are similarly programmed into the product in a way that can become a flywheel that is very difficult to disrupt once it is turning.

A PLG flywheel as a foundation for the revenue stack affords opportunity to build from there (on when to add sales, see Chapter 13: The Enterprise Sales Inflection Point), and we recommend a PLS motion as the second motion where possible. Various motions appropriate for your market can be added in sequence.

Not all businesses are suited for PLG (see Chapter 17: Can PLG Work at a Company Like Mine?), so this is not a one-size-fits-all strategy. One thing is certain, however. When adding additional GTM motions, build from strength to strength. In Chapter 13 we covered why it would make sense to build from PLG to an immediately adjacent GTM motion (PLS), rather than attempting to launch a completely separate enterprise GTM motion for enterprise customers. Similarly, if you started with a classic enterprise GTM motion, selling large contracts to large customers, it is unlikely you would be able to succeed launching PLG as your second GTM motion to acquire new customers all the way at the other end of the market. Perhaps it would be better to begin with self-service renewals for the customers you already have (product-led _X_, covered in Chapter 17).

It is possible and advisable to run multiple GTM motions, but only when following these two basic principles:

1. Do not add a next GTM motion until your current GTM motion is stable.

2. Do not build a next GTM motion far afield from the strength of your current GTM motion.

---

CASE STUDY

**How Figma Deploys Sales within a Product-Led Environment**

Figma is a cloud-first design platform for product designers whose primary GTM is PLG, with PLS picking up very specific PQAs.

Jesus Requena ran growth marketing for Figma from 2021 until Adobe's $20B acquisition offer in 2023.[5]

Figma uses data science to categorize every account in its funnel and treat them with the appropriate GTM approach.

First they divide accounts according to "fit." This is their primary sort, and it puts accounts into a category of either "self-service" or "sales-eligible." For this, Figma uses firmographics, technographics, and other custom data signals.

Within the "sales-eligible" category they further differentiate on what they call "readiness." Readiness at Figma is a function of usage signal.

- Weak usage signal: These accounts may or may not get attention from salespeople (prioritized by score)—if Sales engages, it is to educate and assist with Activation and Engagement—not to sell right away.

- Strong usage signal: These accounts are engaged in a formal process to identify the decision-maker, communicate the advantages of an enterprise contract, and close an enterprise-wide sale.

Of the $400M in ARR Figma had in 2023, 40% was purely self-service, while 60% was sales-assisted. And of the sales-assisted revenue, 70% of that was product-led sales or, in other words, upgrades from "free."

---

## Final Thoughts

Most founders who build a PLG-first company are far more comfortable building products than they are building and managing a sales motion. When the time comes to build a sales motion, however, there are better and worse ways to do it. Having decided to build your sales motion as a "sales assist" or PLS motion adjacent to your PLG motion, you will be in comfortable territory. In this situation, the sales team is just another Monetization channel you can "program" into your current GTM. Salespeople pick up highly qualified accounts (who are current users of your product) and assist them in scaling the impact they are already experiencing. As long as you don't hire faster than can be supported by the product-led machine, this PLS motion can be a highly profitable and effective growth accelerator.

There will be a time to add additional GTMs, including enterprise sales, but if you build methodically, that time will be after you have tuned your PLS motion to be repeatable, scalable, and profitable.

1. PLG

2. PLS

3. Enterprise sales

## Chapter 14 Summary

- All successful PLG companies eventually add a sales GTM.
- Product-led sales leverages product usage to generate sales pipeline.
- PLS is one GTM motion within an overall revenue stack.
- PLS cannot scale faster than PLG can support.

## Manager Minute

Thinking about your own company, take time to reflect on the following questions:

1. What percentage of our new-account sales opportunities are currently sourced via product usage?

   0%                                                                  100%

2. If there is a PLG-to-sales-assist motion in place, how structured are our PLS engagement plays? (check all that apply)

   _____ We identify whether a self-service account is in our ICP or not.

   _____ We measure/score product usage as part of our PQA process.

   _____ We use data to determine whether a self-service account needs Activation assistance or buying assistance.

   _____ We explicitly distinguish between end users and executive decision makers in our PLS playbook.

   _____ N/A: No PLG-to-sales-assist motion in place

3. The next thing we could implement or improve in our PLS journey is:

   _____

   _____

   _____

# FIFTEEN

# Selling Tactics for Product-Generated Leads and Product-Led Sales

## What's Different Tactically in Product-Led Sales?

In 2010, after selling ProfitLogic to Oracle, I lifted my head and looked around to see what was next. ProfitLogic built robust machine-learning models to help brick-and-mortar retailers optimize pricing and merchandise mix. Even though our software was cloud-based, the average ACV (annual contract value) was $1.2M. Like many startup execs, I had played many roles at ProfitLogic: head of marketing, head of product, head of business development. I had helped raise our largest round of funding, I had managed our external relationships with partners, and I had even sold one of our largest deals.

I was anxious to put myself in the mix once again. SaaS companies were hot, with Salesforce leading the way, and I assumed that I would help build another enterprise software company. But enterprise software had changed over the preceding five years. Omniture was selling recurring-revenue deals for tens of thousands of dollars, not millions. Developers could spool up powerful Amazon Web Services without ever speaking with a salesperson. Dropbox, Zendesk, and Basecamp all allowed free trials for their business applications.

If enterprise software was now being sold by way of small, land-and-expand contracts, I would have to learn a new way of going to market. At ProfitLogic, we never provided free trials—we always wanted the customer to have skin in the game. We couldn't negotiate with lower-level people, because they couldn't commit their companies to million-dollar-plus deals. We had to hold out for top-level executives, and we sold exclusively top-down. The last thing we wanted was to spend time and money spooling up an expensive trial with someone who was not empowered to make a commitment.

### In Product-Led Sales, the Product Does the Qualification

Product-led sales takes "no-commitment trials" to the next level. With PLS, no salesperson decides which customers can activate on a free trial. Instead, the self-service motion allows *anyone* to activate on a product, with very few restrictions. As we saw in Chapter 14 (Crossing the Chasm from Pure PLG to PLG-Plus-Sales), a subset of these new free customers become paying customers, and even fewer are customers with whom Sales would want to speak (target ideal customer profile customers with high potential spend). The scoring techniques discussed in Chapter 14 help resolve this for Sales by surfacing the customers with the right fit and readiness to make them ready for a sales conversation.

Further complicating the sales challenge, the users of free trials are almost never decision-makers (DMs) on behalf of a larger team or on behalf of the entire company. Although PLS presents an opportunity for salespeople to work only with customers who are succeeding with the product already, it also presents challenges. Traditional sales playbooks are not suited for these advantages or challenges—they were simply designed for a different situation.

**TABLE 15.1.**  Differences Between Traditional and Product-Led Sales

| Traditional Sales | Product-Led Sales |
| --- | --- |
| • Avoid engaging with non-decision-makers—it is not useful. | • Anyone can begin using the solution. |
| • Identify situation and pain and help the buyer determine potential impact from using the solution. | • Users are already experiencing impact from the solution. |
| • Build a joint impact plan (JIP) that helps the buyer see how to get to impact. | • The current users of the product are non-decision-makers. |
| • Trials can be seen as introducing delay and friction into the buying process. | • Trials are a core part of the process—but not managed by sales. |

### The Basic Product-Led Sales Playbook: How Sales Engages Product-Qualified Accounts

Chapters 13 and 14 covered PLS from a revenue architecture and systems perspective. We covered where, when, why, and how to build PLS into a company's go-to-market (GTM) processes. Having built out the processes and systems appropriately, our product is able to facilitate new customers' self-service journey to impact. We then use scoring and prioritization to get the right subset of those customers (product-qualified accounts) in front of salespeople.

Now what?

Deploying a typical sales playbook that begins with a discovery call and a demo would come across as tone-deaf for a customer who already has the solution. For a customer already succeeding with the solution, we need an entirely new sales playbook—one designed to meet the challenges and opportunities of product-led sales.

When a sales rep engages with an existing customer to help them extend the impact they are already achieving with the product, her intention is to understand the current situation, pain, and impact being experienced by the customer, based on the current use case, and then to explore how to extend beyond the current use. The basic PLS playbook can be simplified into three elemental steps:

FIGURE 15.1.   Product-Led Sales Blueprint

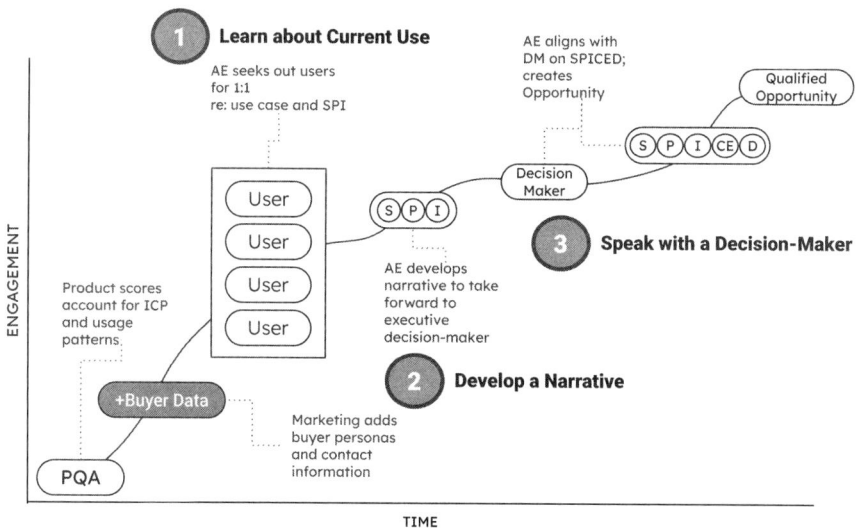

## BASIC PLS PLAYBOOK STEP 1: LEARN ABOUT CURRENT USE

The PLS account executive (AE) first wants to learn about the users and usage patterns within the PQA:

- **Situation:**
  - How many users are there?
  - What is their level of sophistication?
  - How long have they been using the product?
  - What has been the Expansion pattern to date?

Simple data like this should be available via the metrics and instrumentation discussed in Chapter 3: First Principles of Product-Led Growth.

At this point, the AE would ideally like to speak with one or more of the users. The AE is not trying to sell anything—she is simply trying to learn about how the product is being used. If possible, the AE would like to determine the following:

- The **Situation** that caused this solution to be the right answer (Job To Be Done)
- The **Pain** the solution is addressing
- The **Impact** it is having

The more specifics she can learn, the better. It is important, during this process, to develop a good feel for whether, how, and why the solution is delivering impact.

### BASIC PLS PLAYBOOK STEP 2: DEVELOP A NARRATIVE

With metrics gathered from the product itself and the qualitative information learned during user interviews, the AE can begin developing a narrative about how the solution might deliver even more impact if it were deployed to more users in its full Enterprise version. While discussing the use case with end users, the AE may have learned about limitations that could be unlocked if the account were to adopt the higher-tier product. Or perhaps broader adoption would allow for more effective collaboration, delivering more impact. Whatever the case, the AE needs a compelling story for the decision-maker. The more specific the AE can be with this narrative—including names, processes, and data—the more effective she will be in gaining the trust of the DM.

### BASIC PLS PLAYBOOK STEP 3: SPEAK WITH A DECISION-MAKER

Step 3 in the PLS Playbook looks the most similar to traditional playbooks in the sense that AEs are encouraged to locate and get time with a true decision-maker. In the case of PLS, however, there is a major difference vs. traditional sales. At this point, the AE has information the DM does not have regarding *the DM's own team* and its usage of the product. Since this information is valuable to the

DM, the AE channels generosity when sharing it. The focus is on describing the situation, pain, and impact the AE discovered when speaking with the users. At this point we want to validate what we heard and see if the decision-maker views these impacts as something they would want to scale across the company.

---

**PLS Example**

Continuing our example from Chapter 14 (Crossing the Chasm from Pure PLG to PLG-Plus-Sales), imagine our software for hiring temporary workers has been adopted by three hiring managers within a large, multinational organization with revenues exceeding $3B. All three of these managers have achieved First Impact, defined as successfully hiring their first temporary employee. Based on a high fit score and a high readiness score, the account is deemed a product-qualified account (PQA) and flagged for an AE to follow up.

The AE reviews information regarding usage within the account, and she is able to speak to one of the three hiring managers. She is also able to identify a senior vice president (SVP) of talent acquisition for North America, which is where two of the three current users operate.

**AE:** *"Did you know three of your hiring managers are currently using our solution to hire and pay temporary workers?"*

**SVP:** *"I had no idea. That doesn't sound good, to be honest—they shouldn't be subscribing to software on their own."*

**AE:** *"Oh! I don't want to get anyone in trouble. I heard some very interesting reasons why our solution is working well, and I just thought I'd share them with you."*

**SVP:** *"I'm fine hearing what you learned, but don't get your hopes up. We will likely not standardize on your solution—there is a whole process for adopting new human resources (HR) software here."*

Anyone who has worked in sales would love to be in the conversation summarized above. An SVP has agreed to review situation, pain, and impact information we gathered from ongoing current usage of the product. And although the SVP warned us not to get our hopes up, they also signaled there is a process for reviewing and adopting new HR software. They even used the word "standardize." Although we have a lot of selling still to go, we are in the right conversation with the right person, we have the tailwinds provided by three successful users achieving impact, and we have an invitation to explore more. If we play it right and if the impact is compelling, there may even be an opportunity for the company to standardize on our software.

208  FREEMIUM

## Advanced Product-Led Sales

In the examples above, we describe a relatively straightforward approach to PLS, suitable for a situation where individual usage leads to team and enterprise adoption on a uniform path. In some circumstances, the number of users, the variety of use cases, the number of possible upsell paths, or a combination of the above can call for multiple plays, depending on specifics within a given account.

Consider a sales rep with a territory consisting of more accounts than he can reasonably contact in any given year. Within those accounts are both Free and Pro tier users of the product. In addition, his accounts represent companies of various sizes across various industries. In this case, a one-size-fits-all tactic may not make sense for approaching PLS opportunities.

- **Whitespace**: Even though two accounts may have the same number of current free users, if one company is significantly larger than the other, it may have more potential whitespace, and it may therefore be a higher-priority sales opportunity.

- **Industry**: If one account is in the healthcare industry and one is in financial services, the use cases, example case studies, and impact considerations may be different.

- **Product variety**: Depending on which products or which product features are being used, the logical upsell play could be different.

- **Marketing**: Some GTM teams use sales to deliver marketing-generated campaigns to assigned accounts (webinar invitations, new product feature announcements, etc.). These could be appropriate for some but not all accounts in a given rep's territory.

In such situations, we will need more than just fit and readiness scores to prioritize and match accounts with specific upsell plays. Incorporating specifics around whitespace, industry, specific product usage patterns, and company-generated marketing opportunities can create nuanced schemes for prioritizing and planning tailored sales approaches.

**How Miro Manages Sales Within an Install Base of 50M-Plus Users**

Despite its product-led growth (PLG) roots as a digital whiteboard solution, Miro has always relied on its hybrid approach of combining PLG with sales. When Adam Carr joined the company in 2020 as the global head of sales, a fledgling sales organization already existed. Adam's challenge was to harmonize Miro's PLG and sales motions and find a way to prioritize its 50M-plus install base of users so that reps could find upmarket opportunities.

Adam's inclination was to focus on delivering impact to the end user as the main objective. He stated, "From a sales perspective, you can't look at self-service as competition. It's one team. We want to deeply understand the funnel: how do new user signups convert to paid users, how do paid users convert to the team plan, then from teams to the enterprise plan, and finally from the enterprise plan through Expansion?"

The key challenge for Miro's sales team was to leverage existing usage and tie that usage to business outcomes for a top-down sales approach. According to Adam, "Everyone is on a journey, and the key is to reach out to the right person at the right time." For this, Miro uses the concept of product-qualified accounts and product-qualified leads (PQLs). When user activity levels reach certain threshold levels, reps are notified, and they begin the "outbound" approach into these qualified accounts.

Miro uses two motions: a land motion and an expand motion. And they apply these motions with various user types within segments, defined by company size and geography, because, as Adam says, "Each journey is different."

Adam summarized the challenge as follows:

- How do we prioritize our reps' time? Which accounts and prospects should they be working with?

- What signals should we track to determine a prospect's readiness to engage?

- What message or tactic should we use to engage each contact, depending on where they are in their experience?

To manage these various journeys, Miro developed categories of plays, appropriate for different circumstances within target accounts.

Because Miro has been adopted inside many of the world's largest companies, reps often have to navigate a single account with more than ten thousand employees. Miro uses a software solution called Pocus to identify usage patterns and account characteristics, make sense of these signals, and prioritize the right playbook for the right situation. Miro reps enroll target personas in specific plays, managed within

Pocus, depending on account tier, persona, seniority, usage patterns, industry, and available marketing content.

> *"Having the right level of account insights and one aggregated view makes it easy for our teams to know when to engage at the right time. This also gives reps the ability to go a level deeper with more granular insights to uncover things like: where is our penetration within various lines of business? Who are the right senior stakeholders? Who are the power users, casual users?"*
>
> —Adam Carr, Head of Global Sales, Miro

### Final Thoughts

The global market for sales training is over $6B. Hundreds of sales training firms exist, though only a few have methodologies and reputations that have earned them global recognition. All of this industry is ripe for disruption.

As products become more capable of handling portions of the customer journey on a self-service basis, all of the most popular sales methodologies and playbooks will need to be updated. Artificial intelligence (AI) will further increase the percentage of GTM actions that can be automated—from marketing all the way through Retention and Expansion. As mentioned in the preface, I believe 70% of GTM roles as we know them will become unrecognizable, as this inevitable wave of automation gains momentum. As a result, human sellers will elevate their skills. They will let automation do what it does best, and they will step into the role of advisor. No longer will GTM professionals be critical-path for basic Acquisition and Activation tasks (that will increasingly be the domain of the self-service happy path). Rather, GTM professionals will become coaches and concierges. They will consult with customers on how to maximize impact with the solution, advising on best practices, advanced use cases, and strategic opportunities.

I see a future where GTM professionals become the operators of GTM systems and processes, much the same way as factory workers today operate complex systems that include advanced robotics and information systems.

## Chapter 15 Summary

- Product-led sales is different from traditional sales, as the "prospects" are already customers, and they already have experience with the product.

- Individual users of a PLG product are rarely, if ever, the decision-maker for the organization.

- The basic approach to PLS involves three steps:

  - Learn about current use.

  - Develop a narrative.

  - Speak with a decision-maker.

- Depending on the volume and variety of circumstances, PLS plays can be tailored to any level of specificity that makes sense for the business.

## Manager Minute

Thinking about your own company, take time to reflect on the following questions:

1. How do our salespeople incorporate product usage signal into their playbook development?

   _____

   _____

   _____

2. Do our salespeople speak with end users of our product? Why or why not? How might this help them develop better empathy for the situation, pain, and impact involved with product use?

   _____

   _____

   _____

3. How good are our reps at tailoring their approach to the specifics of the opportunity (industry, product usage patterns, persona, etc.)? Could we deliver systematic intelligence/support to help salespeople better meet customers where they are?

---

---

---

# SIXTEEN

# Lessons from Building PLG Within Large, Established Companies

> Three Companies That Succeeded in Adding PLG After Already Achieving $100M-Plus in Sales-Led, Recurring Revenue

Ninety-nine percent of business-to-business (B2B) companies were built without a product-led growth (PLG) go-to-market (GTM) motion.

But 72 of the top 100 up-and-coming private software companies (the Forbes Cloud100) utilize PLG.[1]

We cover this more in Chapter 18 (Product-Led Growth Beyond Software), but non-software companies are getting into the game too: auto companies with free trials, e-bikes with soft upgrades, home automation systems that transform HVAC and hi-fi. . . .

So what if you are one of the 99%? Let's say your business is highly successful with go-to-market strategies that are not PLG. Perhaps despite your success to date, for either offensive or defensive reasons, you believe that you should consider adding PLG.

If you are an existing company operating at scale and considering what it would take to add PLG to your business now—as an additional GTM—this chapter is for you.

### When and Why to Add PLG to an Existing, Successful Sales-Led Company

As we established in Chapter 4, PLG is not a short-term sales tactic. PLG will not replace a sales team, it will not reverse a declining growth rate, and it will not be a "quick fix" for any business. The reasons to consider PLG are in no way gimmicky or surface-level. As you will see from the case studies at the end of this chapter, a decision to add PLG to your GTM motions is a major strategic move—one that can set your company on an entirely new course.

## PLAYING OFFENSE

Sometimes the idea to introduce PLG is motivated by the immense opportunity represented by portions of the market inaccessible via other means. MongoDB was already over $100M in sales-led revenue before they added PLG, and now PLG constitutes over 50% of total revenue, growing at a rate 2x the sales-led side of the business. Unity Software shifted to PLG as part of a wholesale overhaul of its GTM, converting a large, free user base into a self-monetizing revenue machine. And HubSpot—known for its innovative approach to inbound marketing and sales—disrupted itself by adding PLG to its GTM motions after it was already over $100M in revenue. For HubSpot, the lessons learned in PLG were brought back into the core business, streamlining all aspects of its GTM motions.

## PLAYING DEFENSE

Other companies have added aspects of PLG as a defensive response to threats from industry competitors. Microsoft, historically known for its sales-led approach in selling software licenses, has shifted toward subscription-based offerings like Microsoft 365 and Azure. These platforms incorporate self-service features, such as online sign-up and provisioning, to cater to a wider range of customers and fend off PLG challengers. Oracle, a prominent player in enterprise software and cloud computing, launched Oracle Cloud Infrastructure with a focus on self-service provisioning and scalability. By embracing self-service capabilities, Oracle aimed to compete more effectively against PLG-driven cloud providers like Amazon Web Services and Azure. And Adobe leveraged its acquisition of Omniture to accelerate its transition from selling software licenses to offering subscription-based cloud services, such as Adobe Creative Cloud and Adobe Document Cloud. This shift enabled Adobe to provide self-service access to its products, catering to a broader audience beyond traditional enterprise clients.

Given what Zoom was able to do to WebEx and GoToMeeting (these companies were discussed in the Zoom case study in Chapter 1), Slack's ability to put Microsoft on high alert, and Dropbox's achievements in the storage space disrupting long-time players like EMC and IBM, we expect to see a continued trend of enterprise-scale players launching self-service motions to defend against "PLG attackers."

## Product-Led GTM Options for a Large Company

If your company is large, by definition you have existing products and customers as well as established go-to-market motions. Whether you are considering PLG for offensive or defensive reasons, PLG is not an all-or-nothing proposition. You have options for how to pursue a product-led strategy, some of which are outlined here.

### PRODUCT-LED ACQUISITION

To defend against PLG attackers effectively, you will need to build a PLG defense. As Clayton Christensen taught with his disruptive innovation theory, attackers enter markets from the bottom.[2] Beginning with "good enough" products, serving the needs of "low-end" customers, these disruptors gain a foothold and begin to iteratively improve their product, slowly working their way upmarket and causing incumbents to progressively retreat to "better" and "higher-end" customers until there is nowhere left to go. Successful disruptors eventually take over a market, while unresponsive incumbents fail.

The PLG strategies and tactics laid out in this book are essentially a roadmap for disrupting incumbents in digital product industries. If you are under attack from one of these disruptors, you will need a definitive response. Since retreating to "better" and "higher-end customers" is a short-term tactic that eventually leaves an incumbent vulnerable to extinction, the response needs to be something better than "go upmarket."

Launching product-led Acquisition can be an effective way to defend against PLG attackers. Product-led Acquisition effectively protects your flank, cutting off uncontested access to your market from below and offering customers a low-friction, self-service onramp to your product—not just the product from your competition.

Product-led Acquisition will represent a significant commitment of resources—time, talent, and money—so this strategy receives the bulk of our attention in this chapter. It is not, however, the only option for getting started with PLG.

### PRODUCT-LED ONBOARDING

Curtis Cannon, senior product manager at BambooHR, is a true believer in PLG, but BambooHR has historically gone to market via sales. Because of his strong conviction, Bamboo's CEO put him in charge of "figuring out our PLG strategy."

Intelligently, Curtis decided to start as close to the current GTM motion as possible so that his team could work synergistically with the existing business. He chose self-service onboarding as his initial PLG foray.

Whether a customer contract is secured via sales or self-service, nobody likes a clunky onboarding process. What if your customers could self-serve their way to First Impact? Could you identify guides, wizards, tutorials, or templates that could help them be more independent in setting up their new purchase? Curtis made the bet that they could, and his team is seeing good results with customers independently making their way to First Impact. Bamboo already has auto-renewals, so what's the next stop on Bamboo's PLG journey? Product-led Acquisition.

## PRODUCT-LED RETENTION

Almost by definition, any recurring-revenue business relies on its product to secure ongoing Engagement, resulting in long-term Retention and subscription renewal.

In Chapter 11 (Customer Success Without a Customer Success Department), we focused on how to leverage signal from the product to optimize ongoing engagement and recurring impact. And since recurring revenue is the result of recurring impact, recurring impact is the right place to start.

Surprisingly, however, it is not always the case that contract renewals are self-service. Even when a customer displays healthy ongoing Engagement, there are often manual contracting steps involved in renewing a subscription that could be automated via product-led strategies. Many of the same tactics outlined in this and the preceding chapters can be leveraged to build and test a self-service renewal workflow. The starting place for building product-led renewals is the same as with product-led Acquisition: "the self-service happy path."

In any healthy, recurring-revenue business, most renewals are not at risk. As such, a self-service happy path for either auto- or one-click renewal would suffice. If you have humans on your payroll chasing down every single renewal—with both happy and unhappy customers—you are wasting time and money. Not "investing"—wasting. The salary you pay people to pursue renewals manually, when these renewals could be processed automatically, is money you could otherwise invest in product features or other strategic priorities. But as long as you are paying humans to do what the product itself could do, you will not see that money again.

Similar to the Acquisition "self-service happy path," you do not have to let every customer proceed with a renewal unassisted. Whereas the self-service happy path will be sufficient for most customers, other customers will be at risk. Using signal from the product instrumentation, you can identify which customers need attention and then deploy that attention in a targeted way to help return those customers to full health.

## PRODUCT-LED EXPANSION

One argument we've heard against automatic renewals is that it removes an opportunity for a customer success manager or account manager to have a conversation with the customer around Expansion: "Renewals are a perfect time to engage with the customer, assess how things are going, and discuss whether and how to expand their footprint as part of a contract renewal negotiation, therefore, we want human interaction at each renewal."

I reject this premise.

Just as you can leverage signal from the product to inform you of which customer renewals are at risk, you can similarly use signal to indicate opportunities for Expansion. Some Expansion can be processed via automated workflows, while some is achieved more effectively via human assistance. We do not have to wait for the renewal to appear on the calendar to have conversations with customers. Signal-based plays can surface Expansion opportunities throughout a customer's life.

The lowest-friction SaaS contract is for the same user to renew the same product. This is a renewal, and it can be automated as per the above section.

But what about selling *more* of the same to the same user? With a contract already in place and the necessary configurations, integrations, or customization already established, it should also be a "click of a button" to purchase more. That is,

- More seats
- More servers
- More locations

Another type of Expansion is selling to new users. This can be difficult, but as we saw in Chapter 12 (Shifting from Marketing Funnels to Product Loops), this can also be accomplished via product-led strategies. Allowing a new department to take advantage of the same contract for the same product with the same configuration and use case may be the next frontier for product-led Expansion.

The most difficult Expansion is "new product/new user"—a domain likely best left to human-led motions for now.

## PLGTM

The balance of this chapter is dedicated to spooling up the defensive strategies for Product-led Acquisition described above. If for whatever reason your product or customer is not suited for self-service Acquisition, we recommend exploring other product-led options, some of which are outlined in Chapter 17: Can PLG Work at a Company Like Mine?

### Potential Mental Barriers to Adding PLG When Your Business Is Already at Scale

If you read through Part Two (Product-Led Growth Implementation and Tactics), you may have noticed some similarities to your own business. You may have also learned about things that go beyond anything you do today:

- "Marketing-qualified leads seem reasonable, but product-qualified accounts require instrumentation we just don't have."
- "It's hard to imagine a world where thousands of prospects come to us via search engine optimization (SEO) and search engine marketing (SEM), looking for a solution, before we filter them down to the ones who will pay us."
- "Giving things away is easy, but we would struggle to connect that to a viable commercial strategy."
- "The level of precision mechanics built into these PLG businesses is far beyond anything we have—our business is people-driven, and automating those jobs seems like a bridge too far."
- "I'm not sure our customers would want to buy this way. In our industry, people buy from people—that's the way it is, and I don't see it changing for a product as complex as ours."
- "One year is a reasonable timeframe in which to expect results. Three years is too long."

These are legitimate observations, and we do not want to diminish the obstacles that stand in the way of adding a PLG motion to a business already at scale. But the formula for success exists—this has been done before. In this chapter you will learn from the patterns of those who have successfully added a significant product-led Acquisition motion to their businesses that already had over $100M in sales-led annual recurring revenue.

### The Investments Required to Build PLG from Scratch, and How to Justify Them

We have covered the steps for building PLG from scratch:

- In Chapter 6 we covered how to build a minimum viable product (MVP) for freemium adoption.

- In Chapter 4 we outlined the mindset, resources, and timeline required to accomplish the task.

For a newly funded startup, these timelines and resource commitments (1–3 years and 5–7 of the best and brightest people you can find) are not difficult to imagine. In a startup, this is the entire company—of course the only answer is to throw everything at it! In Chapter 4 (Product-led Growth Is a Long-Term Growth Strategy) we saw the startup timelines of Gitlab, Canva, and Twilio, all of which took more than three years from launch to significant revenue growth.

But inside a going-concern company, launching a new PLG motion is not the sole focus. "The best and brightest" resources are needed in many places throughout the company, and the core business—the one currently contributing revenue and profit—is the logical place to continue investing time and energy.

This contention over strategy and resources is expected with any pursuit of innovation within a company. Clayton Christensen often recommended setting up a separate entity within an established company to launch a disruptive pursuit. This concept is known as creating a "disruptive growth engine" or a "disruption incubator."

The idea behind this recommendation is to shield the disruptive initiative from the constraints and processes of the parent company, which may hinder its progress. By creating a separate entity—often with its own team, resources, and culture—companies can foster innovation and agility, allowing the disruptive pursuit to thrive without being suffocated by the bureaucracy or the conflicting priorities of the main organization.

This approach enables the disruptive initiative to operate with greater autonomy and flexibility, experimenting with new business models, technologies, and markets. It also allows the parent company to continue focusing on its core business while simultaneously exploring new growth. In Chapter 4 (Product-Led Sales Is a Long-Term Growth Strategy), we introduced the theory of aggregate project planning, whereby 10% of investments are reserved for pursuing breakthrough innovations. Even if your chief financial officer (CFO) has a strategy like this, it is not a foregone conclusion that a PLG experiment would be funded. And if funded initially, can the organization sustain patience long enough to see financial results? Even though we expect to see leading-indicator results within the first year, if the CFO wants to see a financial return, she will likely have to wait three years.

The key to securing long-term support from the CFO (or other financial approver) is to deliver expectations in her language. Use the language of finance, not the language of growth. The CFO won't have time or motivation to learn about Acquisition, Activation, usage Retention, and the other PLG-specific concepts. The wins you will celebrate in Year 1 and Year 2 are crucial to getting the PLG flywheel going, but they are not compelling to the CFO—she wants to see dollars and cents. Rather than trying to extrapolate from active users to dollars and cents, just set expectations for the CFO in her own language:

These investments are real, but so are the returns. If this investment comes out of the "breakthrough innovation" fund, it can be evaluated on the basis of whether or not it has a chance of producing breakthrough results (not whether or not it is profitable in Year 1). If you can secure this understanding up front, you will have a clear shot on goal.

**FIGURE 16.1.  Sample Investment Case for PLG as "Breakthrough Innovation"**

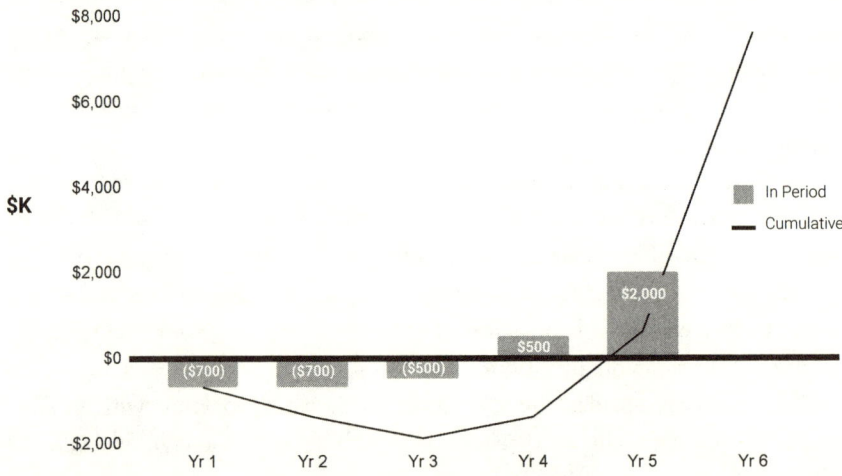

It is responsible to consider the possibility that the experiment fails. Assuming you built your PLG experiment adjacent to the current business, almost everything you built to support your PLG experiment will also benefit the adjacent business: more self-service, more intuitive workflows, easier to use product, and so on.

## The Single Make-or-Break Factor of Successful PLG Pursuits: Growth Teams

In our research, we found a single make-or-break feature of successful PLG pursuits within already established companies: the presence of a Growth Team. As described in detail in Chapter 5 (Creating and Managing Growth Teams), a Growth Team is a small, self-contained, cross-functional team that includes Product, Engineering, Marketing, Design, and Analytics. The existence of a Growth Team is the single distinguishing feature of all mature companies we studied who succeeded at launching PLG.

The larger a company gets, the more difficult it becomes to maintain the agility and collaboration facilitated by small, cross-functional teams. Since PLG depends on ongoing and active collaboration between Marketing and Engineering, Growth Teams are required to succeed with PLG once a company is large enough to have siloed marketing and engineering departments.

## Why You Must Down-Scope Your Product for PLG, and How to Do It

If you would like to launch PLG as a GTM strategy for your existing product, one thing is certain. You will need to down-scope the functionality of your current product.

Why?

Because your product has inevitably become more and more functional as you have built features and capabilities to serve your current customers. These advanced capabilities are not inherently bad, but they can be confusing for a new, self-service user.

Your current product has achieved Product-Market Fit. It has evolved to solve a particular problem for a particular set of customers. You have also achieved Go-To-Market Fit, meaning the way in which your customers prefer to purchase is efficiently accommodated by your current GTM motion.

Now you want to identify a set of customers who would prefer buying your product in a different way—via self-service. These are different customers, with different needs, being served in a different way (see Chapter 6: Building a Minimum Viable Product for Freemium Adoption).

To begin, it is helpful to get into a mindset of pure discovery. Since we are likely building adjacent to our current market, we already know our customers well. But we may not know the self-service use case(s) well, so we need to open our minds to new learnings (discovery).

Discovery starts with a high-level analysis of the target market. We have a general sense of the product and value proposition we want to bring to market, so what does that market look like? How many potential customers exist, beyond our current target market, that we could access with this new GTM approach? How would we reach them? If there are sub-segments in the market (such as industry vertical, geography, or tier), which of these segments is likely an attractive place to start, given size, accessibility, and competition?

In the context of Roger Martin's Playing to Win strategy framework, we ask ourselves the question of "where to play"—which portion of the market do we propose to enter with our self-service proposition?[3]

Having made the decision of "where to play," we need to dig in and get to know the customers in that market. Even if we chose "smaller companies in the same market as our core customers," it is not a foregone conclusion that we understand how these customers think, how they make decisions, or even what their core needs are. We need to get to know and develop empathy for the end users in our target market—the same users we will entice to try our solution (see Chapter 3: First Principles of Product-Led Growth). A useful framework for developing this empathy is the Jobs To Be Done framework[4] first proposed by Clayton Christensen:

> *"In what situation does my user find themself*
> *where they have a Job To Be Done that would*
> *be best accomplished with help from my product?"*

To understand our end users' Job To Be Done (JTBD), we need to understand how they pursue their day. We want to know how they define success and progress in their lives. We want to know what problems and obstacles might prevent them from making the progress they desire. We need to understand how they make decisions—especially purchase decisions. To do this, we embed ourselves in the market we are studying and begin asking questions. These questions are wide-ranging at first and fueled by curiosity. We are trying to get to know the humans in our target market and how they think (on JTBD research, see Chapter 6: Building a Minimum Viable Product for Freemium Adoption).

### The Biggest Trap for Established Companies Wanting to Launch PLG

The balance of the process for building PLG inside a large company follows the same patterns described previously:

- **CHAPTER 4:** Product-Led Growth Is a Long-Term Growth Strategy, Not a Short-Term Sales Tactic
- **CHAPTER 6:** Building a Minimum Viable Product for Freemium Adoption
- **CHAPTER 7:** Filling the Marketing Funnel
- **CHAPTER 8:** Building Self-Service Onboarding into Your Freemium Product
- **CHAPTER 9:** How to Convert Free Users into Large Paying Contracts

In my experience working with dozens of companies, the number one trap into which established companies fall when wanting to add PLG is this: They believe they can skip steps.

There is no skipping steps.

Can it be easy? Yes. Does it follow a formula? Yes. Can we go quickly? Yes! As quickly as we can show success against the metrics outlined in Chapter 4 (PMF, GTMF, Monetization).

But we cannot skip steps. Even if we already have a brand. Even if we already have a product. Even if we already have an installed base of happy customers.

The rest of this chapter is dedicated to companies that built PLG into their businesses after they were already at scale. Internalize the lessons from these cases, and draw inspiration from their successes. Their results were not immediate, but they were definitive. If you don't believe product-led Acquisition is possible for you in your market, consider applying the same principles to product-led renewals or Expansion, per the suggestions above. We outline additional considerations for product-led strategies in Chapter 17 (Can PLG Work at a Company Like Mine?). In all cases, however, a dedicated Growth Team is the first step toward unlocking PLG Success.

### Three Case Studies of Companies That Added PLG After Already Achieving $100M-Plus in Sales-Led Revenue

To illustrate the patterns of success involved in adding PLG as a GTM motion within a large, established company, we studied three examples of companies that did just that.

## MongoDB: $0–$20M PLG Revenue in 18 Months; Over 50% of Total Revenue in Seven Years

MongoDB (Mongo) was founded in 2007 and built early momentum as a pioneer in the NoSQL database market as an open-source database by developers for developers. Since open-source software is free for anyone to download and use, adoption for developers was frictionless. MongoDB's popularity grew rapidly in the tech community, and it soon became one of the most widely used NoSQL databases. Its ability to handle large volumes of data, perform fast queries, and support distributed architectures made it a preferred choice for companies dealing with big data, content management, and real-time analytics.

To Monetize its product, Mongo built an enterprise version of the software. Just like the open-source version, the enterprise version of MongoDB was downloaded and installed on local servers. But the enterprise edition included additional features, including support services and enhanced security. Mongo brought this product to market via an enterprise sales team focused on sectors with high security requirements—primarily financial services, government, and large corporations. This direct enterprise sales motion was highly successful, with attractive unit economics.

Mongo further experimented by adding an inside sales motion. The inside sales team targeted free users of the open-source product and attempted to convert these free users to the paid product. In 2016, this effort was struggling. Developers who were fine using the free product were not concerned with enhanced support or security, and the effort required to find and convert free customers to paying customers was higher than anticipated, resulting in unattractive unit economics (high customer acquisition cost payback).

In 2016, Dev Ittycheria, Mongo's CEO, recruited product leader Sahir Azam to join the company as vice president of cloud products and GTM with the directive to launch a cloud-based product.

At the time, revenue was $100M, with a total employee count of 550 employees. All eyes were on preparing for the initial public offering (IPO), which would happen one year later.

Since the inside sales direct motion had struggled, Ittycheria and Sahir hypothesized that they could launch a cloud version of MongoDB (it later became known as Atlas) to Monetize small and medium business (SMB) customers without incurring the negative unit economics associated with direct sales.

As Sahir puts it, "Atlas was a way to transform and diversify our business." Investors loved the concept.

Ittycheria was so enamored with the idea that he set an aggressive annual recurring revenue (ARR) goal: $20M within eighteen months.

As a first order of business, Sahir set out to get self-service Monetization built, and since the inside sales team wasn't producing desirable results, he decided to redeploy that team. Instead of the inside sales team working on upselling open-source customers to use the enterprise version of installed software, they would now pivot to selling only the new cloud-based product.

The first two years were focused on building bottom-up motions:

1.  Convert current open-source customers to cloud customers.

2.  Drive self-service cloud customers to inside sales for upgrading.

Since the MongoDB website had a lot of traffic based on its popularity as an open-source product, the team leveraged that traffic by adding a "click here" button to buy the cloud product with a credit card.

> "Free adoption of a downloaded product was already built into open source. But Monetization ... that was the difference. We had to figure out how to launch customers on a free cloud-based product, **then convert them from free to paid.**"
>
> —Sahir Azam, CPO, MongoDB

In the beginning, Sahir was the head of product for Atlas. Mongo also hired its first head of growth, and an initial cloud engineering team was named. This was not yet a separate business unit. The mission of the team was to prove out consumption-based pricing and product-led GTM, which would then be used to transform the rest of the organization.

That is—if it worked.

Eighteen months in, the company had reached the $20M ARR goal pursuing self-service Monetization and human-assisted Monetization where appropriate, including conversions from open source to cloud.

At this point, Mongo created a unified Growth Team with Analytics, Product Marketing, Product Management, Performance Marketing, and Engineering. This team is managed with rigor against business and growth objectives.

Today, MongoDB has three distinct GTM motions:

1. Open source
2. Self serve (PLG/PLS)
3. Enterprise

Mongo runs continuous experiments on how to connect the tissue between these GTMs, using "freemium" type plays as a way to work on initial adoption, leading to a potential enterprise sale.

Mongo's management realizes, however, that some accounts will never buy this way. Because of the belief that different customers prefer to buy in different ways, Mongo also maintains traditional outbound (top-down) selling for the Atlas product.

Rather than looking at one GTM as good and another as bad, they ask themselves, "Which customers belong where?" They treat this as an omnichannel GTM, paying close attention to when it would make sense for a customer to transition from one channel to the other and then making that switch seamless. As Azam says, "Much of our invention is around how to get the right customers to the right place."

> "In the early days, sales viewed self service as a threat.... But they soon came around. Free starts are not a threat—they are an opportunity."
>
> —Sahir Azam, CPO, MongoDB

The result? Atlas is now 65% of Mongo's $1.3B in revenue, growing 3.5–4x faster than the rest of the business. Azam says if they were starting today, they would only build Atlas. With open source as demand generation and SaaS as Monetization, there is no need for the in-between step of licensed enterprise software.

For Mongo, the next GTM transformation is optimizing the entire organization around consumption and increasing the velocity of new customer and new workload Acquisition.

---

**CASE STUDY 2**

## Unity Software: $0–$100M Self-Service Revenue in 4 Years

### DEMOCRATIZATION OF GAME DEVELOPMENT

Unity (NYSE: U) is a game development platform founded in 2004 in Denmark. Revenue in 2023 was $2.19B.

In 2016, Unity was the number one game development platform in the world based on game volume. All revenue to that point was perpetual license revenue—secured through a sales-led GTM. Unity had no subscription model.

A few years earlier, founder David Helgason had made the decision to make a free version of Unity and to make it very generous. With this free product, game developers could essentially build an entire game professionally. The mission of the company was to democratize game development. Unity wanted everyone in the world to have an opportunity to build whatever game they wanted.

## SELF-SERVICE

Jesus Requena was brought onboard in 2016 as the director of self-service. His assignment was to grow self-service revenue from $0 to $100M within four years.

Unity launched a subscription version simultaneous to Jesus joining. The subscription business focused on a Premium version, which had additional features that were only appropriate for successful games (e.g., multiplayer services, professional game analytics, version control, etc.). The main difference between the free and paid versions surfaced when the game was published. At this point, if the studio owned the paid version, it could remove the Unity logo from the splash screen and replace it with its own logo. If the game was published using the free version of Unity, the splash screen with the Unity logo remained.

The free version came with an end-user license agreement (EULA). Among other things, the EULA stated that if a customer had more than $200K in revenue or funding, it would be required to use the paid version of Unity. Although this term was stated clearly in the EULA, it was not being enforced.

## GAME STUDIOS

Seventy-five percent of the games built on Unity were mobile games published by game studios.

Game studios generally had three types of professionals working on games:

- **Designers** wrote the plot and designed the game mechanics.
- **Artists** rendered the characters and built out the look and feel.
- **Developers** did the animation and coding to pull it all together.

Most of the direct users of Unity were developers.

Since the free version was so full-featured, developers could complete an entire game with the free software. The only downside to publishing the final version using a free license was that the splash screen still included the Unity logo. Many studios did not care.

Other studios did care about the Unity logo, but they sometimes used a workaround to avoid expense. These studios developed games using free licenses, then bought a single paid license and published their final versions using the paid license, thus eliminating the Unity-branded splash screen.

(Fun fact: Pokemon Go™ was built using free licenses, then utilizing a single paid license to publish without the Unity logo.)

Some studios paid for all their licenses in accordance with Unity's EULA.

## A DISCOVERY

Jesus needed to grow revenue, but he also wanted to be fair to users. After digging into the data, Jesus determined that more than forty thousand businesses were using the free version of the product when (per the terms of the EULA) they should be using a paid license (i.e., these companies had >$200K in revenue or funding).

At 3–4 users per studio on average and $125 per user per month, the potential revenue available to Unity was in the $200M range. These free seats had been acquired through a PLG motion, all bottoms-up, but they had not been Monetized.

## WHAT TO DO?

By this point, Unity had 10M downloads already, and they were getting ten thousand new downloads per day through the self-service flow. Substantially all new downloads were for the free version, with a small subset of those (13.3K total, as of 2016) converting to the paid version.

Unity had also discovered 40,000 additional companies representing over 100,000 seats that should be paying but were not.

Unity was not struggling with Acquisition, but to get from $20M to $100M in self-service revenue Jesus had a Monetization choice to make:

1. Should he go after the 100,000 licenses that were out of compliance and enforce the EULA? If so, how would he do that in a way that would be fair to the users and not offend them?

2. Should he work on the Monetization workflow that was currently only converting a small percentage of free to paid users?

3. Should he continue growing the top of the free product funnel, thereby further cementing Unity's position as the top game development engine and supporting Unity's mission of "democratizing game development"?

Jesus took his cue from logistics and manufacturing and decided to employ what he refers to as the "7–10 Rule."

*7–10 Rule: If you want output to double,*
*don't double the inputs.*
*Find 7 conversion rates in the process*
*and improve each by 10%.*

Jesus decided to work on all fronts: His team notified existing users who were out of compliance with the EULA and worked to improve compliance (and therefore Monetization). The team also worked on improving the Monetization flow during onboarding. Although initially the top-of-funnel flow was not a concern, he eventually steered his team to improve that as well.

**THE TEAM**

Jesus reported to Unity's chief revenue officer (CRO). At the time (2016), the term *product-led growth* did not exist, and the concepts of "growth" and "Growth Loops" were largely business-to-consumer (B2C) concepts, with only a few B2B companies employing these tactics (Unity was watching Adobe and Atlassian). Jesus knew if he was to grow Unity's self-service revenue from $0 to $100M in 3–4 years, he would need developers, designers, lifecycle marketers, and product managers . . . so he asked for them. The CRO approved the hires. In Jesus's words, "It was incredible. As long as we were hitting milestones, the CRO approved whatever we needed, and we built almost a mini-company within Unity."

**RESULTS**

Leveraging the short-term opportunity of EULA compliance, the Growth Team at Unity was able to grow self-service revenue from $0 to $20M within the first year. Further optimization of onboarding and top-of-funnel Acquisition further accelerated this growth. The self-service portion of Unity's business reached $100M within four years.

---

**CASE STUDY 3**

## HubSpot: $0–$10M PLG Revenue via a PLG "Carveout"

Brian Halligan and Dharmesh Shah founded HubSpot in 2006, defining a new "inbound marketing" approach and offering an alternative to marketing platform incumbents like Marketo and Eloqua.

In 2014 HubSpot had reached $100M in recurring revenue and carved out an important niche in marketing technology. Brian had his eye on extending into sales technology, but he was reluctant to take Salesforce head on. He believed that he could address the needs of the individual salesperson and redefine the buying experience in terms of self-service. Brian had the intuition that people wanted to try before they buy, and he had watched the try-before-you-buy motions of Atlassian, Shopify, and Dropbox succeed. He asked himself and his management team—how could they bring that kind of buying experience to marketing and sales?

Halligan, HubSpot's CEO, did not see HubSpot's direct competitors launching self-service buying experiences, so he saw an opportunity to differentiate. He believed it would be easier to adopt a product-led motion in a new market than it would be to retrofit the existing business with product-led motions, so he decided to use HubSpot's launch into sales technology as an opportunity to spool up the first PLG motion. The idea was that if they succeeded, they would then apply the lessons they learned back into the core business.

Brian insisted on running this initiative himself. Since HubSpot had a strong chief operations officer—J. D. Sherman—Brian was confident letting J. D. run the core business, while he assembled a small team of ten people to launch HubSpot's PLG efforts. The team included people from Product, Engineering, Support, Marketing, and Sales.

HubSpot's efforts were quite product-focused in the beginning, since it didn't have a product at all—it relied on its own salespeople to help develop the use cases and the product that would serve them. There was much debate over whether this product would be free or paid. Based on his intention to follow in the footsteps of Dropbox and Shopify, Brian declared that HubSpot would have a free-forever version and a paid version into which users could upgrade ("freemium").

The team knew it wanted to design for rep-centric use cases, not sales-leader-centric use cases. It settled on an initial product called Signals, which was an email-centric tracking and engagement product.

> *"One of the things we learned is that when you are product-led, it forces you to be extremely focused on user experience and customer value—more so than when you are sales-led. You get great feedback from customers, you build better sales motions, and the people who are users of your product become customers at a much higher rate: 4–6 times higher than folks who were not users of your product previous to becoming customers."*
>
> —Kipp Bodnar, CMO HubSpot

The team stayed at 10–15 people until it achieved Product-Market Fit. At this point it began to scale by adding "salespeople." These salespeople were more like coaches—their job was to assist new customers in using the product.

From there, the Signals team built a customer relationship management (CRM) system for sales teams, which they also offered on a freemium basis, and then—at around three years, $10M ARR, and almost 100 people—they folded the sales business back into the core marketing business via an effort they dubbed "One HubSpot."

Since the goal had always been for the core business to adopt PLG, one result of the recombination was that all products now had a "starter" product that could be adopted and purchased without assistance from sales. Because management didn't want salespeople to fight against the starter project, it initially paid sales reps for any sales in their accounts regardless of whether the reps had been directly involved in the transaction or not.

Today HubSpot has 5 "Hubs" (product sets), and all of them have a primary go-to-market that most closely resembles product-led sales: acquire usage first, then deploy sales assistance where and when warranted.

At the time of this writing, HubSpot has revenue of over $2.1B and a market capitalization of $32B. HubSpot is commonly recognized as one of the most successful PLG companies, even though it did not start out product-led.

---

### Final Thoughts

Product-led growth strategies, including freemium, can represent tremendous opportunities for mature companies. In some cases, like the ones presented in this chapter, these opportunities represent growth upside: access to new buyers and new markets by reducing price and friction and introducing a new GTM motion that can extend beyond the current business. In other cases, the opportunity is to defend the business against PLG attackers who may be introducing a low-friction product that threatens to encroach on your base. Whatever the motivation, the benefits of succeeding with PLG can be significant. Addressing a significant opportunity or threat requires a significant approach, but it does not require you to "make it up as you go." The costs, processes, metrics, and timelines are well understood. If your company can carve out the resources and time required (like MongoDB, Unity, and HubSpot did), you can make a legitimate run at getting PLG to work for you.

What's the downside? Let's say you launch product-led Acquisition, you give it a full three years with your best and brightest people, and you cannot achieve liftoff. The consolation prize is that you now have an easier-to-find, easier-to-buy, and easier-to-adopt product. This product can be used in a sales-led or sales-assisted motion and still contribute positively to the business by de-laboring portions of your traditional GTM. Not too shabby!

## Chapter 16 Summary

- For companies in the B2B market, 99% were built without a PLG GTM motion, but 72% of Forbes' Cloud100 (private cloud software companies) now feature PLG.
- There are multiple options for adding product-led motions to a sales-led team, including product-led Acquisition (usually a defensive play), product-led onboarding, product-led renewals, and product-led Expansion.
- If you want to add PLG after the fact, the number one success factor is establishing a Growth Team.
- PLG is a "breakthrough" innovation and needs to be resourced as such.
- Adding PLG at scale may cost you 1–3 years and 5–7 of your brightest people.
- Results will be slow to appear, but they will accelerate quickly once the flywheel gets going.
- Learnings from building PLG in one portion of a business can also be brought back into the core business to streamline and upgrade GTM processes across the board.

## Manager Minute

Thinking about your own company, take time to reflect on the following questions:

1. If we were to add PLG as a GTM motion, what portion of the market would we likely target?

2. What is the "breakthrough innovation" case for PLG in our market?

_____

_____

_____

3. Do we have individuals in product or engineering today who demonstrate the right mindset to build a PLG strategy? Who are they?

_____

_____

_____

4. What executive support would we need to secure to execute a 1–3-year product-led Acquisition strategy to launch PLG within our company?

_____

_____

_____

5. Do we have opportunities to streamline or automate renewals or Expansions in our subscription business using product-led GTM tactics?

_____

_____

_____

6. What lessons emerge from the approaches taken by MongoDB, Unity, and HubSpot to adding PLG after they were already leaders in their respective markets, generating over $100M via existing GTM motions?

_____

_____

_____

### Product-Led Growth Within Large Enterprises

In Part Three we learned that all recurring-revenue growth follows an S-curve: slow to begin while the company is figuring out Product-Market Fit, then accelerating through Go-To-Market Fit, then attenuating as market saturation is reached. Adding additional GTM motions makes sense before saturation is reached, to continue the growth trajectory.

For PLG companies adding sales, the first sales motion to add should be adjacent to PLG so that it can leverage the existing GTM motions and customer base. Product-led sales leverages product-led and freemium adoption to drive opportunities for sales engagement. When Sales engages in these situations, it engages as a coach or consultant, assisting the customer in expanding the impact they are already achieving.

For sales-led growth companies adding PLG, the next motion should also be built adjacent to the existing motion. This usually means building in product-led renewals or product-led Expansion (not product-led Acquisition).

In all cases where PLG is proposed as an add-on GTM for an existing business, the number one success factor is the establishment of a Growth Team. Because the Growth Team will include 5–7 of the "best and brightest" people in the company, working for 3 or more years, an investment case is required. The best way to think about PLG as an investment is in the category of "breakthrough innovation," which in many companies receives roughly 10% of overall investment, according to the theory of aggregate project planning.

And if the PLG experiment doesn't deliver everything in the investment case? Then what? Then you have built ease-of-use and self-service into your business that will benefit your existing GTM and protect you from competitors that have not taken the time to do so. This is a consolation prize we can live with.

**Up Next**

PART FOUR: THE NEXT GENERATION OF PRODUCT-LED GROWTH

Read Part Four for how PLG is working its way into unexpected sectors of the economy. Here we outline decision frameworks for deciding if it's right for you. We also highlight examples of where principles have been applied outside of software, and we consider how AI will accelerate this trend.

# The Next Generation of Product-Led Growth

# SEVENTEEN

# Can PLG Work at a Company Like Mine?

## How to Apply Product-Led Tactics in Any Business

Product-led growth (PLG) isn't for every business—certainly not yet.

While I believe PLG principles will eventually make their way into all corners of the economy (see Chapters 18 and 19), this will not happen wholesale, and it will not happen immediately.

### PLG to Date Has Been Software-Centric, but It Is Underpinned by Core Principles That Can Apply More Broadly

The version of PLG described in this book is largely software-centric and Acquisition-centric. It's the version of PLG that has produced dozens of software unicorns and public companies. The product-led growth we have seen in practice to date has been appropriate for the circumstances of the moment. PLG strategies and tactics have taken advantage of the current state of technology, current customer trends and sentiments, and currently extant ecosystems of software partners that could support rapid product development.

PLG companies have leveraged the state of markets and resources to maximize their ability to address the needs of large groups of customers with favorable unit economics and minimal scale limitations. In an evolutionary sense, it was the correct response to the environment. Those that saw and took advantage of the opportunity to rethink traditional go-to-market (GTM) motions achieved gravity-defying growth at scale and were rewarded by the market:

- Slack was acquired by Salesforce for $27B.
- As of 2024, OpenAI was valued at $90B.
- Adobe offered $20B to acquire Figma.

- As of 2023, Canva was valued at $40B.
- Miro's 2022 valuation was $18B.
- Atlassian's 2024 market capitalization was $51B.

All of these companies took advantage of key factors that in retrospect are conditions favoring the PLG GTM motion:

**TABLE 17.1.**  Ideal Conditions for PLG

| | |
|---|---|
| **Large horizontal market** | Need is shared across industry verticals and geographies. |
| **End-user value proposition** | Product solves a problem for the end user. |
| **Core problem** | Product solves a hard problem—the main problem—for a user's Job To Be Done. |
| **Recurring problem** | Product addresses a user Job To Be Done that presents as part of her regular work (daily, weekly, or monthly). |
| **Self-service** | Users are able to self-serve to experience product value. |
| **Time-to-impact** | Users can see impact immediately. |
| **Single-player mode** | Product can be adopted and used by end users directly (i.e., doesn't require business unit / company-wide adoption such as human resources (HR) system, intranet, etc.). |
| **Software** | The service is delivered via software as a service. |
| **Easy to communicate** | Value proposition can be understood after a few sentences. |

*(We speak of PLG in this and the following chapter instead of "freemium." Freemium as a tactic works best with near-zero marginal cost of delivery for the free offering. Since many physical goods do not have near-zero marginal cost of giveaways, it's best to look at the broader spectrum of PLG for application in non-software industries.)*

### If Conditions in Your Market are Favorable for PLG, Then Establishing a PLG Strategy Is Imperative

Where favorable conditions exist, PLG not only makes sense for your company, it is imperative. In fact, if these conditions do prevail, we confidently predict that your market has already been, or is currently being, disrupted by PLG. In this case, you will be well served to make sure you have a PLG strategy in place—either offensively or defensively.

**OFFENSIVE STRATEGY:**

If you are the "PLG Attacker"—the company offering a PLG alternative to the more sales-led options in your market—then more power to you. May you be the Slack alternative to Microsoft Outlook, the Figma alternative to Adobe's Creative Suite, the Miro alternative to Microsoft's Visio, and the Zoom alternative to WebEx.

Perhaps you are attacking one of the current PLG juggernauts—amazing! Heaven knows that successful PLG companies can also become weighed down by too many features and options and are therefore ripe for disruption from an easier-to-use alternative.

**DEFENSIVE STRATEGY:**

If the above favorable PLG conditions exist in your market, but your company's GTM is sales-led, prepare to defend your position—this is a "perfect storm" for "PLG attackers."

**FIGURE 17.1.   How to Decide If and How PLG Can Work for Your Company**

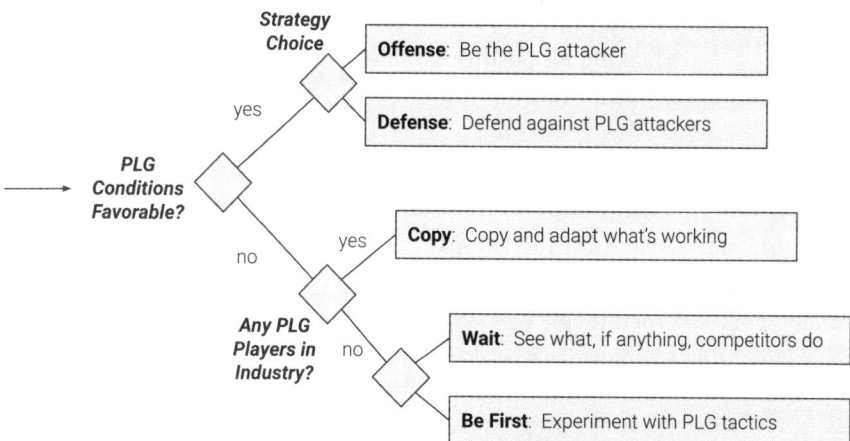

PLG attackers look for large markets with established spending patterns that are served primarily by sales-led companies. They know if they can offer even a fraction of the functionality as the incumbents, but in an easier-to-buy and easier-to-use package, they will win over smaller customers and begin eating their way into the core of the market.

"PLG attackers" are easy to dismiss at first. You might hear people at your company call them "ankle-biters" or "gnats." You might look at the size of their customers and contracts and write them off as irrelevant: "They are doing $1.2K deals. We are doing $1.2M deals. I don't think we need to worry about them."

The problem is, PLG attackers learn as they go. They learn to solve problems with elegant and easy-to-use solutions that end users love. They may not know (yet) how to play the enterprise game, but they can get there. And as they work their way upmarket, they will do so with a streamlined and user-centric product that will likely be more appealing to end users than your product.

So you will need to defend. That means building a new GTM within your existing business that leverages PLG in a way that protects your flank (on how to build PLG into your existing business, see Chapter 16: Lessons from Building PLG Within Large, Established Companies).

### If Conditions in Your Market Are Not Favorable for PLG, You Have Options

*"What if the above conditions are not present in my market? What if I love this whole concept, but I just don't see it for my business?"*

First, a shortcut. We can skip a lot of steps if one thing is true. Ask yourself, "Is anyone in my space making PLG work?"

We are looking for a "yes." We are not looking for confirmation that it's *impossible*—we are looking for positive evidence that it *may be possible*. So look hard. You may have to move a few things around, look in a few corners of your market, or look to other geographies. . . . Is there any evidence of PLG working in your industry?

If there is so much as a PLG heartbeat *somewhere* in your market, that is where you start. You need to study this company in detail. Sign up for the product yourself. Take notes on how easy it was to get started using its product. Look at its pricing page and then toggle over to yours. Notice the options for self-service help. Dive into its knowledge base. Maybe try out its chat function?

Don't get defensive. It won't help you to "explain" the reasons your product is more difficult or more confusing. Right now we are just trying to *learn from* our competition—even if it is serving tiny customers, even if we have never seen it in any of our deals, even if it is in another geography or industry sub-segment.

Inevitably you will see some things you love. Wherever possible, copy these things.

> *"Wait, what? I don't want to copy my competition.*
> *I am the leader in this space—I want to lead out."*

Yes, and . . . begin your leadership journey in PLG by determining what you can copy. Of course, whatever you copy has to fit within your product structure, your flow, and your GTM motion—so it won't actually be a *wholesale* copy. But you can save time by adopting things that are working for someone else. Do this, and build from there. It is almost 100% guaranteed to be easier to clone and adapt something already working than to invent a brand-new product or product experiment. Leverage your competitor's investment of time, energy, money, design, engineering, and testing and then make small adaptations to help the thing you copied fit within your business. (See the Duolingo case study in Chapter 11. Three of the five experiments outlined were straight-up copies from Gardenscapes, Uber, and Farmville 2.)

The PLG competitor you identify may have figured out how to solve the problem of "single-player mode," where it wasn't obvious. Or maybe it figured out how to make an otherwise complex product simple to get started with. It may have figured out how to communicate its value proposition clearly, or perhaps it figured out how to wrap its product or service in software. Whatever its successes on the PLG front, if those successes are out front and visible, they are available to copy.

Consider enterprise resource planning (ERP) systems, which many people believe to be the most complex and monolithic segment of enterprise software. Given how complicated and customized ERP systems are, how could they ever become simple enough to go to market via PLG? Answer: by slimming down to single functions. Concur built very simple travel management functionality and was eventually bought by SAP. Divvy built a simple employee expense management application that was bought by Bill.com. What simple functionality carve-out could make products in your market more accessible?

> *"The imperative here is, if you don't do it, someone else will. They're*
> *going to disrupt you, and you're going to be sold for parts."*
>
> —Kipp Bodnar, CMO, HubSpot

*"Okay, but what if no one in my space is making PLG work?"*

If the conditions in your market are not favorable for PLG and no one in your space is currently making PLG work, this presents a challenge. You essentially have two choices:

1. Do nothing. Wait for others to try PLG, and monitor their success.

2. Be the first in your space to experiment with PLG tactics.

Both of these strategies are fine, and below are some ideas for how to get started with PLG when the conditions are *not* perfect. Each of these tactics can add value to your existing business as well as potentially opening up the possibility for a more comprehensive PLG GTM in the future.

### Product-Led Strategies for When Conditions Are Not Perfect for PLG

If conditions for PLG are not ideal, we have some ideas for how to adopt product-led principles within specific portions of your GTM without embracing PLG entirely. We have seen these tactics put to good use in software and non-software industries alike. If you internalize the core principles of product-led growth and apply them to your industry, you may come up with more ideas. The key is to look for opportunities to de-labor the GTM process while simultaneously making the buying and adoption experience easier and more pleasant for the customer.

#### PRODUCT-LED _X_

Many markets and products do not lend themselves to self-service Acquisition.

- Perhaps the value proposition is too difficult to communicate via digital ads?
- Maybe the initial implementation is too complex to automate?
- Or the product is a platform that requires system-wide adoption?
- Maybe the category is highly regulated, and change is slow?

Okay, if PLG Acquisition is not going to happen, what about somewhere else along your current, sales-led customer journey?

- Product-led renewals?
- Product-led Expansion?
- Product-led onboarding?

FIGURE 17.2.    **The Bowtie**

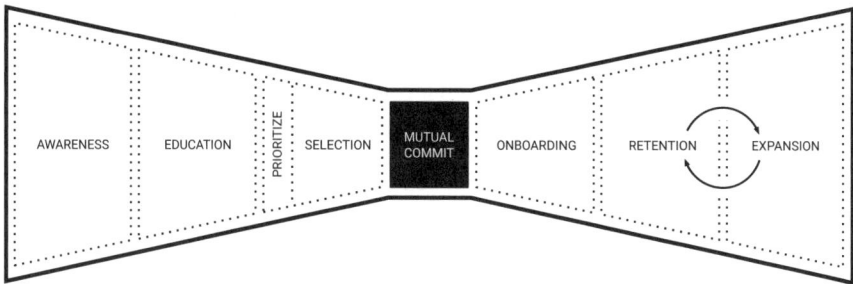

*Source:* Winning by Design

Imagine this: Your sales cycle is long, your implementation is complex, and your pricing model is based on licensed users ("seats"). Now a customer wants to buy more. He has already configured and implemented the software; he just needs to provision a few more users for the exact thing he is already using.

Option A:    Customer talks to his customer success manager, who then creates an "expansion opportunity" in customer relationship management (CRM) and alerts the account executive (AE). The AE contacts the customer, learns of his desire to add new seats. After recording the details of the situation, the AE creates an order and sends it back to the customer for approval, electronic signature, and payment.

Option B:    Customer buys the new seats via point-and-click.

Put yourself in the shoes of the customer. Which option would *you* prefer?

And which options do you currently provide to your customers? If you don't have an "Option B," that may be the easiest place to start: **product-led Expansion**. The configuration is in place, the master contract is in place, the pricing is negotiated—all you need to do is facilitate an Expansion of the existing contract. There are complications to work out, to be sure—this is not as easy as it sounds—but it may be the easiest of all the product-led motions to start with.

Or what about **product-led renewals**? Even easier?

*(On product-led renewals and Expansion, see Chapter 17: Can PLG Work at a Company Like Mine?).*

**Onboarding** is one of the toughest flows to tackle, but it does not require advantageous customer acquisition cost (CAC) via digital Acquisition—the customer in this case has already been acquired via sales. At this point, all you need to do is make it easy to get started with your product. Generally, this means things like:

- An onboarding "wizard" to walk the customer through configuration steps.
- Elimination of confusing configuration options or hiding them until later in the process.
- "Pathing" your customers based on the use case they are pursuing (ask them!).
- Adding in-app help that is easy to find and easy to come back to.
- Templates pre-populated with common or expected content.
- An artificial intelligence (AI) helper bot to answer questions and troubleshoot.

You can measure the results of all these optimizations using the same framework we introduced in Chapter 8 (Building Self-Service Onboarding into Your Freemium Product).

### INTERACTIVE DEMOS

One of the hurdles for product-led Acquisition is the complexity of the trial experience. Let's say a product is easy to understand but hard to test—perhaps because the product would need to be highly configured or would need to connect to multiple systems already in use, in order to present an effective demo?

A solution for this is to offer a realistic experience with the product without configuring it or integrating it into your customer's environment. These experiences are called "interactive demos," and they can be used to deliver self-service exposure to products that otherwise would be difficult to make available via free trial.

**CASE STUDY**

### How Carta Used an Interactive Demo to Demystify a Complex Product

By 2020, Carta had reached over $50M in revenue. Carta's sole go-to-market motion was via a sales-led strategy, owing to the complexity of Carta's product. Carta's core service is capitalization table (cap table) management. The cap table is complex in any company. It calculates ownership percentages (current and pro forma) and tracks the terms, rights, and timelines among various classes of shareholders and various types of equity, including preferred stock, common stock, stock options, warrants, and convertible debt. Each holder of these securities has specific terms associated; some are common to the entire class of holders, and some are specific to one holder (such as required holding period or vesting start date).

If a prospect considering Carta's software wanted to take it for a test drive, the amount of data uploads and configuration required would extend far beyond the scope of a typical "free trial." Furthermore, the data typically loaded into Carta is highly complex. Since the law firm is often the one putting together a pro forma cap table during financing, a founder may not know the differences between preferred and common stock, or PS-1 and PS-2 (used to designate the round an investor participated in). The level of complexity made facilitating a low-friction, free trial difficult.

In 2022, Carta decided to go all-in on PLG. Carta made it easy to purchase, and it created a post-purchase onboarding flow that included an invitation to book an onboarding call so that Carta personnel could help. The streamlined purchase process worked well for second-time users of Carta and for advanced users like VCs or attorneys, since these buyers knew exactly what they were getting.

> "Second-time users wanted to skip onboarding. They were like,
> 'Can we just sign up and go?'
> When we followed up with these users, they had typically already built
> out their system, and they just wanted someone to check their work."
>
> —Angela Winegar, Head of Growth, Carta

For first-time users, however, the process was still difficult. In theory they could begin building a cap table prior to purchase (free trial), but in reality, it was so complicated that they would get stuck. When users got stuck during this free trial period, the only way to speak to a human was to click on "Request a Demo"—a motion that gets a seller involved, instead of a support person.

Prospects not wishing to talk to Sales could read about the product and watch videos about the product, but there wasn't an easy way to *experience* the product without going through the full complexity of setting up a cap table.

To address this deficiency, Carta introduced a product tour in 2023. This call to action (CTA) launches an interactive demo that allows a prospect to explore a pre-configured version of the software, with pop-out explanations for each area of the product. A user can now make an initial assessment of whether the software might meet their needs, prior to purchasing. Demand-generation activities and Loops can also direct prospects to one of these interactive demos and create marketing-qualified leads (MQLs) in a product-supported way.

As of 2024, Carta is working on its second iteration of a PLG product, continuing to simplify the experience of trial, purchase, and onboarding. What was once considered software "too complex" to sell via self-service has been leveraged into an interactive demo to help streamline the introduction to a self-service purchase experience.

**How SAP Made the Most Complex Software Category Self-Service Accessible**

SAP, a global leader in enterprise software, is known for high-precision ERP solutions that run the most complicated businesses on the planet. SAP's go-to-market strategy has always been sales-led, and some of the largest ERP deals in history have been conducted with SAP:

- The US Department of Defense paid over $4B for SAP's implementation of what is known as the Logistics Modernization Program.
- Walmart spent over $1B to install SAP for its global supply chain and retail operations.
- Royal Dutch Shell undertook a multi-billion-dollar SAP project to standardize its global operations.

While SAP is still far from being a paragon of PLG, for years it has been taking deliberate steps to adopt a more buyer- and user-friendly approach to its historically monolithic architecture, allowing the company to address the needs of small and medium business (SMB) customers more effectively.

SAP's PLG efforts have centered mostly on its SAP S/4HANA cloud product. Since ERP is by definition difficult to trial, SAP built and launched an entire suite of what it calls "basic trials," including the ability to "Get hands-on with our software and walk through key workflows and features in a guided manner with restricted administrative rights and sample data."

These basic trials (interactive demos) correlate to the next level of trial, "advanced trials," where a customer can begin using software for a limited time with her own data, as well as a free tier of software (freemium) that allows a customer to begin for free and then "pay as you go" for features or usage as they are consumed.

While the overall success of SAP's PLG efforts has yet to eclipse its formidable sales-led go-to-market approach, it is clear that SAP is committing significant resources to building a PLG bulkhead in order to protect SAP's core business against intrusion from PLG attackers.

### When Your Core Product Is Not PLG-Ready: Sidecar Products

One of the more successful workarounds in recent years for a non-PLG-able product has been the sidecar product. A sidecar product is a standalone product that is adjacent to the main product but not dependent on it.

A sidecar product is designed to leverage all the advantages of a PLG product, including the list above (end-user value proposition, single-player mode, etc.). We want the sidecar product to solve an important problem, but the problem doesn't necessarily have to be recurring.

---

**CASE STUDY**

### How HubSpot's Website Grader Became a Wildly Effective Pipeline Builder

HubSpot famously introduced WebSite Grader as a free product to help marketers identify strengths and weaknesses of their current website regarding keywords, search engine optimization (SEO), and search rankings. WebSite Grader evaluated over 4M websites for free from its launch date in 2006 through 2011. Marketers (the same users who might be interested in HubSpot's core marketing platform) could enter their URL into HubSpot's Website Grader and get a grade as well as an evaluation of weak spots that theoretically could be addressed by HubSpot's paid products.[1] Even though HubSpot employed a sales-led GTM at the time, Website Grader was distributed digitally via self-service, and its usage helped develop a sales pipeline for the paid product—a perfect example of a sidecar product.

---

**CASE STUDY**

### How MuleSoft's Salesforce Data Loader Unlocked
### Pent-Up Demand for Data Automation Tools

MuleSoft is a data integration and automation platform that competes with Boomi, IBM, TIBCO, and Informatica. MuleSoft was founded in 2006, based on the Mule Project, a lightweight and flexible integration framework that had been developed under an open-source license beginning in 2003. From its initial launch, data administrators loved working with the MuleSoft product. Its arrival was met with widespread support among technical users.

MuleSoft's strong launch onto the scene was difficult to maintain, however, because the product was hard to purchase. For companies interested in benefiting from its services, MuleSoft represented a large purchase with a decent amount of friction in the buying process. To install MuleSoft within a company's data architecture required approval from the chief information officer and the information security office.

Because of its price, further approvals were required from finance, procurement, and legal. These hurdles hindered MuleSoft's growth, and MuleSoft struggled to get the new-customer traction it wanted. To address this friction, in 2017 MuleSoft launched a sidecar product called Salesforce Data Loader (dataloader.io).

MuleSoft had identified a core pain point for data operations people: getting data in and out of Salesforce. Every analyst interested in combining Salesforce data with data from other sources struggled to get data in and out of Salesforce in a seamless way. Getting data in and out of Salesforce was so cumbersome, it had become a well-known pain point among data analysts. MuleSoft suspected if it could solve this one isolated pain point, analysts would flock to the solution.

MuleSoft developed a standalone product designed only to address the issue of getting data out of Salesforce. It offered the solution for free, and the product did not carry the brand "MuleSoft"—it was simply called Salesforce Data Loader.

> *"As soon as we released Salesforce Data Loader, we knew we had a hit. Everyone wanted to get their hands on it, and it became the number one app on the Salesforce AppExchange for a long time. The trick then was translating that organic adoption of a free product into revenue and opportunities for our sales team to engage around our fully featured MuleSoft Platform."*
>
> —Ken Yagan, head of product, MuleSoft

The use of Data Loader did not require all the approval and installation steps of MuleSoft core, nor did it depend on already owning MuleSoft. It functioned independently and just did what it claimed it would do—no muss, no fuss.

As adoption grew, MuleSoft added a paid tier and began monetizing the free Data Loader users without traditional sales and marketing expenses.

But ...

Use of Data Loader also placed new users *adjacent to* MuleSoft. The Data Loader experience was able to highlight what the next steps *could be* if MuleSoft were installed, and it planted MuleSoft into the mind of these users. Not only did the sidecar product drive accelerated growth for MuleSoft, it also sparked an acquisition offer in 2018 by Salesforce itself for $6.5B.

Both these companies' primary GTM was sales-led, but their sidecar products opened an entirely new funnel for them that was product-led.

*"So is PLG for me? Net it out, my friend."*

**Short answer:** Yes, PLG in some form is likely for you.
**Longer answer:** ... but maybe not right away ...
**Even longer answer**: ... and it's not all or nothing.
You can figure out ways to "de-labor" your GTM today.
You can employ Loops today. You can make your product easier to discover/install/use today.

Whether or not your market is ideal for PLG, you can apply *some* PLG principles today. Even traditional sales-led software companies are getting into the action via product-led renewals and Expansion, interactive demos, free trials, and sidecar products. In non-software companies, we've also seen adoption of select PLG principles to accelerate growth and separate from the competition. This is the topic of the next chapter.

## Chapter 17 Summary

- Product-led growth isn't for everyone in every space, at least not immediately.
- However, if anyone in our space is currently making PLG work, we should study and copy what we can or risk being disrupted.
- Even if we can't enable PLG fully, we could consider:
  - Product-led _X_.
  - Sidecar products.
  - Interactive demos.

| Manager Minute |
| --- |

Thinking about your own company, take time to reflect on the following questions:

1. Which of the following PLG-favorable conditions exist in our market?

   Y  N  **Large horizontal market.** Need is shared across industry verticals and geographies.

   Y  N  **End-user value proposition.** Product solves a problem for the end user.

   Y  N  **Core problem**. Product solves a hard problem—the main problem—for a user's Job To Be Done.

   Y  N  **Recurring problem.** Product addresses a user's Job To Be Done that presents as part of her regular work (daily, weekly, or monthly).

   Y  N  **Self-service**: Users are able to self-serve to experience product value.

   Y  N  **Time to impact**: Users can see impact immediately.

   Y  N  **Single-player mode:** Product can be adopted and used by end users without involvement of HR, IT, etc.

   Y  N  **Software:** Service is delivered via Software as a Service.

   Y  N  **Easy to communicate**: Value proposition can be understood after a few sentences.

2. Which competitors in our space are making PLG work today?

   _____

   _____

   _____

3. What is the most appropriate PLG strategy for us to pursue now? (check all that apply)
   - Pure PLG
   - Product-led _X_
   - Sidecar products

- Interactive demos
- Other: _____

_____

_____

_____

# EIGHTEEN

# Product-Led Growth Beyond Software

How PLG Is Extending to Unexpected Places

### How Embedded Software and "Smart Products" Make PLG Possible Everywhere

Marc Andreessen (co-founder of Netscape and Andreessen Horowitz) famously blogged that "software is eating the world."[1] He explained that large portions of the value chain for all industries—including non-technology industries—were being overtaken by software. Andreessen pointed to automotive, defense, retail, logistics, oil and gas, agriculture, healthcare, and education as being industries where major portions of production, operations, analysis, control, and distribution were already being managed via software. That was 2011.

As software becomes more and more embedded into all products, those products become capable of selling themselves—or at least capable of selling feature upgrades, content, information, service contracts, or integrations. Because of this ongoing trend, PLG could impact all aspects of industry within the next thirty years.

Predictive artificial intelligence (AI) further empowers intelligent products to anticipate needs, and generative AI helps create an interface with the customer that can approximate human interaction. The more prevalent embedded software becomes in a product, and the more capable that software becomes at anticipating and meeting the needs of customers, the better that the product will become at selling itself.

## How Product Can Participate in Its Own Go-to-Market

A key element of PLG is the product growth model discussed in Chapter 5 (Creating and Managing Growth Teams). The product growth model (owned by the Growth Team) describes how the product grows, identifying the primary and secondary strategies for:

- Acquiring customers
- Monetizing customers
- Retaining customers
- Expanding customers

Sometimes growth strategies and tactics are product-led (meaning the product takes a primary role), and sometimes they are marketing- or sales-led. The combination of these decisions comprises your product growth model, which will serve as your True North as you grow the business.

What if the product is not software? Could the product still play a role in acquiring customers? Consider the freemium strategy—where a product or service of real value is given away with no obligation to the customer. The objective here is to let potential customers directly experience the positive impact of that product or service in the hopes they will become longer-term customers. This freemium Acquisition and Monetization strategy is not limited to software only.

## Six Key Hallmarks of Product-Led Growth

In this book we have looked at a number of hallmarks of product-led growth, including the following:

- *Self service*: A de-labored/self-service go-to-market (GTM) motion at any point along the customer journey (Discovery, Acquisition, Activation, First Impact, Habit, Monetization, Retention, Expansion)
- *Freemium*: A product experience where users experience impact before purchase
- *User-centric*: A product that is easy for end users to find, understand, and use
- *Product-driven*: A GTM motion where the product itself is the primary driver of customer Acquisition, Retention, and Expansion

- *Instrumented*: Instrumented products that send signal back to the product provider about how and where and when the product is being used

- *Self-propagating*: Growth Loops that bring new customers to the product and existing customers back to the product

As we have defined it, "pure PLG" is recognizable as the primary or secondary GTM motion at many software companies. There is no reason, however, that a product would need to be primarily software to profitably take advantage of *select PLG tactics*.

Consider the following non-software examples of these principles in action.

### Self-Service: How Self-Service Shows Up in Non-Software GTM

How do you buy a new Tesla? On the app. The preferred purchasing experience is on the app, with a credit card. This works as well on mobile as it does on the web. For Tesla (an admittedly expensive purchase), everything is built to be fully automated and self-service. You shop, configure, purchase, and pay online. You learn about the car's features from the car itself. Your driving patterns are tracked, and you are reminded about service, features, and upgrades based on your driving history.

Lynk & Co.—a Chinese car manufacturer—goes one step further. Its model is not for you to own the car but to subscribe to it. One monthly payment covers the lease, the insurance, and the maintenance—all you do is drive the car. Everything is managed through the app: self-service and via credit card. Furthermore, if you want to lend your Lynk & Co car or borrow a Lynk & Co car, you can—just use the app to identify a car that is available, an electronic key updates to your phone, and you drive the car away.

### Free: "Free" as a Marketing Tactic for Products and Services of All Kinds

"Free" has been a strategy to entice potential buyers for as long as we can remember. Free samples, free program weeks, free consulting . . . all designed to deliver impact before the purchase decision.

As the economy continues to trade more in attention, loyalty, and information, free is something we have come to expect in business-to-consumer (B2C) life:

- Free streaming entertainment (YouTube)

- Free internet, seating, restrooms, and air conditioning (Starbucks)
- Free first month at the gym (Crunch Fitness)
- Free food samples (Costco)
- Free birthday dessert (Applebee's)

Some free experiences are offered prior to the first purchase, and some are interspersed throughout the customer lifetime. In all cases, the inclusion of "free" is designed to create an experience that feels empathetic and generous—two core tenets of product-led growth.

**CASE STUDY**

### How Oak Wood Fire Kitchen Uses "Free" to Optimize for the Return Visit

In the restaurant business, return visits are the key to financial success. Earning return business can cost 1/25 to 1/5 what it costs to attract a first-time visitor, so restaurants that figure this out tend to succeed, and those that don't often fail.

Michael McHenry is the restaurateur behind Oak Wood Fire Kitchen in Draper, Utah. McHenry had the instinct that he could and should treat first-time diners differently if he wanted them to become regular visitors. McHenry put his mind to designing a specific first-time dining experience that would surprise and delight diners, such that they would be highly likely to return.

As guests are seated, McHenry's staff asks whether this is their first time dining at the restaurant. If so, the guest is provided with a distinct placemat—often a different color—to subtly signal to all staff that this is a first-time visitor. The team is then encouraged to offer enhanced service for these guests, such as a free appetizer, customized menu recommendations, a detailed introduction to the restaurant concept, and even a tour of the kitchen.

When the guests' dining experience begins to wind down, the server presents one final offer. The conversation might go something like this: "You had the steak tonight—how did you enjoy it? I know you were deciding between steak and chicken, and I really want to make sure you get a chance to try the chicken—it's also wonderful. I'm going to write 'chicken' down on this business card. Bring this in on your next visit, and the chicken is on me."

McHenry knows that a delightful hospitality experience is likely to engender loyalty. He also knows that a returning diner is likely to bring friends who may be new to the restaurant. By building specific features into his restaurant's dining experience, McHenry has architected in key PLG principles:

- First Impact—a differentiated first-time experience
- Freemium—a free entree that will likely be accompanied by paid sides, drinks, and desserts
- Growth Loops
  - Retention Loop—the free voucher encourages a repeat visit
  - Acquisition Loop—a returning diner is likely to invite friends who may not have previously experienced Oak Wood Fire Kitchen
- Retention—focusing on recurring business takes a full-lifetime-value view of each diner
- Customer acquisition cost (CAC)—securing a return visit from an existing diner can cost 1/5 to 1/25 as much as attracting a new visitor

---

The B2C world is full of examples of free samples, and this extends to the business-to-business (B2B) world as well. Sometimes the B2B "free sample" becomes a feature of a longer-term relationship, whereby goods or services of value are given away as part of a longer-term service contract.

- *Printer and Copier Companies*: Xerox offers free hardware with service contracts.
- *Point of Sale (POS) Systems*: Square provides free or discounted equipment with software and merchant processing contracts.
- *Fleet Management Solutions*: Verizon Connect supplies free GPS tracking devices with service agreements.
- *Medical Equipment and Software*: General Electric Healthcare provides medical hardware at a reduced cost with software or maintenance contracts.
- *Industrial Equipment and IoT (Internet of Things) Solutions*: Siemens bundles free hardware with IoT services for industrial contracts.
- *Office Furniture and Workspace Solutions*: WeWork offers free or discounted furniture with office space or co-working service agreements.
- *Educational Hardware and Software:* Both Apple and Google have employed aggressive give-away strategies for educational institutions. Hardware is donated to schools, provided that students use the provider's free software. In the process, students become comfortable with Google/Apple software and become lifelong customers.

To embrace the concept of "free" requires a mindset shift from transactional ("How can I maximize this transaction?") to relational ("How does this transaction contribute to a long-term customer relationship, and how do I maximize the lifetime value of that relationship?"). The best and highest emotional quotient (EQ) marketers have good instincts about designing customers' experiences that engender loyalty (including free experiences), and the best marketing analysts are able to integrate free components and paid components in customer relationships that are highly profitable over their lifetime.

## User-Centric: How Modern Product Companies Circumvent Traditional Purchasing Using User-Centric Design and Marketing

In their ongoing competition for market share, modern B2B manufacturers have gone out of their way to appeal to end users. This goes beyond appealing to corporate buyers, who often sit in the procurement department and may never directly experience the product. The strategy is to go around the procurement department and appeal to end users directly.

---

**CASE STUDY**

### How Stryker Corporation Works Directly with End Users to Disrupt Traditional Hospital Purchasing

Most medical equipment manufacturers and distributors sell large contracts to hospital systems, with many organizations standardizing on certain vendors by category, e.g., GE Healthcare for imaging equipment, Becton Dickinson for infection prevention supplies, and DePuy Synthes (Johnson & Johnson) for orthopedic implants and devices.

Stryker Corporation is well known for circumventing hospital purchasing and developing relationships directly with orthopedic surgeons. To this end, Stryker representatives schedule regular demonstration and educational events in local markets. These events can last anywhere from a few hours to multiple days. At the events, Stryker scientists, inventors, and surgeons demonstrate the most recent equipment, train surgeons on technique, and solicit feedback for ongoing product development. Some workshops are designed to provide continuing medical education (CME) credit for surgeons, in some cases even providing cadavers for surgical practice, using Stryker implants.

Stryker's direct engagement with orthopedic surgeons builds familiarity, trust, and relationships that can influence not only those surgeons' individual preferences but also the purchasing patterns of the healthcare systems within which they work. According to a 2017 study by Bain & Company, more than 80% of surgeons and procurement officers say they work in collaborative partnerships to make purchasing decisions regarding medical equipment, weighing clinical and economic value together.

More than 60% of surgeons rank "strongest existing relationship" with a manufacturer as a key purchasing criterion.[2]

---

Designing for, building for, and developing a relationship directly with the end user can create significant "pull" that influences corporate purchasing decisions. B2B supplies and equipment in all industries are selected at least partially on the basis of how they appeal to end users.

## Product-Driven: How "Smart Products" Participate Directly in Product-Led Growth

As software is more often embedded into durable equipment, what once were one-and-done purchases can now be evergreen sources of revenue for the manufacturer. "Soft updates," feature improvements, and even parts replacement, supplies, or maintenance can be ordered and paid for via interfaces built right into the product itself or via a Bluetooth- or Wifi-enabled ability to "log in" to the product and make such purchases.

A relatable B2C example is the home laser printer, which communicates with a connected computer and alerts the user when to order new cartridges. Industrial equipment is rife with examples of similar opportunities to upgrade and resupply in response to prompts generated by the equipment itself.

## Instrumented: How "Smart Products" Are Instrumented for Signal-Based Commerce

Software and communications-enabled products can send data about usage patterns back to the manufacturer, which can in turn be used to improve the user experience.

- **Commercial HVAC Systems** (e.g., Trane): Manufacturers of commercial HVAC systems rely on data for optimizing energy efficiency, enhancing product performance, and reducing maintenance costs, which appeals to corporate buyers seeking cost-effective solutions.

- **Heavy-Duty Trucks** (e.g., Volvo Trucks): Manufacturers of heavy-duty trucks use data to improve fuel efficiency, predict maintenance needs, and develop safer and more reliable vehicles, ultimately benefiting fleet operators and the manufacturer.

- **Agricultural Machinery** (e.g., Case, International Harvester): Companies producing agricultural machinery leverage data to refine equipment designs, increase crop yield, and reduce downtime for farmers, which enhances their products' effectiveness and reputation.

- **Construction Equipment** (e.g., Caterpillar): Manufacturers of construction equipment collect data to monitor machinery health, improve safety features, and enhance equipment performance, benefiting both corporate buyers and construction professionals.

In addition to the equipment examples listed above, traditionally nontechnical products will continue to become "wired." Consider sensors in tires, roofing materials, pavement, pipes. . . . Almost all durable equipment can and will be outfitted with sensors in the future. Even disposables (like vaccines, expensive perishable foods, etc.) are packaged with sensors to ensure consistent temperature throughout the distribution process.

### Self-Propagating: How Loops Are Built into Product and Services of All Kinds

Software-based PLG products feature Growth Loops, whereby existing users are brought back into the product and new users are invited to create accounts. Marketers of non-software products employ similar incentives to drive increased adoption:

- **VIP Access**: Regus offers exclusive benefits to engaged B2B customers, such as priority services, access to premium workspace, and the ability to invite guests. The strategy is to turn these customers into product advocates.

- **Partner Collaborations**: FedEx collaborates with existing B2B customers for joint marketing campaigns, encouraging them to engage its business network in exchange for incentives.

- *Tiered Rewards*: American Express Business creates progressive referral programs for B2B clients, increasing incentives as they introduce more businesses to drive continued engagement.

- *Customer Success Stories*: Grainger showcases satisfied B2B customers' stories to inspire new business clients and highlight positive outcomes from using your products.

## Three Case Studies of Non-Software Companies Actively Using Product-Led Principles to Drive Growth

Once you've seen examples of product-led principles in action, you'll begin seeing them everywhere. "Isn't this just good product management?" a friend asked me. Yes, it is just good product management. But since not all product management is good product management, the product-led growth principles in this book provide structure and language for doing a better job. Taking a growth-oriented approach to product management is unfortunately not the norm. We hope these insights can help you broaden your thinking about how to take your products to market and what role they themselves can play in GTM.

Below are three additional case studies across three non-software industries. We hope these get your ideas and creativity flowing!

---

**CASE STUDY 1**

### How Kiln Uses Community-Plus-an-App to Aim a Real Estate Company at Product-Led Growth

When Arian Lewis founded Kiln in 2018, he had the aspiration to "elevate the quality of life at work" for all its members.

Kiln is a co-working-space company that offers memberships ranging from "club" membership (offering access to flex desks and common areas) to dedicated single desks or offices to full office suites across multiple geographies.

But Arian's vision extends far beyond co-working space.

Each of Kiln's fourteen locations has approximately 600–700 paying members, but each location receives an additional 15–20K visitors per year. How do they do that?

- Kiln actively encourages its members to host outside guests free of charge.

- Kiln helps organizations organize events to be held in the Kiln "theater," a space designed to host presentations and meetups.

- Kiln's common spaces, including outdoor decks, stand-up meeting rooms, kitchens, and lounges, encourage teams to gather and include colleagues who don't yet have a membership.

Each time a visitor checks in at the front desk, Kiln collects an email address, which allows them to market community events and other opportunities to return and experience Kiln.

For members, all Kiln services are accessible via an app installed on the member's phone. The app boasts 100% Activation rates, since it facilitates electronic access to the building, access to offices, reservation of conference rooms, and so on. The app also allows community members to market services and gatherings to other community members.

In what ways is Kiln product-led?

- Its Acquisition funnel begins with free usage.

- It moves users through the funnel by continuing to engage them in community events.

- Its initial tier of paid usage is extremely inexpensive ($250 per month), with additional tiers extending all the way to $20K+ per month.

- The Kiln app has user profiles, permissions, and payment information stored so that upsells and extensions are friction-free transactions.

- The Kiln app has notifications that allow for ongoing Engagement and re-Engagement.

> "We regularly host community events like lectures, forums, and meetups. This gets people into our buildings. We simply began asking ourselves, 'How can we lead with generosity in such a way that people will default to us when they need flex space?'"
>
> —Arian Lewis, CEO Kiln

As Kiln continued to think about the principles of empathy, generosity, and metrics, ideas for future roadmap flowed freely.

- What if we built a free tier of membership that gave individuals (users) access to Kiln community facilities and events?

- Would free-tier members download the app to access services?
- What if we created incentives around inviting new members to experience a Kiln membership on a free trial basis?
- What if we encouraged teams to host offsite meetings in our space, even if they are not members?
- Could we monitor the use of our services (internet, gym, office space, food, meeting rooms), such that we could spot patterns and identify opportunities for upsell?

In this way, a real estate business—a business that revolves around fixed assets—becomes highly self-service and product-led.

---

**CASE STUDY 2**

### How John Deere Is Betting Its Future Growth on Converting From "Big Iron" to "Smart Iron"

In January of 2023, the keynote speaker at the Consumer Electronics Show (CES) in Las Vegas represented one of the oldest and most storied brands in agricultural equipment and manufacturing: John May, CEO of John Deere. Why was John Deere kicking off the world's largest and most influential technology trade show? For the same reason we are including it here as a case study—its investment and ambitions in AI, machine learning and computer vision (MLCV), and the internet of things (IoT) are both surprising and mind-blowing. John Deere (known as "Deere" to insiders) calls this strategy *Leap Ambitions*, and it aims to lead the agricultural industry into the fourth industrial revolution.

As of 2023, the average American farmer was 58 years old, still largely relying on in-person advisory services to make decisions about seed, crops, yields, and fertilizers.[3] Trends showed the average farmer getting younger and more technically savvy.

Meanwhile, John Deere was actively investing in technology to change all this, by embracing "precision farming," an approach to farming that targets "plant-by-plant precision" when it comes to managing soil, water, and nutrient conditions. John Deere's journey to precision farming began in the 1990s, when a small group of engineers was separated out from the main group and moved to Des Moines, Iowa, where they began working to incorporate GPS technology into tractors.[4] Since then Deere has added geographic information system (GIS) data, IoT sensors, computer vision, precision sprayers, and AI models to its most advanced tractors. The fully autonomous tractor demonstrated at CES 2022 can be operated from a farmer's phone. Using computer vision, it can navigate fields in perfect lines, identify obstacles, recognize each plant as being a desirable plant or a weed, and, through the use of precision sprayers, it can apply fertilizer or weed control as necessary. Simultaneously, the tractor can read moisture and nutrient levels in the soil and adjust fertilizer composition accordingly. When water levels are too high or low, it can communicate with the irrigation system. When pests are detected, it can apply pesticide. Soil and moisture data from the tractor is uploaded to the cloud, where it is combined with weather, geographic, and other third-party data, and analyzed for seed and yield optimization. Supply orders for fertilizer, pesticide, and seed are semiautomated.

These capabilities are delivered to farmers via the John Deere Operations Center and the AutoTrac™ guidance system. Farmers who use these advanced features save up to 20% on fertilizer (by avoiding overlaps and gaps) and experience better crop yields.[5]

The John Deere system is a "walled garden." The hardware works with the software, which in turn integrates with external services and data sources—all in an internally consistent—and proprietary—way.

To make this work, John Deere has introduced subscription-based services like Machine Sync and AutoTrac, offering ongoing value to users and incentivizing repeat purchases and upgrades. John Deere's corporate goal is for its software and subscription revenues to exceed 10% of total revenue by 2030.

By embedding subscription services into its products, Deere shifts from a one-time sale to a recurring revenue model, much like how SaaS companies operate. The ongoing value these services provide (such as reducing machine downtime and improving efficiency) keeps customers engaged with the brand.

John Deere is not without competition. BlueWhite, an Israeli company, offers subscription-based farming-as-a-service (on-demand smart tractors), boasting 35%–75% savings for farms served.[6] AGCO and Sabanto approach precision farming from a retrofitting perspective, outfitting *existing* equipment with computer vision, navigation, and precision sprayers. Software and analysis services are then delivered on a subscription basis. These vendors claim their solution can cost only a fifth of the total expense of purchasing a new smart tractor from John Deere.

**How a Physical Photobook Company Built Its Entire
Business Around Social Growth Loops**

In 2021, Nate and Vanessa Quigley, founders of Chatbooks, took their entire company to Lagoon for an offsite. Lagoon is an amusement park in Farmington, Utah, and home of Colossus, one of two Anton Schwartzkopf double-looping roller coasters in the United States. Nate and Vanessa issued the team a challenge and offered a prize for the winner: Who could ride Colossus the most times in a day? The objective of this challenge was to cement in the minds of Chatbook employees the importance of "Loops" (see Chapter 12: Shifting from Marketing Funnels to Product Loops). The thought was, if Chatbook employees physically experienced a looping roller coaster, they would have a hard time forgetting the idea of Loops when designing and delivering the Chatbooks experience.

On the surface, Chatbooks is a photo book company. But everything about the company—its origins, its structure, its Monetization, and its roadmap—looks more like a software company than a printing company.

Chatbooks was founded in 2014 as a way to "print your Instagram." Users (also called Chatbookers) could create a Chatbooks account online, connect their Instagram account, and then subscribe to a series of 6x6, perfect-bound, 60-page, white numbered volumes that would be printed and shipped automatically each time 60 new photos were posted to Instagram. Before approving a book, Chatbookers could re-caption, rearrange, or delete photos. Over time, editing and layout options were added, allowing Chatbookers to be as automated or as hands-off as they wanted in the design process.

Chatbooks quickly became popular with Instagram micro-influencers and "millennial moms," who would proudly share their "shelfies," photos of themselves with their "shelf full of Chatbooks"—often with as many as a hundred Chatbooks proudly displayed. Sharing these "shelfies" created awareness of Chatbooks, encouraging followers to create their own Chatbooks account (Loop). Chatbooks awarded customers whose photos they re-shared, creating a feeling of community among fellow Chatbookers and instilling a "fear of missing out" (FOMO) in Instagram friends who had not yet subscribed to the service (Loop).

Photo memories are inherently social, making a photo book in *theory* a highly shareable thing. But since a book is physical and sitting in your house, the only way to share across distances would be to re-digitize. Chatbooks does this by turning each Chatbook into a "Mini Movie," stitching together the "live photo" versions of the printed pictures from each book. Mini Movies can then be shared via Instagram Reels or directly via messaging. Mini Movies are incredibly popular with Chatbookers—over

30% of people who make a book also opt to download and share their Mini Movies. Each Mini Movie has a call to action (CTA) at the end, inviting viewers to create their own Chatbooks account (Loop). In 2024, the feature became even more popular and more shared, as Chatbooks gave customers the option to add AI-generated, custom soundtracks to their Mini Movies. Chatbooks uses computer vision to log details about the photos in the movie, combines those details with captions and any specific key-word the user wants to add (names or places or occasions, e.g., "Mike and Toni's 15th Wedding Anniversary") and then writes a custom song in the style requested by the Chatbooker (e.g., country, rap, rock, pop, ballad). This feature increases sharing and resharing, creating more exposure and more FOMO (more Loops).

Chatbookers are extremely loyal, with a long average lifetime driven by the "story of our lives" nature of the Job To Be Done (JTBD) and small product design details. It is not uncommon for a Chatbooker who meets Nate or Vanessa to break down in tears, thanking them for helping capture and preserve memories in such a unique way.

As Chatbooks continues to look to the future, it has become less dependent on Instagram and more focused on being a complete "Family Memory System." Chatbooks has built a platform called HeyFam, which is essentially "Slack for Families," allowing memories to be directly shared with family members, including the option to also automatically upload photos to Chatbooks for further printing, movie-making, and sharing (more Loops).

By wrapping itself in software and explicitly architecting subscription and Loops into its business model, Chatbooks has morphed a manufacturer and distributor of physical goods into a product-led company that hits all PLG notes:

- **Self service**: Chatbookers design, create, and share books on their own.
- **Freemium**: It is free to design a Chatbook and even to create a Mini. Movie. The only cost is for printing and shipping the physical Chatbook.
- **User-centric**: Chatbooks invests an inordinate amount of energy understanding and designing for the needs of its end users.
- **Product-driven**: Using "memories" as the primary "shareable" currency, Chatbooks uses its own product to drive over 30% of its new user Acquisition.
- **Instrumented**: Chatbooks measures each portion of its funnel (Bowtie), including Discovery, Acquisition, Activation, First Impact, Habit, Monetization, Retention, Expansion
- **Self-propagating**: Growth Loops are built throughout the Chatbooks experience.

P.S. The winner of the 2021 Chatbooks Lagoon challenge rode Colossus a mind-boggling forty-five times in a single day (ninety Loops).

## Going Forward

It does not take an overly active imagination to envision a world where usage patterns are tracked; reorders, replacements, and upgrades are semiautomated; and products themselves are central to this process—even for traditionally non-technical products.

We believe this trend will be limited only by manufacturers' creativity and the unit economics of incorporating PLG tactics into customer Acquisition, Monetization, Retention, and Expansion.

Generative AI will only accelerate this trend, as it can put an interactive front end on the experience of discovering, using, and purchasing products and services as well as product extensions, upgrades, and associated consumables.

"Looks like you are low on soy sauce. Should I add it to your Amazon order?"

The line between software and non-software is blurring. And we believe that it behooves the makers of non-software products to consider PLG principles as part of the argument for adding intelligence to their products.

Ask yourself: What would be the economic benefit of having intelligence embedded into our <xyz> such that we could employ the product to collect information about usage, sell its own extensions/upgrades/replacements, propagate itself via invitations and collaboration, and so on?

As systems get more connected, more intelligent, more predictive, and more conversational, selling capabilities will become embedded into more traditionally non-software products. Successful product-led strategies for non-software products will follow the same core principles as software-only PLG: empathy, generosity, and metrics. Product manufacturers that are able to program these principles into their products in a natural way (without crossing into the uncanny valley) will prevail in their respective markets, taking advantage of PLG's natural economic leverage.

### Chapter 18 Summary

- Core principles of PLG can be applicable to products beyond software.

- As purchasing power shifts to the end user and software continues to be embedded into more and more products, we have seen computer hardware and networking markets and even consumables and durable equipment markets introduce recurring, software-based services.

- It behooves managers to think about how they can "hire" their products to do some of the work of GTM, leveraging core PLG principles and tactics.
- Advances in predictive and generative AI make it possible for embedded software to anticipate needs and have conversations with product owners, including conversations about upgrades, re-supplies, and other services related to product ownership.

## Manager Minute

Thinking about your own company, take time to reflect on the following questions:

1. How could intelligence be built into our products or packaging to enable PLG-type instrumentation or GTM enhancement?

_____

_____

_____

2. What are some ways we could apply the following principles in our GTM motions?

*Self service*: A de-labored/self-service GTM motion, at any point along the customer journey (Discovery, Acquisition, Activation, First Impact, Habit, Monetization, Retention, Expansion)

*Free*: A product experience where users experience impact before purchase

*User-centric*: A product that is easy for end users to find, understand, and use

*Product-driven*: A GTM motion where product itself is the primary driver of customer Acquisition, Retention, and Expansion

*Instrumented*: Instrumented products that send signal back to the product provider about how and where and when the product is being used

*Self-propagating*: Growth Loops that bring new customers to the product and existing customers back to the product

# NINETEEN

# The Role of Humans and Artificial Intelligence in Product-Led Growth

> Go-to-Market Automation Is Becoming the Norm; AI Will Blend with PLG to Accelerate the Trend

### Will AI Replace All Humans in Sales and Marketing?

Elon Musk is wrong.

In a 2023 interview with Rishi Sunak, Great Britain's prime minister, Elon Musk declared there would be a time when "no job is needed," thanks to an AI "magic genie that can do everything you want." Musk added that as a result, "we won't have universal basic income, we'll have universal high income."[1]

Musk is not the first smart person to make such a bold jobs declaration. In 1930, British economist John Maynard Keynes warned that the economy was "being afflicted with a new disease" called technological unemployment. Labor-saving advances were, he wrote, "outrunning the pace at which we can find new uses for labour." At the time, machinery was transforming factories and farms. One of the most common jobs for young American women—telephone operator—was being replaced by mechanical switching. And in the context of the great depression and its accompanying 20% unemployment rate, the situation seemed dire.[2]

Unlike Musk, Keynes predicted this would only be a "temporary phase of maladjustment."[3] He believed new jobs would emerge, and as a whole, employment would remain intact.

Earlier in the book, I made the claim that 70% of go-to-market (GTM) jobs as we know them will change. I do not believe jobs will go away; rather, they will be transformed. Why? Because machines will improve the way buying and selling happens.

### How GTM De-Laboring Has Progressed from Freemium to PLG to Automated GTM

Product-led growth is part of an overall trend of GTM automation that empowers the customer to choose how and when they engage in the buying process. This automation also provides leverage to the seller by "hiring" products to accomplish certain GTM roles. In general, the GTM trends of the past three decades point toward autonomy and self-service.

**In Part One** of this book, we established a trend toward the "de-laboring" of GTM, evolving from shareware to Freemium to PLG. In PLG-enabled software markets, the product itself took on some of the traditional GTM roles of acquiring and expanding customers, by enabling self-service options for purchase and use.

**In Part Two**, we examined the mechanics that underpin PLG. We established the PLG Bowtie as a way of organizing the customer journey. We studied customer Discovery, Acquisition, Activation, First Impact, Habit, Monetization, Engagement, Retention, and Expansion as specific objectives within the Bowtie. We also looked at Growth Loops as a means for this system to reinforce itself by acquiring new customers, re-engaging customers, and expanding customers via its own mechanisms.

**In Part Three,** we pushed the boundaries of product-led growth, looking at ways it has been adapted for use in large enterprises. In this section we examined the hybrid GTM motion of product-led sales, and we looked at applications and techniques that require extensions of the core PLG models—such as sidecar products, interactive demos, and product-led GTM.

Now we look to the future and consider where things might go from here. What are the opportunities for GTM innovation across the economy, and what boundaries and conditions will govern this evolution? What role will freemium, self-service, PLG, and AI play? Will we, as Musk posits, succeed in completely de-laboring GTM to the point where no humans at all are involved in marketing, sales, or customer success (CS)? Or will we experience, as Keynes observed, only a "temporary phase of maladjustment," while the humans involved in go-to-market learn new tools, techniques, and tactics?

I believe the latter will be true. And if I am right, all GTM professionals are on notice, starting now, to begin learning the tools, techniques, tactics, and strategies of a new era.

**FIGURE 19.1. What Comes Next in the GTM De-Laboring Trend?**

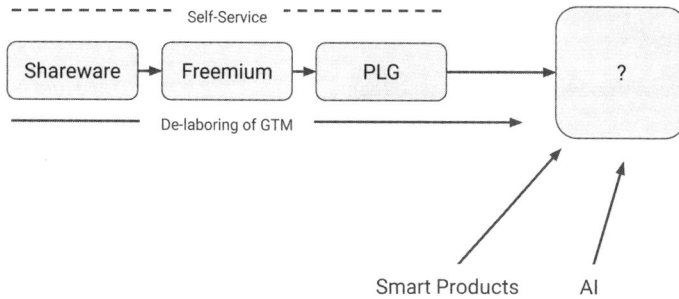

## With Smart Products and AI, What's Next in the GTM De-Laboring Trend?

In this book we have touched on three converging trends:

1. The de-laboring of software GTM via PLG

2. Physical goods becoming "smart" by incorporating software and sensors ("smart products")

3. Artificial intelligence performing complex tasks and mimicking human interactions

Where do these trends lead? What comes next in the de-laboring of GTM? The answer to this question can be informed by both buyer preferences and technical capabilities, governed by economic forces.

## Buyer Preferences: Buyers Prefer Human Assistance in Some Instances and Computer Assistance in Others

Finnish GTM strategist Sara Eklund recently asked me: "As a buyer, in which situations would you rather deal with a human, and in which would you rather deal with a robot?"

In general:

- People trust humans with intuition, creativity, strategy, extrapolation, and empathy.

- People trust robots with facts, transactions, details, and calculations.

So if we were designing the perfect buying experience, we might employ humans to do what humans do best, and machines to do what machines do best. Logical, right?

- If you wanted to know about the technical specifications of a product, you might trust a bot, designed to deliver such answers. If you wanted to run a return on investment (ROI) calculation, you might like to interact with an unemotional calculation machine vs. a quota-carrying rep.

- But if you wanted to know, "What other questions should I be asking that I haven't asked yet?" well, a human with empathy and insight might do a better job responding to that inquiry.

To better consider "who does what" in a GTM process, let's break down the various components of a GTM stack.

### Tech The Technical Capabilities of a Human-Machine "GTM Stack"

Consider the full GTM apparatus—including humans and machines—as a stack.

### THE HUMAN GTM PROFESSIONAL

The human GTM professional (sales, marketing, CS) is at the top of the stack, representing capability for nuanced perception, judgment, intuition, empathy, and creativity. GTM professionals interact directly with customers and often work according to priorities and processes documented in GTM systems like customer relationship management (CRM; see below). GTM pros consume information from and contribute information to these systems, while they manage relationships and interactions with customers.

### GTM SYSTEMS

GTM systems are product-agnostic. They are built to support the GTM motion regardless of product specifics. GTM systems are highly configurable software, and they are programmed to house the logic that defines GTM processes for a particular business. GTM Systems include software with which our customers interact directly (e.g., websites, marketing automation tools, sales engagement

FIGURE 19.2.   The Human-Machine GTM Stack

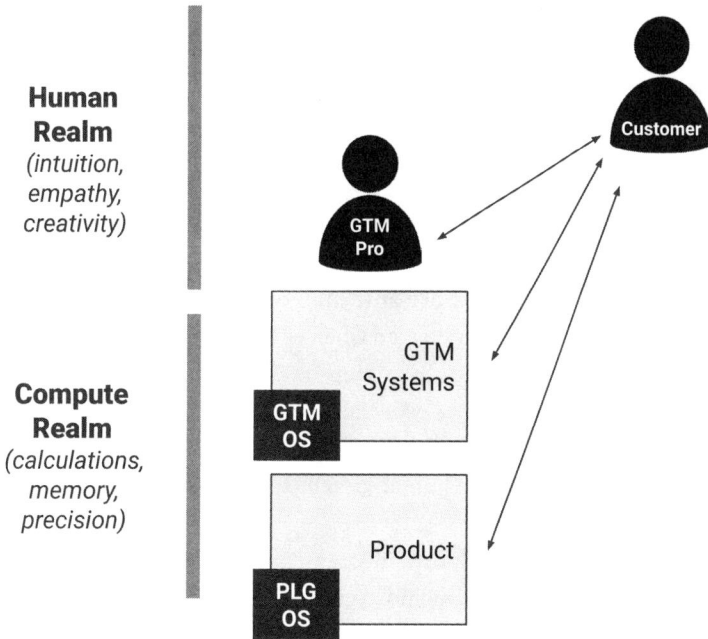

platforms, websites, and chatbots) and software used internally (e.g., CRM, customer success platforms, sales enablement platforms, and revenue intelligence platforms).

### PRODUCT

Products can also house GTM logic and perform GTM tasks. In product-led growth, the product itself manages Acquisition, Expansion, and so on. Product Growth Teams run experiments to optimize for desirable outcomes. A new category of software systems has emerged to support the data and processes involved in PLG, including customer data platforms (CDP), product analytics platforms, user onboarding and engagement platforms, and product experimentation/feature flagging platforms. These systems make it easier for product managers to adhere to a common operational framework for product-led GTM.

### Human Realm vs. Compute Realm in the GTM Stack

Customers can interact with any portion of the GTM stack:

- They can work directly with the human seller or other GTM professional.
- They can interact with elements of the GTM system, such as websites or chatbots.
- They can self-serve within the product itself.

Because the human intelligence at the top of the stack is more nuanced, human-to-human interaction is preferred when emotion impacts a buyer's decision process. Human buyers tend to make decisions based on a combination of intuition, experience, and emotion—especially when the stakes are high. The more concerned a customer is about making a mistake, the more emotional the decision becomes. In these cases, a human coach (seller) can be helpful in guiding a customer toward a decision.[4]

Humans, however, have limitations compared with computers. Humans have slower processing speed, memory constraints, and personal financial motivations. If these limitations would inhibit a purchasing decision that could otherwise be better supported by a computer, then a computer is preferred. Customers, therefore, would rather trust a computer with things like data, analytical deductions, unbiased ROI analysis, and even step-by-step advice on adoption or recommended use cases.

### How to Program the Human-Machine GTM Stack

Let's say you agree that "humans are better at feelings and computers are better at math" (a gross oversimplification). So it's solved then, right? Computers will do all the technical stuff, and humans will be there for intuition and moral support.

Ideally, yes, but not so fast . . .

I once sat in a San Francisco Starbucks and slid a napkin and pen across the table to Salesforce executive Shahan Parshad. I asked him, "How would you instruct a computer to do your team's work?"

Shahan is a smart guy—Stanford, McKinsey, Salesforce—but my question stumped him. If he could write down instructions for a computer to do anything he wanted it to do—what would that be? We worked on that problem for a while.

The truth is, we have the luxury *right now* of being able to "program" computers to do whatever we want them to. Today's computers are highly capable order takers—they follow instructions and predefined algorithms to accomplish tasks. Computers can also handle most of the data acquisition, pre-processing, and algorithm selection necessary to complete even tasks that are quite vague.

So *hypothetically*, one could say, "Computer, send personalized check-in emails to the most engaged customers," and the computer could make all the calculations and assumptions needed to complete the task. *Hypothetically.*

Two problems exist with this scenario:

1. Is that really what you wanted? Did you really want the computer to select the appropriate customers and send customized emails to them, based on vague instructions?

2. Do we have GTM systems designed to operate at that level? Yes, we have generative pre-trained transformers (GPTs) that can carry out generic tasks based on instructions from humans. And some GPTs are trained specifically to execute within a particular domain, such as legal (document drafting and review), software development (code generation, debugging, and documentation), and education (personalized tutoring and practice question generation). But do we have GTM systems that have been trained to execute with precision *in the GTM domain*? Do systems exist to retrieve the right data from the right GTM systems and execute GTM tasks at the right level to follow instructions like the ones above? Spoiler alert: whatever we have now, it's about to get a whole lot better.

At this point, the limitation is not in the computer realm. We're not constrained by not whether or not a computer *could* do it. The limitation is in the human realm. *Computers and robots will do anything we want.* But can we articulate what we want?

> "If you can't describe what you're doing as a process,
> you don't know what you're doing."
>
> —W. Edwards Deming

### Growth Architects Needed to Unlock the GTM Stack's Full Potential

Who programs the GTM stack? Who decides what GTM strategy and process we want to pursue and how that gets programmed into the GTM stack? We might call people with this role "growth architects." The role is highly needed, because as W. Edwards Deming reminds us, if we can't describe what we are doing as a process, we don't know what we are doing.

In product-led companies, the growth architect function lives within the product organization. Here, Growth Teams operate to bring to pass the overall growth objectives housed in the product growth model (see Chapter 5: Creating and Managing Growth Teams).

In sales-led companies, the growth architect function lives within Revenue Operations (RevOps). RevOps is typically responsible for defining the desired GTM processes, programming them into GTM systems, and measuring and optimizing them over time.

In an ideal state, the role of growth architect spans both product-led and human-led GTM motions. The growth architect programs a GTM stack that is vertically integrated. Sales-oriented GTM systems take handoffs from product-oriented systems (e.g., product-qualified accounts, or PQAs). Both product-oriented and sales-oriented systems adhere to a common language and common data model, constituting what is in effect a single "GTM operating system" (GTM OS). The GTM OS is PLG-aware, and its data model is robust enough to bridge product-led and human-led growth.

With a common GTM OS, PLG-defined user states such as "activated" or "engaged" can be systematically aggregated with account-level data such as "fit score." PQAs can be seamlessly managed and handed to sales for engagement. Whether a renewal should be processed automatically or receive personal attention can be informed by activity within the product. From an internal, GTM perspective, the growth architect has full rein to program the GTM stack top to bottom, and the GTM pro herself (sales, marketing, CS) is reserved for highest and best use.

More important, the vertical integration of the GTM stack benefits the customer. In this world, the same customer who takes advantage of self-service during a free trial is able to seamlessly join a team or enterprise plan and get personal help with purchasing or upgrading when needed. Customers can seamlessly transition between self-service and human assistance without being needlessly pigeonholed into one or the other. This removes internal

FIGURE 19.3.   Integrating the GTM Stack

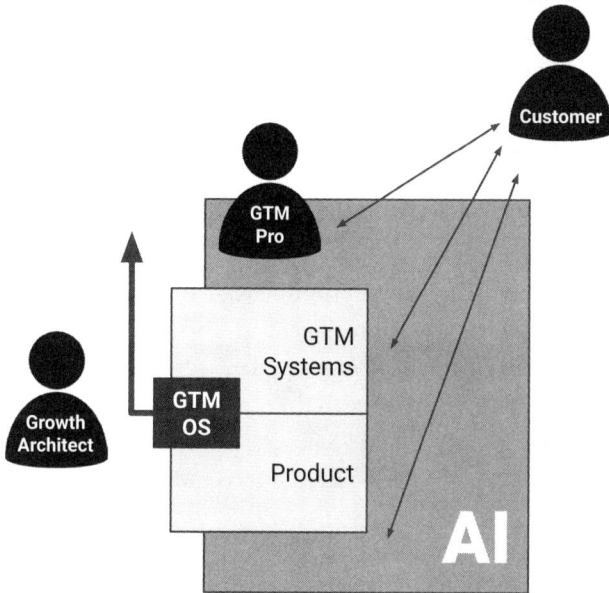

competition between sales and product, and it centers the buyer experience as the primary concern. As multiple protagonists in this book's case studies have stated, human-led and product-led motions need not compete with each other. Product-led motions can help the human GTM pro do their job more effectively, as long as the processes are synchronized (see the MongoDB case study featuring Sahir Azam in Chapter 16 and the Miro Case study featuring Adam Carr in Chapter 15).

### And Along Comes AI: How AI Helps Execute a Well-Defined Strategy

Once we have a single, defined GTM strategy in place, AI has a clear role: help execute the strategy.

For companies that have not taken the time to define and document their GTM strategy to the level of process, it is quite difficult—impossible, even—to expect help from AI. AI is a great order taker. But until our processes and objectives are defined and documented, it is impossible to expect a computer to read our mind and accomplish the job effectively.

→ Process first, AI second.

As we document GTM processes, some of the prescribed tasks will only be executable by humans. These are tasks that require empathy, judgment, intuition, and creativity. Human buyers need human sellers to help them finalize certain types of decisions—especially when the stakes are high. This level of emotional support and guidance will always be best delivered by a human, and we should not attempt to automate it.

Some tasks performed by GTM pros today are mundane. They are required to keep commerce flowing, but with current advances in AI, they are highly automatable: e.g., note taking, CRM record updating, task scheduling, reminders, emailing, customer background research, sequencing, and forecasting. If these tasks are defined and sequenced into a process, AI can automate many of them. These AI-enabled tasks can be integrated into GTM-system processes that are product-agnostic.

Still other GTM functions are so product-specific, they can be incorporated directly into the product itself, e.g., onboarding, upgrades, renewals, extensions, and configurations. For these tasks, the "self-service happy path" (see Chapters 4 and 14) can be sufficient to allow a customer to move forward with minimal friction.

Deciding which tasks fall into which category, designing those tasks, and programming them into an overall process belong to the domain of growth architects. Growth architects work across the entire GTM stack and answer the question posed to Shahan, "How would you instruct a computer to do your job?" Once this question is answered, we are well on our way toward enabling a truly de-labored and automated GTM.

> "At Canva, nearly 200 million users embark on unique design journeys each month. While our product often guides them, there are times when our sales and customer support teams step in to show customers all that is possible. We prioritize genuine, human connections, and we use process, AI, and a product-led growth motion to clear the path for meaningful interactions."
>
> —Rob Giglio, Chief Customer Officer, Canva

## A View into the Future of PLG

One can imagine a scenario like the following:

*"Hey, Siri. Restock my refrigerator."*

It's much more difficult to imagine:

*"Hey, Siri. Fix my depression."*

The latter situation is complicated by nuance. It requires perception and intuition that stretch beyond the current capabilities of computers.

But the former situation relies only on technical capabilities already available. These capabilities could theoretically be combined today into a set of AI-enabled processes to facilitate the appropriate workflow, e.g., computer vision or near-field communication (NFC) to detect what's in the fridge, AI to compare current inventory to historical purchase and consumption patterns, and a buying agent to find the restock items needed and order them for delivery.

This business-to-consumer (B2C) example, while possible, may take some time to impact most refrigerators in most homes. But in business-to-business (B2B) buying, I believe reorders will quickly become automated—as will preventative maintenance, service calls, and upgrades (for examples, see Chapter 18: Product-Led Growth Beyond Software). The economics of automating these mundane aspects of commerce (especially where prices and fulfillment logistics have already been established), will pull us to this world sooner than later.

> *"If humans can buy from machines, what is preventing machines from buying from machines?"*
>
> —Dunigan O'Keefe, Global Strategy Lead, Bain & Co.

In the future, buying agents will manage many of our purchasing processes—both B2B and B2C—operating within parameters we set, negotiating with selling agents, and automating much of what is routine about commerce.

But since not all commerce is routine, not everything will be automated (sorry, Elon). Many of our largest purchases require judgment, intuition, foresight, and strategy. In these situations, the human GTM professional plays an important and vital role.

Even in these instances, where the GTM professional is front-and-center, artificial intelligence can support the GTM pro by pre-processing large amounts of data, running simulations, and providing reasonable options from which to choose. This level of decision support also enhances the interaction between buyer and seller, lifting the ethos from transactional to strategic.

### Final Thoughts

When I told my fellow board members at Forrester I was taking a break from operating companies to write a book on product-led growth, the general response was, "I think I know what that is, but just in case, can you explain it to me?" When I realized that the concept and principles of PLG, while deafeningly omnipresent in Silicon Valley, were less well known in the "capital-E Economy," I knew there was an arbitrage opportunity. One of the board members, Neil Bradford, suggested that I begin with the term *Freemium*. "Everyone knows what freemium means," he said, "and from there you can explain the rest of PLG."

The principles of product-led growth have been tried and tested for over a decade. Dozens of multi-billion-dollar companies have been built, leveraging PLG as their primary go-to-market motion, and thousands more are being built today. Combining PLG with human-led motions has allowed these companies to break through growth and scale barriers and redefine what is possible in terms of efficient growth (for the relative performance of product-led and sales-led companies, see Chapter 4: Product-Led Growth Is a Long-Term Growth Strategy).

Product-led growth is a strategy that to date has been the nearly exclusive domain of software entrepreneurs. To their credit, these entrepreneurs have refined the techniques, the language, and the processes of PLG. They have developed a structured discipline called "Growth," which, if mentioned in the right circles, evokes an entire set of understanding. Growth frameworks and tactics are taught in places like Reforge Academy and leading business schools, and they have been documented in books and blogs by and for tech entrepreneurs (see the Resources appendix). Adding the word "growth" to your job title—assuming you can back it up—can add $50–100K to your commandable income (similar to "machine learning" or "AI").

Whereas PLG techniques have been somewhat constrained to software to date, the emergence of smart products makes it possible to program and automate GTM for software and non-software products alike. As products become more intelligent and more connected, these same growth principles will be applied across all product sectors.

Making products and services easier to discover, easier to buy, easier to adopt, and easier to expand is indeed, as my friend said, "just good product management." But since growth hasn't historically been programmed into most products, PLG frameworks offer a useful and helpful guide to do just that.

All product managers in the future will instrument products to actively participate in their own distribution—to make themselves easier to discover, buy, adopt, and expand. As we do this, we will also integrate the operating systems that orchestrate product-led and human-led GTM motions. This integrated approach to go-to-market has proven to be the most efficient and effective way to scale companies, and it is the way of the future.

As self-service buying options and automated GTM proliferate, the customer's buying experience appropriately takes center stage. The buyer is able to choose which portions of her experience she would rather self-direct and when she would like assistance for larger or more complex decisions. AI will continue to assist growth architects and product managers in designing commerce experiences that are smoother and more convenient for both buyer and seller.

PLG pioneers have demonstrated how to make freemium and self-service a profitable pursuit. Thanks to their work, we now have a fully developed, refined, and documented methodology for managing growth via product-led motions. As product-led growth further permeates the "capital-E Economy" and as it becomes integrated with traditional sales-led motions, augmented by AI, tomorrow's version of commerce holds unlimited promise.

> *Here's to a future that is bright and shiny*
> *on the other side of software's Industrial Revolution.*
> *Here's to a new and highly de-labored version of GTM*
> *across industries beyond software.*
> *And here's to you and I being on the right side of history,*
> *as we innovate our way into the future.*
>
> XOXO,
> —dave

## Chapter 19 Summary

- GTM automation has progressed from shareware to freemium to PLG.

- The emergence of smart products and AI will continue the trend of de-laboring GTM.

- Buyers prefer human interactions for emotional decisions and computer interactions for rational and data-driven input.

- The GTM apparatus (including humans and machines) can be viewed as a single stack, operating in concert to deliver seamless customer experiences.

- To optimize GTM for both seller and buyer, processes must be defined that integrate product-led and human-led motions. This job is best performed by a growth architect.

- With processes defined, AI can streamline, automate, and improve experiences for both buyer and seller.

## Manager Minute

Thinking about your own company, take time to reflect on the following questions:

1. Which portions of our business today are product-led? Which pieces are human-led?

2. Given the answer to the first question here, what is our strategy with regard to GTM automation? Which pieces should be handled by the product itself, by GTM systems, and by humans?

**3.** What opportunities do we have to better define processes, such that AI could help automate portions of our GTM?

_____

_____

_____

### The Next Generation of Product-Led Growth

In Part Four we took a look at PLG through the front windshield. Where does it go from here? Can GTM capabilities be programmed into our product? Can they be programmed into our GTM systems? Are these strategies applicable to my company? If so, how would I add them? What about in a non-software environment? And with the advent of AI, when does PLG/GTM automation become the *de facto* standard?

We learned that PLG in its purest form is not for every company. Certain conditions make PLG an obvious choice in some industries, while in industries where those conditions are absent, PLG is more difficult. If any company in your space is making PLG work, however, you must strongly consider adopting it too or risk becoming irrelevant. We also learned about PLG-adjacent strategies such as product-led _X_, sidecar products, and interactive demos.

We looked at how core PLG principles are being applied beyond software—largely by using embedded software as a "Trojan horse." Apps that communicate with sensors in a product can turn that product into a "smart" product that can participate in its own GTM.

Finally, we asked ourselves what the role of AI would be in next-generation GTM. We looked at an integrated GTM "stack" consisting of product, GTM systems, and humans, and we considered a future where that stack is fully integrated and coordinated by a single GTM operating system, and in which any given step in a GTM process is performed by the human or machine best suited for that step.

# Acknowledgments

Here's to the *true believers* who were willing to bet on me, writing my first book. You generously gave time, talent, insight, ideas, and resources to help me get my arms around a topic so large, it required all our collective contributions. I will forever be grateful to you.

Winning by Design
  Jacco van der Kooij, Dan Smith, Dominique Levin, Andrew Parry, David Gordillo, Walter Taboada, Roee Hartuv, Sari Green, Shari Johnston, Harry Rogiers, Fiona Chiu, Derek Sather

Brigham Young University
  Dan Snow, Brigitte Madrian, Jeff Larson, Lexis Pearson, Preston Lyman, Tony Kent, Evan Parry, Court Lykins, Christine Roundy, Jake Adams

Harvard Business School
  Frank Cespedes, Mark Roberge, Clayton Christensen

Forrester
  George Colony, Rob Galford, Yvonne Wassenaar, Carrie Johnson, Lisa Singer, Neil Bradford

Collaborators and Editors
  Jared Davis, Ben Williams, Jesus Requena, Sandy Mangat, Leah Tharin, Kyle Poyar, Wes Bush, Dave Sundahl, Dave Grow, Jordan Roper, Ben Brown, Gabriel Elizondo, Calvin Boyce, Jacob Boyce, Jordan Callister, Mitchell Beck, Jeff Angerbauer, Greg Pal, Paul Baltes, Alex Bilmes, Sahir Azam, Elena Verna,

Kipp Bodnar, Jorge Mazal, Rob McFarland, James Citron, Sara Eklund, Anil Somaney, Kate Syuma, Dan Cook, Nate Quigley, Arian Lewis, Ken Yagan, Tandra Bidyananda

Stanford University Press
  Richard Narramore, Natalie Rovero

Levine, Greenberg, Rostan Literary Agency
  Jim Levine, Neil Hoyne

# Appendix A

Below are some of my favorite resources for product-led growth (partial list). Find links to these and other resources at: DaveBoyce.substack.com/resources

## PLG/Growth Blogs and Newsletters

- Dave Boyce's *Product-Led GTM*
- Kyle Poyar's *Growth Unhinged*
- *Lenny's Newsletter*
- Ben Williams's *The Product-Led Geek*
- *ProductLed.com*
- *Elena's Growth Scoop*
- *Leah's ProducTea*
- Drew Teller's *TheProductLed*

## PLG/Growth Books

- *Product-Led Growth* by Wes Bush
- *Hacking Growth* by Sean Ellis and Morgan Brown
- *The Product-Led Organization* by Todd Olson

## Product Books

- *Inspired* by Marty Cagan
- *The Four Steps to the Epiphany* by Steve Blank
- *The Lean Startup* by Eric Ries

## Strategy Books

- *Competing Against Luck* by Clayton Christensen et al.
- *Playing to Win* by Roger L. Martin et al.
- *Crossing the Chasm* by Geoffrey A. Moore

## Revenue/Growth Books

- *Revenue Architecture* by Jacco van der Kooij
- *The Sales Acceleration Formula* by Mark Roberge
- *The High Growth Handbook* by Elad Gil

# Appendix B

## Acquisition Metrics

1. *Website Traffic*

   - **Definition**: Total visits to the product's website or landing page

2. *Sign-Up Conversion Rate*

   - **Definition:** Percentage of website visitors who sign up for the product

   - **Formula:**

   $$\text{Sign-Up Conversion Rate} = \left( \frac{\textit{New User Sign Ups}}{\textit{Total Website Visitors}} \right) \times 100\%$$

3. *Customer Acquisition Cost (CAC)*

   - **Definition**: The total cost associated with acquiring a new customer, including all marketing, sales, and associated expenses

     This usually refers to the cost of acquiring a paid user.

4. *Product-Qualified Leads (PQLs)*

   - **Definition:** Users who have engaged meaningfully with the product and show potential to convert to paying customers

5. *Referral Rate*

   - **Definition:** Percentage of users who refer others to the product

   - **Formula:**

   $$\text{Referral Rate} = \left( \frac{\textit{Users Who Refer Others to the Product}}{\textit{Total Users}} \right) \times 100\%$$

6. *Virality Coefficient (R-Factor, or Ro)*

   - ***Definition***: A measure of how many additional users each existing user brings to the product through referrals

- *Formula*:

$R_o$ = Average Number of Invitations Sent by Each User × Conversion Rate

## Activation Metrics

1. *Activation Rate*

- *Definition*: The proportion of new users who experience a defined First Impact event (e.g., using a key feature) demonstrates that they have experienced the product's core value

  Activation Rate is often calculated by cohort, where the denominator represents the total number of cohort members (e.g., new users who created an account in a certain period) and the numerator represents the cumulative number of users who have activated by the end of a certain period. This can be expressed as, e.g., "Week Three Activation Rate."

- *Formula*:

$$Activation\ Rate = \left(\frac{Number\ of\ Activated\ Users}{Number\ of\ New\ Users}\right) \times 100\%$$

2. *First Impact Success Rate (FI Success Rate)*

- *Definition*: The percentage of new users who achieve First Impact within a specified time period

- *Formula*:

$$FI\ Success\ Rate =$$
$$\left(\frac{Number\ of\ New\ Users\ Experiencing\ First\ Impact\ within\ Time\ (t)}{Total\ Number\ of\ New\ Users}\right) \times 100\%$$

3. *Daily active users (DAU)*

- *Definition*: The number of unique users who engage with a product or service on a daily basis

4. *Weekly active users (WAU)*

- *Definition*: The number of unique users who engage with a product or service on a weekly basis

5. *Monthly active users (MAU)*

- *Definition*: The number of unique users who engage with a product or service on a monthly basis

## Monetization Metrics

1. *Monetization Rate*

   - **Definition**: The percentage of users who convert from free to paying customers within a given period

     Monetization Rate is often calculated by cohort, where the denominator represents the total number of cohort members (e.g., new users who created a free account in a certain period), and the numerator represents the cumulative number of users who have Monetized by the end of a certain period. This can be expressed as, e.g., "Six-Month Monetization Rate."

   - **Formula**:

     $$\text{Monetization Rate} = \left( \frac{\textit{Number of Paying Users}}{\textit{Total Number of Users}} \right) \times 100\%$$

2. *Customer Lifetime Value (LTV)*

   - **Definition**: The total revenue a company expects to earn from a customer over the duration of their relationship

   - **Formula**:

     LTV (in years) = ACV (Annual Contract Value) × Customer Lifetime (in years)

3. *LTV: CAC (Customer Lifetime Value to Customer Acquisition Cost)*

   - **Definition**: The ratio of the average customer lifetime value to the amount of sales and marketing expense required to acquire a new customer

   - **Formula**:

     $$\text{LTV : CAC} = \left( \frac{\textit{Customer Lifetime Value (LTV)}}{\textit{Customer Acquisition Cost (CAC)}} \right)$$

4. *CAC Payback Period*

   - **Definition**: The time required for customer-generated revenue to replenish the expenses incurred acquiring the customer

   - **Formula**:

     CAC Payback Period (months) =

     $$\left( \frac{\textit{Customer Acquisition Cost (CAC)}}{\textit{Monthly Recurring Revenue (MRR)per Customer}} \right)$$

## Retention Metrics

1. *Usage Retention Rates (DAU, WAU, MAU)*

   - ***Definition***: The percentage of users who continue to engage with a product or service over a specific period after their initial use

     Usage Retention is often calculated by cohort, where the denominator represents the total number of cohort members (e.g., users who activated in a certain period), and the numerator represents the number of active users in the current period. This can be calculated for DAU, WAU, or MAU.

   - ***Formula***:

$$\text{Usage Retention Rate} = \left( \frac{\text{Number of Active Users in a Period}}{\text{Number of Active Users in a Previous Period}} \right) \times 100\%$$

2. *Customer Retention Rate (CRR)*

   - ***Definition***: The percentage of customers who continue to use the product over a given period

   - ***Formula***:

$$\text{Customer Retention Rate} = \left( \frac{\text{Number of Customers at End of Period}}{\text{Number of Customers at Start of Period}} \right) \times 100\%$$

3. *Gross Revenue Retention (GRR)*

   - ***Definition***: The percentage of customer revenue retained from one renewal cycle to the next

   - ***Formula***:

$$GRR = \left( \frac{\text{Revenue from Existing Customers at End of Period (excluding upgrades)}}{\text{Total Revenue at Start of Period}} \right)$$

## Expansion Metrics

1. *Expansion Rate*

   - ***Definition***: The percentage growth in revenue from current customers due to additional purchases, upgrades to higher-priced plans, or increased usage of the product or service

- *Formula*:

$$\text{Expansion Rate} = \left(\frac{R_b - R_a}{R_a}\right) \times 100\%$$

Where Ra = Revenue from Existing Customers at Beginning of Period

Rb = Revenue from Existing Customers at End of Period

2. *Net Revenue Retention (NRR)*

- *Definition*: Measures the retained portion of existing contracts plus the expansion of those same contracts

Note that Net Retention can be greater than 100%.

- *Formula*:

$$NRR = \left(\frac{\textit{Revenue from Existing Customers at End of Period (including upgrades)}}{\textit{Revenue from Existing Customers at Start of Period}}\right) \times 100\%$$

# Notes

**Introduction**

1. Adam Schoenfeld, "Cloud 100 List," PeerSignal, 2024, https://peersignal.org/cloud100/.

2. Throughout this book, when the acronym GTM is used as a modifier, it stands for "Go-to-2 Market," and when it appears as a stand-alone acronym, it represents "Go-to-Market motion."

**Chapter 1**

1. Eugene Kim, "No Salespeople for Us, Says CEO of $4 Billion Startup Slack," Business Insider, March 16, 2016, https://www.businessinsider.com/slack-ceo-stewart-butterfield-no-salespeople-2016-3.

2. Dina Bass, "This $5 Billion Software Company Has No Sales Staff," Bloomberg, May 18, 2016, https://www.bloomberg.com/news/articles/2016-05-18/this-5-billion-software-company-has-no-sales-staff.

3. Kyle Poyar, "How Supermetrics Grew to €50m+ 🚀," Growth Unhinged, September 21, 2022, https://www.growthunhinged.com/p/how-supermetrics-grew-to-50m-and.

4. Barbara Findlay Schenck, "Freemium: Is the Price Right for Your Company?" Entrepreneur, February 7, 2011, https://www.entrepreneur.com/business-news/freemium-is-the-price-right-for-your-company/218107.

5. Sam Richard, "The Product-Led Growth Market Map," OpenView, October 25, 2022, https://openviewpartners.com/blog/the-product-led-growth-market-map/.

6. Adam Schoenfeld, "Cloud 100 List," PeerSignal, 2024, https://peersignal.org/cloud100/.

7. Mickey Alon, "Product-Led Growth Index 2022," Gainsight Software, June 7, 2022, https://www.gainsight.com/blog/product-led-growth-index-2022/.

8. "Product-Market Fit," Wikipedia, June 18, 2024, https://en.wikipedia.org/wiki/Product-market_fit. A more technical definition is provided later in this book.

9. Lori Wizdo, "The Ways and Means of B2B Buyer Journey Maps: We're Going Deep at Forrester's B2B Forum," Forrester, August 21, 2017, https://www.forrester.com/blogs/the-ways-and-means-of-b2b-buyer-journey-maps-were-going-deep-at-forresters-b2b-forum/.

10. Kate Sukhanova, "Video Conferencing Market Statistics," The Tech Report, July 22, 2024, https://techreport.com/statistics/software-web/video-conferencing-market-statistics/.

11. Curt Townshend, "Product-Led Growth Index," OpenView, 2022, https://openviewpartners.com/product-led-growth-index/.

## Chapter 2

1. Hiten Shah, "How Atlassian Built a $10 Billion Growth Engine," Nira, 2020, https://nira.com/atlassian-history/.

2. Endgame Product-Led Sales Summit, Los Angeles, California, November 2022.

3. Revenue and growth rates, Pitchbook Data, varying time periods based on public availability.

4. As of December 2022.

5. As of January 2022.

6. As of June 2021.

7. As of August 2021.

8. As of December 2022.

9. As of January 2023.

10. As of December 2022.

11. As of June 2022.

12. As of January 2023.

13. Kyle Poyar, "How Product-Led Growth Went from Idea to the Biggest Trend in Software," OpenView, May 2, 2022, https://openviewpartners.com/blog/inventing-product-led-growth/.

14. Jitender Miglani, "2022 Online Retail Forecast, US," Forrester, August 2, 2022, https://www.forrester.com/report/2022-online-retail-forecast-us/RES177791.

15. Michael Pietroforte, "IaaS, SaaS, PaaS, and XaaS," 4sysops, December 3, 2013, https://4sysops.com/archives/iaas-saas-paas-and-xaas/.

## Chapter 3

1. "Empathy Definition: What Is Empathy?" Greater Good, accessed September 5, 2024, https://greatergood.berkeley.edu/topic/empathy/definition.

2. Clayton M. Christensen, Taddy Hall, Karen Dillon, and David S. Duncan, Competing Against Luck: The Story of Innovation and Customer Choice (New York: HarperBusiness, 2016).

3. A great resource for understanding this mentality is Steve Blank, Four Steps to the Epiphany: Successful Strategies for Products That Win (K & S Ranch, 2013).

4. Janelle Teng and Ethan Kurzweil, "10 Product-Led Growth Principles," Bessemer Venture Partners, March 8, 2022, https://www.bvp.com/atlas/10-product-led-growth-principles.

5. See Ben Williams, "The Importance of Trustworthy Data," The Product-Led Geek, March 5, 2023, https://www.plg.news/p/the-importance-of-trustworthy-data

## Chapter 4

1. Kim B. Clark and Steven C. Wheelwright, Managing New Product and Process Development: Text and Cases (New York: Free Press, 1993).

2. See Gary P. Pisano, The Development Factory: Unlocking the Potential of Process Innovation (Boston: Harvard Business School Press, 1996).

3. For a terrific article on this concept, see Mark Roberge, "The Science of Re-Establishing Growth: When and How Fast?" Stage 2 Capital, 2023, https://www.stage2.capital/blog/the-science-of-re-establishing-growth-when-where-how.

4. Kyle Poyar, Tom Holahan, and Sean Fanning, "OpenView's 2023 SAAS Benchmarks Is Here!" OpenView, 2023, https://openviewpartners.com/2023-saas-benchmarks-report/.

## Chapter 5

1. Steven G. Blank, The Four Steps to the Epiphany: Successful Strategies for Products That Win (Hoboken, NJ: John Wiley & Sons, 2020).

2. Sean Ellis and Morgan Brown, Hacking Growth: How Today's Fastest-Growing Companies Drive Breakout Success (New York: Crown Business, 2017).

## Chapter 6

1. Geoffrey A. Moore, Crossing the Chasm: Marketing and Selling Disruptive Products to Mainstream Customers (New York: HarperBusiness, 2014).

2. Marty Cagan, Inspired: How to Create Tech Products Customers Love (Hoboken, NJ: John Wiley & Sons, 20180.

3. On jobs theory, see Clayton Christensen, Competing Against Luck: The Story of Innovation and Customer Choice (New York: HarperBusiness, 2016).

4. Chris Speiek and Bob Moesta, Jobs-to-be-Done Handbook: Practical Techniques for Improving Your Application of Jobs-to-be-Done (Createspace, 2014).

5. On the concept of an MVP, see Eric Ries, The Lean Startup: How Today's Entrepreneurs Use Continuous Innovation to Create Radically Successful Businesses (New York: Currency, 2011).

6. Marty Cagan, Inspired: How to Create Tech Products Customers Love (Hoboken, NJ: John Wiley & Sons, 2018).

## Chapter 7

1. Jacco Van der Kooij, Revenue Architecture (Winning By Design, 2023).

2. Benchmarks for SaaS performance across the Bowtie are available here: https://bench sights.com/wbd-benchmarks/.

3. Mina Alaghband, Nina Panagiotidou, Paul Roche, and Jeremy Schneider, "From Product-Led Growth to Product-Led Sales: Beyond the PLG Hype," McKinsey & Company, August 8, 2023, https://www.mckinsey.com/industries/technology-media-and-telecommunications/our-insights/from-product-led-growth-to-product-led-sales-beyond-the-plg-hype.

4. Lauren Simonds, "Figma's Dylan Field Will Discuss Evolving as a Leader and Why Fun Is an Essential Company Value at TechCrunch Disrupt," TechCrunch, June 8, 2022, https://techcrunch.com/2022/06/08/figmas-dylan-field-will-discuss-evolving-as-a-leader-and-why-fun-is-an-essential-company-value-at-techcrunch-disrupt/.

5. Kyle Poyar, Tom Holahan, and Sean Fanning, "OpenView's 2023 SAAS Benchmarks Is Here!" OpenView, 2023, https://openviewpartners.com/2023-saas-benchmarks-report/.

6. Kyle Poyar, Tom Holahan, and Sean Fanning, "OpenView's 2023 SAAS Benchmarks Is Here!" OpenView, 2023, https://openviewpartners.com/2023-saas-benchmarks-report/.

7. Esteban Domingo, Virus as Populations: Composition, Complexity, Quasispecies, Dynamics, and Biological Implications (Amsterdam: Academic Press, 2019).

## Chapter 8

1. Anna Fitzgerald, "What Is the Average Time Spent on a Website? [+How to Improve It]." HubSpot Blog, 2021, https://blog.hubspot.com/marketing/chartbeat-website-engagement-data-nj;

Jakob Nielsen, "How Long Do Users Stay on Web Pages?" Nielsen Norman Group, 2011, https://www.nngroup.com/articles/how-long-do-users-stay-on-web-pages/.

2. Wes Bush, Product-Led Growth: How to Build a Product That Sells Itself (Burlington, VT: Author's Republic, 2019).

3. Kyle Poyar and Kate Syuma, "The Evolution of Miro's User Onboarding," Kyle Poyar's Growth Unhinged, August 23, 2023, https://www.growthunhinged.com/p/the-evolution-of-miros-user-onboarding.

4. Kim Flaherty, "Diary Studies: Understanding Long-Term User Behavior and Experiences," Nielsen Norman Group, March 29, 2024, https://www.nngroup.com/articles/diary-studies/.

## Chapter 9

1. Kyle Poyar, "Free Is Here to Stay," Kyle Poyar's Growth Unhinged, March 11, 2021, https://kylepoyar.substack.com/p/free-is-here-to-stay.

2. Hannah McGrath, Curt Townshend, and Kyle Poyar, "OpenView 2023 Product Benchmarks Is Here!" OpenView, 2023, https://openviewpartners.com/2023-product-benchmarks/.

3. Hannah McGrath, Curt Townshend, and Kyle Poyar, "OpenView 2023 Product Benchmarks Is Here!" OpenView, 2023, https://openviewpartners.com/2023-product-benchmarks/.

## Chapter 10

1. "Uncanny valley" is a term from the world of computer graphics to express the revulsion the viewer feels when a human simulation is close to real-life—but not quite enough. See https://en.wikipedia.org/wiki/Uncanny_valley.

## Chapter 11

1. "Duolingo Hits 100m Maus, Reports 59% Dau Growth and 41% Revenue Growth in Second Quarter 2024," Duolingo, Inc., August 7, 2024, https://investors.duolingo.com/news-releases/news-release-details/duolingo-hits-100m-maus-reports-59-dau-growth-and-41-revenue.

2. Sondra Orozco, "How to Explode Growth Twice. Duolingo—Jorge Mazal," YouTube, September 5, 2023, https://www.youtube.com/watch?v=BIagRI_uQ3w.

3. Jorge Mazal, "How Duolingo Reignited User Growth," Lenny's Newsletter, February 28, 2023, https://www.lennysnewsletter.com/p/how-duolingo-reignited-user-growth.

4. Sondra Orozco, "How to Explode Growth Twice. Duolingo—Jorge Mazal," YouTube, September 5, 2023, https://www.youtube.com/watch?v=BIagRI_uQ3w.

5. Ben Williams, "Product Qualified Accounts at Risk of Churn (aka the Inverse PQA)," The Product-Led Geek, April 21, 2023, https://www.plg.news/p/product-qualified-accounts-at-risk.

## Chapter 13

1. Jacco Van der Kooij, Revenue Architecture (Winning By Design, 2023).

## Chapter 14

1. "2023 PLG Index," Peersignal, 2023, https://app.peersignal.org/datasets/plg.

2. Kyle Poyar, "Your Guide to Product Qualified Leads (Pqls)," OpenView, 2022, https://openviewpartners.com/blog/your-guide-to-product-qualified-leads-pqls/.

3. For clarity, this refers to a "Sales ICP" account—one we hope to engage with a contract beyond the scope of PLG.

4. Hannah McGrath, Curt Townshend, and Kyle Poyar, "OpenView 2023 Product Benchmarks Is Here!" OpenView, 2023, https://openviewpartners.com/2023-product-benchmarks/.

5. This acquisition was subsequently canceled in the wake of increasing pressure from regulatory bodies in the EU and the UK.

## Chapter 16

1. Kenrick Cai and Alex Konrad, eds., "Forbes Cloud 100 2024 List—Best Cloud Computing Companies Ranked," Forbes, August 6, 2024, https://www.forbes.com/lists/cloud100/; Adam Schoenfeld, "Cloud 100 List," PeerSignal, 2024, https://peersignal.org/cloud100/.

2. Clayton Christensen, The Innovator's Dilemma: When New Technologies Cause Great Companies to Fail (Boston: Harvard Business Review Press, 1997).

3. A. G. Lafley and Roger L. Martin, Playing to Win: How Strategy Really Works (Boston: Harvard Business Review Press, 2013).

4. Christensen, Clayton M., Taddy Hall, Karen Dillon, and David S. Duncan, Competing Against Luck: The Story of Innovation and Customer Choice (New York: HarperBusiness, 2016).

## Chapter 17

1. Morgan Brown, "How Hubspot Grew a Billion Dollar B2B Growth Engine," GrowthHackers, 2023, https://growthhackers.com/growth-studies/hubspot/.

## Chapter 18

1. Marc Andreessen, "Why Software Is Eating the World," Andreessen Horowitz, August 20, 2011, https://a16z.com/why-software-is-eating-the-world/.

2. Deborah Chiaravalloti, "Surgeons and Purchasing Decisions: Their Power Is Increasing," BoardVitals Blog, January 5, 2018, https://www.boardvitals.com/blog/surgeons-purchasing-decisions-power/.

3. Belle Lin, "America's Farmers Are Bogged Down by Data." Wall Street Journal, August 22, 2023, https://www.wsj.com/articles/americas-farmers-are-bogged-down-by-data-524f0a4d.

4. Kannan Ramaswamy and William E. Youngdahl, "The Strategic Transformation of John Deere: Precision Agriculture, AI, and the Internet of Things," Thunderbird School of Global Management, November 5, 2023, https://www.thecasecentre.org/products/view?id=194676.

5. Amanda Ashworth and Philip Owens, "Benefits and Evolution of Precision Agriculture," Argicultural Research Service, U.S. Dept. of Agriculture, July 12, 2023, https://www.ars.usda.gov/oc/utm/benefits-and-evolution-of-precision-agriculture.

6. Dan Crummett, "Weighing the Viability of an Autonomous Future," Precision Farming Dealer, March 27, 2023, https://www.precisionfarmingdealer.com/articles/5320-weighing-the-viability-of-an-autonomous-future.

## Chapter 19

1. Zoe Kleinman and Sean Seddon, "Elon Musk Tells Rishi Sunak AI Will Put an End to Work." BBC News, 2023, https://www.bbc.com/news/uk-67302048.

2. David Rotman, "People Are Worried That AI Will Take Everyone's Jobs. We've Been Here Before," MIT Technology Review, January 27, 2024, https://www.technologyreview .com/2024/01/27/1087041/technological-unemployment-elon-musk-jobs-ai/.

3. John Maynard Keynes, "Economic Possibilities for Our Grandchildren," marxists.org, 1930, https://www.marxists.org/reference/subject/economics/keynes/1930/our-grandchildren .htm.

4. Matthew Dixon and Ted McKenna, The JOLT Effect: How High Performers Overcome Customer Indecision (New York: Portfolio, 2022).

# Index

Skype: early internet success of, 1; free software, 128; sales motions complementing
freemium models, 136
Slack: acquisition of by Salesforce, 239; as B2B
software, 30; freemium, 18, 131; as leveraging multi-sided task of communication
as, 166; as putting Microsoft on high alert,
214; use of PLG by, 1, 11, 28
smart products: attributes of, 20; as instrumented for signal-based commerce, 260–
61; as making PLG possible everywhere,
254; as participating directly in product-led
growth, 260
Snowflake, use of PLG by, 19
Snyk: case studies, 81–82, 158–60, 159f, 160f;
Impact and Learnings Review (I&L),
86–87; use of PLG and enterprise motions
by, 19
software: advances in ability to distribute
itself, 14, 18, 30; enterprise software, 28,
36, 203; history of freemium tactics in, 1;
line between software and non-software
as blurring, 268; PLG as dominant GTM
model for emerging companies, 28; PLG as
expanding beyond, xvii, 2, 6, 21, 254–68;
PLG as industrial revolution of, 31–34;
self-service models built into, 2, 3
Software as a Service (SaaS), 32
SOM (serviceable obtainable market), 92
Somaney, Anil, 14
Spotify, early internet success of, 1
Square, free as marketing tactic of, 258
Starbucks, free as marketing tactic of,
257
startup phase, 178
Stripe, use of PLG and enterprise motions by,
18
Stryker Corporation, case study, 259–60
Sunak, Rishi, 271
Superhuman, as example of freemium, 18
Supermetrics, use of PLG by, 11–12
sustainable, defined, 63
Syuma, Kate, 123, 125

talent: identifying the right talent for PLG
team, 56; required for launching credible
PLG initiative, 49, 54, 66, 73
TAM (total addressable market), 92
Team, as tier of PLG products, 140, 142, 143
technology-powered life, case study, 29–30
Tesla, 256
timeline: overview, 59–60; required for
launching credible PLG initiative, 49, 51,
54, 66, 73; what to measure when, 60–65,
61f
total addressable market (TAM), 92
total recurring revenue, measurement of, 168
traps, biggest trap for established companies
wanting to launch PLG, 223
Twilio: founding of, 12; free software, 128;
PLG company revenue growth patterns,
52f; sales motions complementing freemium models, 136; startup timeline, 219; use
of PLG by, 28

UberConference, 16
unit economics (for Acquisition): as everything during scaling, 113–15; as mattering
less at launch, 113
Unity Software: case study, 226–29; use of
PLG by, 66, 214
usage retention: measurement of, 151; as more
important than dollar retention, 150–62
use-case fit, 195
user-centric: circumventing traditional
purchasing using user-centric design and
marketing, 259–60; as key hallmark of
PLG, 255
user experience (UX), 123
users: cautions against confusing user with
buyer in PLS, 194–95; converting free
users into large paying contracts, 128–37;
end users, 37–39, 92–93, 108–9; inviting
them to return again and again, 151; new
user onboarding, bowling with bumpers
analogy for, 122f; product-led user journey
to First Impact, 110f; use of growth loops